Layman's (Laywoman's) Study of the Parables of Jesus Christ

Mary Bullock Carter

WestBow
PRESS
A DIVISION OF THOMAS NELSON

All Quoted Scripture From:
The Open Bible
New King James Version
Thomas Nelson Publishers
1997 Edition

WestBow Press books may be ordered through booksellers or by contacting:

WestBow Press
A Division of Thomas Nelson
1663 Liberty Drive
Bloomington, IN 47403
www.westbowpress.com
1-(866) 928-1240

ISBN: 978-1-4497-1103-0 (sc)
ISBN: 978-1-4497-1104-7 (hc)
ISBN: 978-1-4497-1102-3 (e)

Library of Congress Control Number: 2011920321

Printed in the United States of America

WestBow Press rev. date: 01/26/2011

From the Four Gospels of the New Testament of the Holy Bible
Matthew
Mark
Luke
John

The Words of Jesus, Our Lord are in Italics

With Recognition and Love for all their Assistance and Patience:

REV. MIKE CATOE... My Human Spiritual Guide, my Most
Honored Pastor, and my Christian Brother
and
INA RABON BULLOCK... my First Sunday School Teacher,
my Christian Sister, and my Most Beloved Mama

Thank you Both !

DEDICATION

To those who are truly seeking the wisdom
that God has promised to all of us:
It is my testimony that this is indeed a promise
that He will keep, if you simply ask !

"For do I now persuade men, or God? Or do I seek to please men?
For if I still pleased men, I would not be a bondservant of Christ.
But I make known to you, brethren, that the gospel
which was preached by me is not according to man.
For I neither received from man, nor was I taught it,
but it came through the revelation of Jesus Christ."

Galatians 1:10-12

CONTENTS

FOREWORD

I have known Mary Carter for approximately five years. Most of this time she has been a member of my church, and I have had the privilege of being her pastor. About a year ago she asked my opinion about her writing a laywoman's interpretation of the parables of Jesus. Since I already knew she was a good Sunday School teacher and that she really put herself into it, I knew she would do an excellent job with this project. I encouraged her to do it.

The finished product that you are about to read confirms my original confidence in her ability. While writing her understanding of the parables, she has also been teaching them in her Sunday School class. The response of her students has been overwhelmingly positive, and attendance has grown in the process.

You will really enjoy the way Mary puts her life experiences into her interpretations. She does this in a unique way while staying true to the scriptures. I have learned things about Jesus' parables that I had never thought of as Mary shares her Holy Spirit inspired interpretation. I'm sure you will be inspired and may learn something, too. Mary's work has been a blessing to me. May it also be to you!

Reverend Mike Catoe, Pastor
Mount Arnon Baptist Church
Allendale, South Carolina

PROLOGUE

Parable:

(1) an illustration: an earthly story with a heavenly meaning:

(2) a teaching tool:

(3) a description of facts that compares the world of nature to the human experience:

(4) a narration of human experience compared to a natural fact:

(5) usually used in an oral lesson following the words, For Example:

(6) a short story that explains a complicated idea:

(7) the Greek translation is to lay one thing down beside another:

(8) a short and simple story teaching a moral lesson:

(9) an allegory (a description to convey a different meaning than that which is expressed) conveying a moral message:

I found all these definitions, and more in various dictionaries and Bible glossaries. And I asked a number of people what the word meant to them. I know, that as a teacher in Sunday School, first young teens and later adults, a parable is a tool that just comes out of your mouth when you see the blank look of "I don't understand" reflected in your students' eyes! As a teacher, you WANT them to take in and soak up every thought you present. Often I try to explain a point by taking something familiar to my students and showing them the likeness to the idea I am trying to explain. All teachers and public speakers do this! I am NOT surprised that the Greatest Teacher, with the Most Important Message, Jesus Christ, teaching the Plan of Salvation, used this tool in His ministry. There is a question of how many parables He used. But there is no question that He used them effectively.

There are parables throughout the Bible, Old and New Testaments. There are at least ten parables in the Old Testament (I will list them at the end this paper) but I will limit this study to the parables that are found in the books of Matthew, Mark, Luke and John. Those are the books that quote Jesus' words more directly so that is where we will look for His teachings. I will occasionally refer to the other books for a clearer understanding of His words. It is my goal to find and identify all the parables Jesus used, if I can. I guess I have bitten off a big mouthful to even attempt this, but for some reason, I think I am supposed to try.

God has been preparing me for a while. He has given me the education I need. He has given me the computer and printer I need, and the ability to use them, and He has blessed me with the time. I will have to say that this is the most exciting project I have taken on since my babies were new and I could see the future of raising them. So with the leadership of the Holy Spirit I will continue. I beg you to be patient with me and watch my opinions develop as I work through this project. It is my prayer that it will help someone reach an understanding of Jesus and His love. Even through my study so far, I have come to see Him and those around Him as real people. They are no longer people in an old, old story that I heard when I was a little girl. I hope through this study you too can get to know them on a personal basis as I have.

So here goes! I will limit my study to the parables that Jesus used in His ministry as we have it recorded in the four gospels. We know there were teachings He gave the disciples that were not told in the scriptures. Each writer mentioned this at one time or another; but John was very clear about this:

> (JOHN 21:25) "AND THERE ARE ALSO MANY OTHER THINGS THAT JESUS DID, WHICH IF THEY WERE WRITTEN ONE BY ONE, I SUPPOSE THAT EVEN THE WORLD ITSELF COULD NOT CONTAIN THE BOOKS THAT WOULD BE WRITTEN. AMEN."

I have learned that He also used a number of different literary tools in His speaking. The samples I have listed here are just that, 'samples', and not a complete list. All of these are from Matthew. There are many more in all four of the gospels, as well as the rest of the Bible where other speakers or writers used them.. (I have underlined the actual tool I am demonstrating):

PARALLELISM...(the state of being equally compared... by comparison when two or more sentence parts of equal rank are equally stated... Usually joined by a correlative conjunction) this tool often makes the sentence more clear.)

MATTHEW 13:13

"THEREFORE I SPEAK TO THEM IN PARABLES, BECAUSE SEEING THEY DO NOT SEE, AND HEARING THEY DO NOT HEAR, NOR DO THEY UNDERSTAND."

METAPHOR...(implied comparisons of things that are not basically alike, expressed without use of a comparing word such as "like" or "as")

MATTHEW 15:14

"LET THEM ALONE. THEY ARE BLIND LEADERS OF THE BLIND. AND IF THE BLIND LEADS THE BLIND, BOTH WILL FALL INTO THE DITCH."

SIMILE...(a figure of speech that makes a comparison between two things to exist between those things which ordinarily differ completely expressed with the use of a comparing word such as "like" or "as")

MATTHEW 13:47

"AGAIN, THE KINGDOM OF HEAVEN IS LIKE A DRAGNET THAT WAS CAST INTO THE SEA AND GATHERED SOME OF EVERY KIND."

PARADOX...(a statement that seems impossible but really founded on the truth)

MATTHEW 11:30

"FOR MY YOKE IS EASY AND MY BURDEN IS LIGHT."

HYPERBOLE…(statement or figure of speech that states much more or much less of the truth, for the sake of exaggeration)

MATTHEW 19:24

"AND AGAIN I SAY TO YOU, IT IS EASIER FOR A CAMEL TO GO THROUGH THE EYE OF A NEEDLE THAN FOR A RICH MAN TO ENTER THE KINGDOM OF HEAVEN."

SIMILTUDE…(the state of being alike or similar…a parable)

MATTHEW 5:14

"YOU ARE THE LIGHT OF THE WORLD. A CITY THAT IS SET ON A HILL CANNOT BE HIDDEN."

As you can see, we have worked our way right back to the parable, the most often used and most effective tool that a teacher or speaker has at hand. The truths that Jesus taught during His ministry are timeless in the sense of being universally true… but they are not timeless in the sense of being fully understandable out of their historical context. We can only totally see the absolute meaning that Jesus intended if we see the situation in which He presented His teachings. We must understand the words used as well as the events surrounding His words in order to get the depth of understanding He wanted His disciples to have. And we are His disciples for today's time.

Some times I think, "It would have been easier to be what I need to be if I could have lived then. If I could have walked with Him and talked to Him in the flesh, I could have understood it all." I know that is not the truth; it is probably easier now. I know the whole story. Those folks back then still had a lot to see. But either way, now or then; Jesus set pretty high standards for all of us; so we must dig and study to do the best we can.

It was my original idea to write this in a very formal and professional manner. I thought that more people might take it as a serious work. But somewhere along the way I have come to believe that since God chose me to do this, He must have wanted me to be in it. He apparently trusted me because I am me, so I should too. Anyway, it's much easier to speak as I would normally and not to have to worry about how I word something. I have enough trouble with spelling, much less wording. I do pray this is a blessing to you. And I do pray it is interesting enough to hold your attention. It certainly has been interesting to me thus far and I'll never be able to count the blessings I have already seen!

One of the things I have always believed is that a writer's emotions show in his work. If that is true you will want to read this a second or third time! All my heart and thoughts have been in this work since I began it (February 2010). I know that the work here is my own and that everyone will not agree with all I have to say. As much as I respect our pastor's education and life experiences to interpret the Word for us, sometimes I see something in a different light. Usually I can see his views too, so I seldom disagree with him, I just see an additional light. And I know that will happen with this project and those of you that might read it. I think that is all of us growing. I don't believe you are wrong and I am right, nor the other way round. I think we are learning, together. And I think that any work that makes us search in our heart for God's will for our life has to be good. I think He wants us to discuss and study; and I know He wants us to think about His word. Else He would never have given us the parables to ponder.

I think to learn we need ALL the information available. After that we can form opinions and develop knowledge and wisdom. With only bits of information we have only bits of opinions or worse yet, wrong opinions! If we base our eternal life on a few verses or a small amount of understanding we are taking a BIG chance on where we will spend our ETERNITY. We had certainly ought to pick the right few verses if that is what we think we can do. Now, I know I have said that my study on this has already shown me the "real men" and not the story-men I knew before, but thank God, I had the background and could add to that. I didn't start out completely blank and without hope. But in the process of trying to give you all the information you need for complete understanding (Now, wouldn't THAT be nice? To have complete understanding?) Well, in the steps toward that goal, I think to understand the words, we need to know the writers. After we know who, what, where, when and why of the men that wrote about Jesus, then perhaps, we can better know Jesus, The Man, as well as Jesus,

Our God. Therefore I am giving you a short biography of each writer. Referring to it occasionally during your study of the parables later might help you understand why a writer would word something in such a way as he does.

Each of the gospels shows a different form and style of the writer. Some of the authorities of Biblical study use symbols to represent the different men and their personalities. Matthew is presented as a Lion. That shows strength and royal authority. Mark is represented by the Bull, showing power and service. Luke is shown as a young man, standing for wisdom and compassion. And John's symbol is the regal Eagle, representing the Deity of God. I don't know where the symbols came from or who chose them, but in a small way they do tell us a bit about each man.

All four gospels depict Jesus as a Great Teacher. He was a Master at all the literary tools used to teach: poetry; metaphors; similes; paradoxes; as well as others. He used real historic events; He used the traditional story-telling methods; He used the narrative view, and He used dialogue. He told of miracles and other super-natural events. And He always spoke with authority, both the authority of true knowledge and the Authority of God.

So in addition to the fact of beautiful words, there is the undeniable truth of the story of Jesus told to us by four of His greatest earthly friends! The four gospels reflect both the style and standpoint of four very special men chosen by God to write His story and they show the teachings of God's only Son. By studying those teachings, we can't help but be closer to God. We will come much nearer to the person He wants us to be.

ABOUT THE FOUR WRITERS

MATTHEW

Matthew means Gift of the Lord / Levi means Joined.

Matthew Levi was a most disliked man in his day. His father was a man named Alphaeus, of the Levite family. His family name indicates he was probably well educated; at least in the Jewish laws. His chosen career made him extraordinarily disliked within his community. He worked for the Roman government as a tax collector. Tax collectors aren't really liked today but in those days, they had a lot of authority, above and beyond what we would accept today before we chased them out of town. Taxable areas, (townships- counties- states- etc) were franchised or sold to an individual. That man was responsible to turn in a certain amount of money to the Roman officials every year for ownership of the tax rights of that area. Anything else he could collect was his share. They had a pretty loose set of rules on how they collected or the amount they could name as "fair tax". No doubt, Matthew was a successful collector. He had an office; he didn't just work from his home or the local street corner. But the job he did for the Romans, made him hated by the Jews and just the fact that he was a Jew made him hated by the Romans.

His tax post was the city (or parts of the city) of Capernaum. Jesus had chosen Capernaum as His base town for His ministry. There are a number of possible reasons that would explain to us why He chose that area. It seems to have been the home of most of His disciples. It was a trade city with connections to the sea and trade routes across the land areas. It was the big city nearest His home in Nazareth. But right now, we are talking about Matthew and his life. I expect he was a very unhappy man. I think he had a family, but if people were then as they are today, I'd think his family was disliked too. That would make a man feel miserable, wouldn't it? But like us, today, he was probably sort of trapped by the financial need to keep that job and unhappy with the thought of it. I never had a job where the very nature of it encouraged me to take from others but I have certainly been in situations where I had to stay at a job I disliked, at least for a while. And to think that what I did for a living might have influenced people to dislike or mistreat my babies would have been nearly unbearable.

Apparently Matthew had been following Jesus' ministry and listening to a few of His "sayings" . He had been hearing what Jesus was teaching. And he realized the law was not enough to answer the needs in a man's heart. When Jesus walked by and called Matthew, he responded without delay or worry! There was no concern for his job or how he might earn a living. There was no question in his heart that this Man was the Prophecy fulfilled! He then gave a dinner party; we would call it, to introduce his new Friend to all his old acquaintances.

Bible scholars are not sure when Matthew wrote his gospel. There are a few verses saying things like 'to this day' and 'until this day' that are phrases that we would use to indicate some time had passed. And we think Matthew probably used those words in the same context. But there are phrases that indicate it was written before the fall of Jerusalem in AD70. Most authorities also believe that more than likely the book of Mark was written prior to Matthew and that Matthew used the book of Mark as a guide to write his work. That gives the idea that it was written somewhere between the years of AD58 and 68. Even though this book was written after Mark's was, those that put the Holy Bible together chose Matthew to be presented first. He had written the story that tied the Old Testament and the New Testament together. He bridged the four hundred years that was not mentioned by any of the prophets.

He was living in either Palestine or Syrian Antioch at the time he wrote it. In the *Ecclesiastical History* written by Eusebius (AD323) a statement by Papias (AD140) was quoted that said Matthew wrote 'sayings' in Aramaic. However, no gospel in Aramaic by Matthew has ever been found. Most Scholars do not believe that he ever wrote the whole gospel in any language other than Greek. He may have written shorter versions or chapters for specific people as time passed but it is accepted that Greek was the language of choice to reach the greater number of people.

The Christ that Matthew came to know, and tried to show his readers, was the Holy Christ. He was the Messianic King that had been promised since the beginning of time. Matthew used the words "the kingdom of heaven" over 30 times and it is used nowhere else in the New Testament that I have been able to find. Matthew quotes or refers to Old Testament scripture over one hundred twenty times to show that Jesus fulfills the qualifications to be the Messiah. The main point that Matthew continues to try to portray to his readers is that *Jesus is King*. This is a Jewish tax collector trying to convince a Jewish audience that the prophecies have been fulfilled!

There are several key verses within Matthew. One grouping is chapter 16:16-19. In these verses Peter recognizes Jesus for Who He is; "You are the Christ, the Son of the living God." And Jesus responds by recognizing Peter:

> *"YOU ARE PETER, AND ON THIS ROCK I WILL BUILD MY CHURCH..."*

There are other key thoughts expressed by Matthew and one of those is in Chapter 12. In this chapter the Pharisees and other leaders of the formal Jewish church rejected Jesus as the Messiah and accused Him of being from the Devil. At this point Jesus stepped up His ministry and began to show an increased importance to His teachings. He started to give more attention to the education of the disciples, both as a group and as individuals.

Some of the teachings that Matthew gave us are in the other gospels, along with others that Matthew did not cover. Each writer gives us his own version, or memory, of the separate teachings. It is an absolute that each writer was inspired by the Holy Ghost, so each version gives us something that we need to learn. I have no problem studying the different writers and knowing that each might tell the story a bit differently from another. For example, Matthew tells us that during the Sermon on the Mount, Jesus spoke of showing your faith to the world and not hiding it like a lamp under a basket (Matthew 5:14-16). Then in Mark (4:21-23), Jesus spoke of this same parable during a sermon from a boat at the edge of the sea. This is not an example of two writers using the same story to make their point; but it is an example of one Teacher using the same story to two different audiences. Any teacher that would teach the same lesson two times might do the same as Jesus did that day, word them just a bit differently.

The book of Matthew can be divided into several different themes. First, he tells the birth story of Jesus, or the presentation of the King. Next he proclaims Jesus is King and shows His power through examples of His works. At that point we read of the rejection of the King as it begins. His story then turns to the preparation of the disciples. Matthew then tells of the final rejection of the King and His death; and at last Matthew shows us proof that Jesus is King! And He is Alive! One of the most special characteristics of Matthew is that it shows the role we, as the Gentiles, will have in the kingdom of God. The story of the centurion (8: 5-13) is and should be a precious story to those of us not born to one of the chosen Israelite tribes. This story gives us, as non-Jews, the assurance of God's love, saying that we, too, can be children of God.

Matthew has become real to me. I can almost see him. I picture, not a big man, but an average sized person, Maybe about five feet ten inches tall and weighing about 180 pounds. In fact I see him as a neatly dressed man with intelligent brown eyes. He was Levite so he probably had facial hair but he kept it neatly clipped and combed. I see his skin tone as an olive tan, both from his birth and from his work taking him outside often. I see him at about forty to forty-five years old, so he was old enough to question some of the 'laws' but perhaps not old enough to find the answers yet. And we know he could not have found the answers without knowing Jesus. I see him as a man that has been prepared by God; both in his education and in the way that he has been treated by his fellow countrymen, to be ready to accept and recognize the Son of God. I see a man that was ready to be a true and loving disciple and a man that was chosen by God to later record the earthly life of His Son. Oh my, what an honor!

(Now, I hope you know that every word about his physical being that was just printed was from my wild imagination! It is just my way of making Matthew a person I can relate to. So you picture your own version of him but know that the words he quoted that we are going to study are from Jesus and as real as the grass on this earth!)

MARK

Mark means polite or shining / John means Yahweh has been gracious

Mark was known by his Latin name *Marcus*. He was also called by his Hebrew name of *John*. And in the book of Acts, he was called "John, with the surname of Mark". So actually we would call him John Mark today. He lived with his mom (Mary) in a big house in Jerusalem. They often had meetings there with the other believers. Peter was a close friend. And Mark was a cousin to Barnabas. He traveled with Paul and Barnabas on mission trips. Sometime during an early mission trip, he and Paul had a disagreement and they no longer traveled together. However, somehow, they ended up in jail together about twelve years later.

Most scholars believe that Mark wrote his gospel before any of the others were written. His has written the book that was the shortest and the simplest to read. We recently studied Mark as part of our Sunday School class and he very quickly became a favorite of mine! He is easy to read and he says what he means. He did not try to write his work as a piece of literature, but more as a historical fact. He was trying to tell exactly what happened during the earthly life of Jesus. His writing style leads me to believe he was less educated than Matthew or Luke. He was more of a down-to-earth ordinary man and he wrote his book for no other purpose other than people needed to know what he could tell them.

It is thought that Mark wrote this to a Roman audience. That would explain why he seldom made reference to the Jewish Laws. He did not mention Jewish customs or prophesies nearly as often as the other gospels. He knew that the Romans would not understand nor appreciate the importance of those references. Maybe that is one of the reasons that I, as a non-Jew, enjoy reading Mark so much. He used Latin terms more often than Greek or Hebrew. That again might be one reason he seems more familiar to me. I took Latin in school, but I certainly did not have any chance to study Greek or Hebrew.

There are some questions about the date it was written, it seems to be before the fall of Jerusalem in AD70 but it is believed to be after Peter was put to death; therefore, the range would be between AD55 and AD65

Mark told the story of Jesus by showing us a Man of action. He told of some of His discourses but more often, Mark told of His work: His miracles and His healings and His service. One of the key verses in Mark states his opinion of Jesus in as few words as possible:

> *"FOR EVEN THE SON OF MAN DID NOT COME TO BE SERVED, BUT TO SERVE, AND TO GIVE HIS LIFE AS A RANSOM FOR MANY."*

This was a quote from Jesus (Mark 10:45) but Mark carried that theme through out his book. Mark skipped the birth and early years of Jesus all together. He started his gospel with the beginning of Jesus' ministry. He followed the teachings and travels during the last three years of Jesus' life on this earth. As in Matthew, the key change in His ministry came when Peter declared that Jesus was the true Son of God (chapter 8). At this point Jesus intensified His teachings.

When you read the book of Mark it is easy to picture Jesus as a real person. I can't explain it exactly; but Mark makes Him seem so human…is that wrong for us to think? Is it disrespectful? Or does that make it easier to relate to Him? Mark shows Jesus' compassion and love. We see His pain and distress in the Garden and we see His determination to carry out His Father's wishes. It is a perfect example of how we SHOULD behave in times of stress and grief. And the fact that Mark makes Jesus appear more human is exactly <u>not</u> what Mark intended to do. It was his purpose to show Jesus as the Son of God. One of the key verses tells us clearly, (Mark 15:39) "Truly this Man was the Son of God!" as a quote of a Roman soldier, it shows us that even the Gentiles could recognize Jesus!

How do I see Mark? A young man, compared to Matthew, maybe in his mid to late twenties. His Mom was a believer and raised her son in the company of other believers. I picture him as a clean-shaven man of small build, full of energy, and always busy. Everything he did, he did in a hurry. You have known people like that. Just the fact that he used the word immediately more than 40 times in his work tells us that he put great store and value in the use of his time.

(Please do not forget that these ideas that I present concerning the physical and personal knowledge of these men is simply me and mine. I like to know who I am studying and if that is not possible, I use my God-given imagination to get to know them! You have one too, so use yours. Do what ever you need to do to make this a real experience that will help you understand the words of Jesus that these men have brought to us.)

LUKE

Luke means to give off light

Luke was a physician and writes much of his book as if he were an old family friend talking to young people. His compassion and warmth as a man shows through as he tells a family history to those that might not otherwise know it. Luke and Paul were close companions and traveled most of the mission trips together. Often we see them both in jail at the same time and place.(That's a fine way to describe their friendship, isn't it?)

It is believed that he was a Greek physician that had belonged to a Roman family as a slave and was freed at some point. Because he was a non-Jew,(and unlike Mark, who just skipped the problems of explaining the laws and traditions); he carefully <u>did</u> explain the Jewish faith to his Gentile audience. Scholars think he remained unmarried and was one of the very few disciples (though he was not of the original twelve) that died of natural causes at the age of eighty-four in Syrian Antioch.

Luke was not an eyewitness to the events he tells us about, but through his friendships with the witnesses, he has given us a very detailed account of the life of Jesus. He researched and investigated the testimonies of those that were witnesses to the events of Jesus' life. He carefully listened and studied and then told the story in chronological order. He gave details to the life of Jesus that is not available in any of the other gospels. That is proof of how well Luke interviewed so many people that had known Jesus in person. He was determined that his gospel be accurate as well as beautiful. His writings remind us of classic Greek literature. His style and form of writing was graceful and beautiful.

He wrote it for a specific person named Theophilus, whose name means Friend of God. His title as Most Excellent, indicates he was a man of high-standing, either political or financially. The book of Luke and the book of Acts were written as two parts to one book. It was separated later. It is believed that

Theophilus trusted Luke and trusted that he wrote the truth with the authority blessed by God. With that faith in Luke's work, Theophilus published both books so that the gospel would be available to the Greeks. It was probably written in the early AD60's.

Luke shows us the compassionate Man that identified with the sorrow of the sinful man. The key verses are found in chapter 15. The three parables told there express Jesus' need to let people know forgiveness is available to all God's children. We are assured in these stories that the purpose of Jesus' life here was to seek and save those lost to sin.

Luke tells his friend, Theophilus, (and us) that without Jesus, there can be no forgiveness. Jesus is the ONLY PERFECT sacrifice to be offered and accepted by God for the forgiveness of sin. Luke is the longest and most complete story of Christ among the gospels. Sections of it are probably among the most quoted verses when men of today decide to tell a part of Jesus' story.

Luke also emphasizes the work of the Holy Spirit, and tells of His importance as a part of the Trinity. He shows us that we cannot function as Christians without the help and support that He gives to us. And we don't have to try. He is ALWAYS there for us!

(Luke is a bit harder for me to picture. I guess that is a compliment to his work. When I read his book, I was thinking of the work, not the writer! I guess he can be a short version of Doc Adams on 'Gunsmoke'. Yes, that seems as good a picture as any for him. He would be comfortable to be around and more than willing to answer any question you could think of. I suppose I am picturing him as a kindly grandpa. So, in my mind, I like Luke, as a person, I just don't know what he looks like for sure. When I read Luke's gospel, I see pictures of the Christ child, the mother; as she loves her new baby; I visualize a new dad realizing the responsibility that has come to his shoulders: and then I watch the Young Man grow into His work and the love He has for the men that walked with Him. And I see the perfect example God meant for us to learn from. I see Jesus and His life, not Luke…he showed me what he set out to do…<u>Luke</u> <u>showed</u> <u>me</u> <u>Jesus!</u>

JOHN

John means Yahweh has been gracious

The book of John is written in a simple style that makes it easy to read and understand. The powerful language makes a statement of testimony from a man that was with Jesus during most of these events. John's work focuses on the theological meaning behind Jesus' actions. John was a Palestinian Jew, so he was familiar with all the Jewish traditions and laws that concerned Jesus. He was a true eyewitness so he could speak with the absolute authority of knowledge.

When John called himself 'the one Jesus loved', I first thought of it like I was hearing a young child say, "I'm my Mom's favorite." It endeared John to me beyond measure because we all want to be 'the favorite'. (I have always known I was my Daddy's favorite. But I know at least three of my sisters think they were his favorite… and my one brother, he thinks so too.) It is sort of sad for them because as the oldest, I know the truth. And John had those same feelings toward Jesus…

John was the last of the four gospels written, and since his other three letters (John I, John II, and John III) as well as the book of Revelation were written at an even later dates, it is assumed the dates for this book were somewhere between AD60 and AD90.

John wrote the strongest case of Jesus as a Deity. There was no question from his first words that Jesus Christ is the Son of God. John showed the Power of God with the miracles that Jesus performed. John (5: 30-40) told of the witness of John the Baptist and the witness of God to confirm Jesus as the Son of God.

The first verse… "The Word was God…" (1:1) and with the words… "The Word also became the flesh…" (1:14) it was John's total testimony that Jesus was sent to earth to tell us the entire total of all that God wanted said to us. As the "Word" in the flesh God spoke to us in the only way we could truly understand Him, through the life of Jesus.

John also showed us an intimate view of Jesus when he told us of His weariness (4:6) and His human need of thirst (4:7). With John we learn that Jesus could suffer the same disappointment(11:35) and loneliness (12:27) that we suffer…

The most quoted verse in the entire Bible is from the Gospel of John. From a child I was taught this verse as the base of all Christian faith. It shows the love of Christ as the only way to salvation. Nothing I can do or say, nothing I can think or desire can take me to the Kingdom of God; except the love of Jesus, as John 3:16 so clearly tells us. We must believe in Jesus, that's all! John specifically wrote his gospel to tell people about Jesus and to lead them to salvation. John spoke more of Jesus and His relationships with individuals than the other gospels did. He told of the works of Jesus. He spoke of the teachings of Jesus in a clear and informative way.

Some Biblical scholars say that there are no parables in John but there are two sets of verses that I have always been taught that are very basic parables. One of these, "The Good Shepherd" (10:1-18) is confirmed by the use of the word *parable* in the verse 10:6 (King James Version). Since I used that as my way of confirming some of the parables, I cannot now at this late date in my life begin to question the translation of the King James Version! And the second teaching I have included from John is the "The True Vine / Branches" (15:1-11). I cannot imagine studying parables and leaving that teaching out! It is the very essences of a parable! And it is essential to the teachings of Jesus. I have had a great deal of trouble trying to decide which teachings are really parables and which are some other figure of speech but these two in John, have not bothered my heart at all. Whatever one might call them, they are the words of Jesus and the messages are precious. And together, we will study them…call them *parable* or *teaching*. It simply does not matter to me!

I really do see John as a young man. He ran all the way to the tomb on Easter Sunday morning. That for sure would have to be a young man! He would have a ruddy complexion and a slim frame. His eyes would be dark and he probably was too young for a lot of facial hair. He was extremely intelligent to understand and be able to explain the theology behind words of Christ. It does seem strange to me that he quoted extensive discourses of Jesus, mostly longer and more detailed than any of the other gospels. He understood the teachings with a depth that was not matched by any one else, and yet, he seldom even mentioned the parables. He honored the commitment Jesus told us about in Matthew (28:18-20) to spread the gospel. The following quote sums John's purpose for writing his gospel:

> *"BUT THESE ARE WRITTEN THAT YOU MAY BELIEVE THAT JESUS IS THE CHRIST, THE SON OF GOD, AND THAT BELIEVING YOU MAY HAVE LIFE IN HIS NAME."*
> JOHN: 20: 31

WHY DID JESUS USE THE PARABLES?

I think one of the first things we need to look at...is why did Jesus use parables? We can look to that by reading His words when the disciples, more than confused, asked Him, "Why do You speak in parables?"

MATTHEW 13: 10-17

"AND THE DISCIPLES CAME AND SAID TO HIM, "WHY DO YOU SPEAK TO THEM IN PARABLES?" HE ANSWERED AND SAID TO THEM, *"BECAUSE IT HAS BEEN GIVEN TO YOU TO KNOW THE MYSTERIES OF THE KINGDOM OF HEAVEN, BUT TO THEM IT HAS NOT BEEN GIVEN. FOR WHOEVER HAS, TO HIM MORE WILL BE GIVEN, AND HE WILL HAVE ABUNDANCE; BUT WHOEVER DOES NOT HAVE, EVEN WHAT HE HAS WILL BE TAKEN AWAY FROM HIM. THEREFORE I SPEAK TO THEM IN PARABLES, BECAUSE SEEING THEY DO NOT SEE, AND HEARING THEY DO NOT HEAR, NOR DO THEY UNDERSTAND. AND IN THEM THE PROPHECY OF ISAIAH IS FULFILLED, WHICH SAYS:*

HEARING YOU WILL HEAR AND SHALL NOT UNDERSTAND, AND SEEING YOU WILL SEE AND NOT PERCEIVE; FOR THE HEARTS OF THIS PEOPLE HAVE GROWN DULL. THEIR EARS ARE HARD OF HEARING. AND THEIR EYES THEY HAVE CLOSED. LEST THEY SHOULD SEE WITH THEIR EYES AND HEAR WITH THEIR EARS. LEST THEY SHOULD UNDERSTAND WITH THEIR HEARTS AND TURN, SO THAT I SHOULD HEAL THEM. (ISAIAH 6: 9- 10)

BUT BLESSED ARE YOUR EYES FOR THEY SEE, AND YOUR EARS FOR THEY HEAR; FOR ASSUREDLY, I SAY TO YOU THAT MANY PROPHETS AND RIGHTEOUS MEN DESIRED TO SEE WHAT YOU SEE, AND DID NOT

SEE IT, AND TO HEAR WHAT YOU HEAR, AND DID NOT HEAR IT."

The disciples were very confused. It seemed to them (and me too) that you would think Jesus would speak very clearly to the crowds. It seems that it would be His goal that EVERY soul would understand every syllable He uttered. But Jesus, being considerably wiser than the disciples (or me...to be sure!) knew that no matter what He said or how He worded it, there would be many that could not or would not have any idea what He meant. There would be those that would mock His teachings and by their behavior would lead others to disbelief, rather than belief. Their laughter might shame those that were just beginning to see the truth of His words. So knowing that, lets try to break down the words here and see if we can understand His teaching.

First He tells the twelve that they have been chosen to receive the understanding they seek. The mysteries of the kingdom of heaven have always been just that until now. Very few were taught to read, and most of them were part of the Levite tribe. And even those that could read had very little access to books. The Bible consisted of the first few books of what we call the Old Testament. (Most authorities say it was the first five books only.) The only way it could be reproduced was to be hand-written. The copies that were in the temples were often chained to a speaker's podium in the building. That placed a mysterious aurora around the Word of God. The books were precious and dear.

The people heard it read in temple but don't you expect it was really hard to follow and comprehend like that? Today I seldom see our pastor read scripture that we, as the congregation, don't follow in our own Bibles. It is much easier to understand that way! Plus we all read on our own and are a little bit familiar with most any scripture that our pastor might choose to speak about. Those people back then did not have that luxury. So it is easy for me to imagine that the Word was a true mystery to them. Jesus knew that it was time that people understood the spirit of the word as well as the words themselves; but He knew that there were people that were not ready yet. He knew that if He gave them the meaning of the words they would use it and twist it. He knew that so many misunderstanding that He was Truly the Son of God, and not believing He was the prophesied Messiah, would mock and reject everything He tried to teach.

He told us in the Sermon on the Mount (Matthew 7:6) to be aware of giving anything Holy to those not ready to accept it. Those that are not willing to admit they are sinners are far more likely to resent some one telling them that they are. We have the responsibility to warn them of their need for God's love and forgiveness but if they reject us at that point, there is no purpose in continuing the conversation that day. Jesus did not want to force them to take a stand with the frame of mind they had then. But He planted a seed… and He would give it time to grow.

As a Teacher, Jesus was also what we call today, a Student of human nature. He was aware that there were members in any crowd that heard Him that could understand what He was saying. They were listening with a heart that had been softened by the Holy Spirit. They were ready to recognize Him and His love. They were ready to accept more and a deeper knowledge of God's will. And He wanted to share that with them, without opening Himself or His teachings to ridicule; so parables were the answer to that.

Those that listened with their heart would learn more of what Jesus felt they needed to know. Those that did not understand would just simply not understand. There was nothing there they could question or make fun of! One cannot argue with a story about spreading seeds in the garden (as in Parable #1 "The Sower"). In the scripture Jesus quoted we can see that Isaiah prophesied this attitude of the people toward Jesus hundreds of years earlier. In Matthew 13:17, Jesus blessed the disciples with the gift of understanding. And that blessing holds true for us today if we are honestly seeking His wisdom for the purpose of spreading the gospel!

MATTHEW 13:34-35

"ALL THESE THINGS JESUS SPOKE TO THE MULTITUDE IN PARABLES; AND WITHOUT A PARABLE HE DID NOT SPEAK TO THEM, THAT IT MIGHT BE FULFILLED WHICH WAS SPOKEN BY THE PROPHET, SAYING:

"I WILL OPEN MY MOUTH IN PARABLES; I WILL UTTER THINGS KEPT SECRET FROM THE FOUNDATION OF THE WORLD." (EPH. 3:9)

One of the things we need to pay attention to right now, is that any quotes accredited to Jesus from the Prophets and scriptures, is not ever an exact quote like you or I would do if we were quoting scripture (Proverbs 30:6). This is something we will be seeing throughout this work. Any one quoting God's Word would not dare to misquote a single word. But when Jesus quoted someone, He gave the essences of the meaning, not necessarily an exact quote. And He did not use the phrase "Thus says the Lord" like anyone else would have. (Remember when we studied the Prophets; they spoke with God's authority and <u>exactly</u> as it had been spoken to them). Jesus did not have to acknowledge the authority of God in His speech. He was and is the authority of God! When He quoted someone, He gave the essences of the meaning but the words may or may not be an exact quote.

MARK 4:10-12

"BUT WHEN HE WAS ALONE, THOSE AROUND HIM WITH THE TWELVE ASKED HIM ABOUT THE PARABLE. AND HE SAID TO THEM, *"TO YOU IT HAS BEEN GIVEN TO KNOW THE MYSTERY OF THE KINGDOM OF GOD; BUT TO THOSE WHO ARE OUTSIDE, ALL THINGS COME IN PARABLES, SO THAT 'SEEING THEY MAY SEE AND NOT PERCIEVE, AND HEARING THEY MAY HEAR AND NOT UNDERSTAND, LEST THEY SHOULD TURN AND THEIR SINS BE FORGIVEN THEM." (ISAIAH 6:9-10)*

I think one of the things we might consider while we are trying to understand these words is: the crowds would have been made up of all peoples in the area: Jewish farmers, political officials, Roman soldiers, townsmen, visitors from other cultures, a large variety of people. And this variety would have included gentiles and pagans. (That sounds like a bunch of today's motorcycle groups, doesn't it?) Jesus was there at that point of His ministry to speak to the Jews. It was His goal, right then to bring the Jewish community back into fellowship with God. Later He did include the rest of the world of people, but at first He was trying to reach the Jewish nation.

MARK 4: 21-25

"ALSO HE SAID TO THEM, *"IS A LAMP BROUGHT TO BE PUT UNDER A BASKET OR UNDER A BED? IS IT NOT TO BE SET ON A LAMP STAND? FOR THERE IS NOTHING HIDDEN WHICH WILL NOT BE REVEALED,*

NOR HAS ANYTHING BEEN KEPT SECRET BUT THAT IT SHOULD COME TO LIGHT. IF ANYONE HAS EARS TO HEAR, LET HIM HEAR." THEN HE SAID TO THEM, *"TAKE HEED WHAT YOU HEAR. WITH THE SAME MEASURE YOU USE, IT WILL BE MEASURED TO YOU; AND TO YOU WHO HEAR, MORE WILL BE GIVEN. FOR WHOEVER HAS, TO HIM MORE WILL BE GIVEN; BUT WHOEVER DOES NOT HAVE, EVEN WHAT HE HAS WILL BE TAKEN AWAY FROM HIM."*

In these verses Jesus tells us that the mysteries of the Kingdom of God will be revealed to those that listen. <u>There is nothing that we need to know, or want to know, that He will not show us if we truly seek the answers.</u>

He does not want us to walk in ignorance but to walk with wisdom and knowledge! But Jesus warns us in these verses that we are to be careful how we listen, and to what we listen. If we misunderstand or misinterpret or even worse, choose to alter what we hear to suit our own needs when we are looking at someone else; well, rest assured that those are the same terms God will use when He looks upon our deeds! If we seek that knowledge with a pure heart, God will make more available to us; but if we seek knowledge for a selfish benefit for ourselves, or for harm to someone else; it seems to me, He is promising here to take what good sense you thought you had away! (Not that you had much to begin with if you tried to pull such a stunt.)

MARK 4: 33-34

"AND WITH MANY SUCH PARABLES HE SPOKE THE WORD TO THEM, AS THEY WERE ABLE TO HEAR IT. BUT WITHOUT A PARABLE HE DID NOT SPEAK TO THEM. AND WHEN THEY WERE ALONE, HE EXPLAINED ALL THINGS TO HIS DISCIPLES."

Jesus wanted His disciples to get the tiniest syllable of understanding of His teachings. So He often explained the parables to them when they were alone. He was training them from the beginning of His ministry to carry on after He was back in heaven. Even though they had not the slightest idea that He would be leaving them, He knew. And it was His plan to have them prepared to teach the world of that day and of the future. There would only be the twelve of them to start and spread to truth of the gospel for that day and for every day of the future. The responsibility was heavy! They needed <u>all</u> the understanding they could possibly have.

JOHN 3:12

"IF I HAVE TOLD YOU EARTHLY THINGS AND YOU DO NOT BELIEVE, HOW WILL YOU BELIEVE IF I TELL YOU HEAVENLY THINGS?"

Such a simple question that Jesus asked in this verse! If the people He was teaching could not learn from the stories that were facts of nature, how could they ever understand things that were of a spiritual realm? Things of nature are just facts that we only have to watch to know the truth. But thoughts of an inner spiritual knowledge can only be accepted by faith and trust of the One giving us the message. This simple question is the basis of all His teaching! It must be answered before we can proceed any further. So look deep in your heart and answer this question with prayer. Then we (you and I) can continue this study.

JOHN 20:30-31

"AND TRULY JESUS DID MANY OTHER SIGNS IN THE PRESENCE OF HIS DISCIPLES, WHICH ARE NOT WRITTEN IN THIS BOOK; BUT THESE ARE WRITTEN THAT YOU MAY BELIEVE THAT JESUS IS CHRIST, THE SON OF GOD, AND THAT BELIEVING YOU MAY HAVE LIFE IN HIS NAME."

These parables were written that <u>we</u> might believe that Jesus is Christ, the Son of God and that <u>we</u> might understand His will more completely!

Introduction:
PARABLES AND COMMENTARIES

At this point of my study I have decided there are 46 parables to include in this project. One thing for sure I have discovered is that everyone has a different opinion on that! I have found from 39 to 59 on different lists. Some were separated that I think should be one. Some were neglected that I think need to be mentioned. In other words, I don't think anyone knows for sure how to count them or list them. Some had a title that was entirely different from another man's version. And the verses that were used for each one were all different! For example 'The Seed' might be called 'The Man's Garden' by another authority. And the verses might be 1-3 on one and 3-10 on the other! All are the words of Jesus, that part is consistent. And they all need our attention. So if I have listed some that you disagree with, that's all right. We will study it as words of Our Christ, and we will know those words are among the things that He wanted us to learn!

All scripture quotations are from the New King James Version, *The Open Bible.* I used that because it is both, the nearest to the original King James Version that I could find and the closest to the language we use today. There is no purpose in trying to understand the parable if we are fighting with the use of a word such as *thee* or *thou*. This was the first place I had a tough decision to make, so it was the first place I had to trust my instincts or the judgment of the Holy Spirit. (I think, or at least I certainly hope that my instincts and the Holy Spirit are one and the same!) This project would not have even gotten started if I had not made a decision of some sort.

The second decision I needed was to determine which verses in the Bible are parables. I used several different ways to make those decisions. The first was if, in the Holy Bible (King James Version) the word *parable* was used either by Jesus or by the writer in describing the verses, then that was one I later will call *Confirmed.* A second method I used was if the set of verses in question appeared on all the lists I found in my resources, then I agreed and used them. The third way was if the set of verses were generally accepted by most people (including my Mama and my pastor)as a parable, then I included it.

The last decision that I had to make before I could start this work was the order of presentation of the parables. I did that by use of the word *parable* too. According to the number of times the word was confirmed in the different books became the rank of the story. There are none of the parables more important than another, but somehow one had to be listed first. I have asked the Holy Spirit for guidance, the best I know to do now, is trust Him.

PARABLE SCRIPTURES

TITLE	MATTHEW	MARK	LUKE	JOHN
1-THE SOWER	13:1-9 13:18-23 confirmed	4:1-9 4:13-20 confirmed	8:4-8 8:11-15 confirmed	
2--WICKED TENANTS	21:33-46 confirmed	12:1-12 confirmed	20:9-19 confirmed	
3-THE FIG TREE	24:32-44 confirmed	13:28-37 confirmed	21:29-36 confirmed	
4-MUSTARD SEED	13:31-32 confirmed	4:30-32 confirmed	13:18-19	
5-INTO/OUT OF MOUTH	15:10-20 confirmed	7:14-23 confirmed		
6-PATCHED GARMENTS & NEW WINE-SKINS	9:14-17	2:18-22	5:33-39 confirmed	
7-HOUSE DIVIDED	12:24-32	3:22-30 confirmed	11:14-23	
8-SPECK IN EYE	7:1-5		6:37-42 confirmed	
9-LEAVEN	13:33 confirmed		13:20-21	
10-LOST SHEEP LOST COIN	18:10-14		15:1-15 confirmed	
11-MARRIAGE FEAST / GREAT SUPPER	22:1-14 confirmed		14:15-24	
12-TEN TALENTS	25:14-30		19:11-27 confirmed	
13-WHEAT & TARES	13:24-30 13:36-43 confirmed			
14-HIDDEN TREASURE	13:44 confirmed			
15-PEARL OF VALUE	13:45-46 confirmed			

TITLE	MATTHEW	MARK	LUKE	JOHN
16-DRAGNET	13:47-50 confirmed			
17 HOUSE-HOLDER	13:51-52 confirmed			
18-RICH FARMER			12:13-21 confirmed	
19-BARREN FIG TREE			13:1-9 confirmed	
20-AMBITIOUS GUEST			14:7-11 confirmed	
21-WIDOW & JUDGE			18:1-8 confirmed	
22-PHARISEES & TAX COLL-ECTOR			18:9-14 confirmed	
23-GOOD SHEPHERD				10:1-18 confirmed
24-SALT	5:13	9:49-50	14:34-35	
25-THE LAMP	5:14-16	4:21-25	8:16-18	
26-THE PHTSICIAN	9:10-13	2:15-17	5:29-32	
27-TREASURERS OF THE HEART	6:19-21		12:33-34	
28-GOOD FATHER	7:7-11		11:9-13	
29-GOOD FRUIT BAD FRUIT	7:15-20		6:43-45	
30-TWO HOUSES ON ROCK & SAND	7:24-37		6:46-49	
31-FAITH AS A MUSTARD SEED	17:18-21		17:56	

TITLE	MATTHEW	MARK	LUKE	JOHN
32-FAITHFUL AND WISE STEWARD	24:45-51		12:35-40	
33-PROFANING THE HOLY	7:6			
34-UNMERCIFUL SERVANT / INSOLVENT DEBTOR	18:21-25			
35-LABORERS IN VINEYARD	20:1-16			
36-TWO SONS	21:28-32			
37-TEN VIRGINS	25:1-13			
38-GROWING SEED		4:26-29		
39-TWO DEBTORS			7:36-50	
40-GOOD SAMARITAN			10:25-37	
41-MIDNIGHT FRIEND			11:5-8	
42-COST OF TOWER/ WAR			14:25-33	
43-PRODIGAL SON			15:11-32	
44-UNJUST STEWARD			16:1-13	
45-RICH GLUTTON & LAZARUS			16:19-31	
46-TRUE VINE & BRANCHES				15:1-11

1- THE SOWER

MATTHEW 13:1-9 (Confirmed)

Sermon by the Sea. Taught to the Multitudes

"On the same day Jesus went out of the house and sat by the sea. And great multitudes were gathered together to Him. So that He got into a boat and sat; and the whole multitude stood on the shore. Then He spoke many things to them in parables saying: *"Behold, a sower went out to sow. And as he sowed, some seed fell by the wayside; and the birds came and devoured them. Some fell on stony places, where they did not have much earth; and they immediately sprang up because they had no depth of earth. But when the sun was up, they were scorched, and because they had no root they withered away. And some fell among thorns, and the thorns sprang up and choked them. But others fell on good ground and yielded a crop: some a hundredfold, some sixty, some thirty. He who has ears to hear, let him hear!"*

MARK 4:1-9 (Confirmed)

Sermon by the Sea. Taught to the Multitudes

"And again He began to teach by the sea. And a great multitude was gathered to Him, so that He got into a boat and sat in it on the sea; and the whole multitude was on the land facing the sea. Then He taught them many things by parables, and said to them in His teaching: *"Listen! Behold, a sower went out to sow. And it happened, as he sowed, that some seed fell by the wayside; and the birds of the air came and devoured it. Some fell on stony ground, where it did not have much earth, and immediately it sprang up because it had no depth of earth. But when the sun was up it was scorched, and because it had no root it withered away. And some seed fell among thorns; and the thorns grew up and choked it, and it yielded no crop. But other seed fell on good ground and yielded a crop that sprung up, increased and produced, some thirty fold, some sixty, and some a hundred."* And He said to them, *"He who has ears to hear, let him hear!"*

LUKE 8:4-8 (Confirmed)

Place unknown. Taught to the Multitudes

"And when a great multitude had gathered, and they had come to Him from every city, He spoke by a parable: *"A sower went out to sow his seed. And as he sowed, some fell by the wayside; and it was trampled down, and the birds of the air devoured it. Some fell on rock; and as soon as it sprang up, it withered away because it lacked moisture. And some fell among thorns, and the thorns sprang up with it and choked it. But others fell on good ground, sprang up and yielded a crop a hundredfold."* When He had said these things, He cried, *"He who has ears to hear, let him hear!"*

The following verses are Jesus' own words of interpretation of this parable. These verses were spoken to the disciples when they were alone with Jesus.

MATTHEW 13:18-23

"Therefore hear the parable of the sower. When anyone hears the word of the kingdom, and does not understand it, then the wicked one comes and snatches away what was sown in his heart. This is he who received seed by the wayside. But he who received the seed on stony places, this is he who hears the word and immediately receives it with joy; yet he has no root in himself, but endures only for a while. For when tribulation or persecution arises because of the word, immediately he stumbles. Now he who received seed among the thorns is he who hears the word, and the cares of this world and the deceitfulness of riches choke the word, and he becomes unfruitful. But he who received seed on the good ground is he who hears the word and understands it, who indeed bears fruit and produces: some a hundredfold, some sixty, some thirty."

MARK 4:13-20

"And He said to them, "Do you not understand this parable? How then will you understand all the parables? The sower sows the word. And these are the ones by the wayside where the word is sown. When they hear, Satan comes immediately and takes away the word that was sown in their hearts. These likewise are the ones sown on stony ground who, when they hear the word,

immediately receive it with gladness; and they have no root in themselves, and so endure only for a time. Afterward when tribulation or persecution arises for the word's sake, immediately they stumble. Now these are the ones sown among thorns; they are the ones who hear the word, and the cares of this world, the deceitfulness of riches, and the desires for other things entering in choke the word, and it becomes unfruitful. But these are the ones sown on good ground, those who hear the word, accept it and bear fruit; some thirty fold, some sixty, and some a hundred."

EXTRA READING

GENESIS 26:12	JEREMIAH 4:3	LUKE 11:28
LUKE 21:34	JAMES 1:18	I PETER 1:22-23

Matthew and Mark tell us that Jesus and the twelve were down by the sea when a crowd began to gather around them. Luke does not tell us exactly where they were but he does tell us that the twelve, with Jesus, had been traveling and visiting several cities and villages in the area. A crowd began to gather about them. As Matthew explains to us, the crowd became massive, so Jesus got into a small boat at the edge of the water and the people crowded to the edge of the sea to hear what He had to say. After all had settled down, Jesus began to tell a story. Of course you realize that people will stay and listen to a story much quicker than they will stay and listen to someone preaching at them.

It appeared from the first words to be a simple story that everyone could relate to...a story about a farmer planting his crops. In times then or in today's time, we all can still relate to a story like that. It would not matter if you were a big commercial landlord or a poor tenant farmer or a widow lady with a small kitchen garden. A story concerning planting seeds to grow into food for our table is a story we all would pause from our busy lives to listen to.

We need a little background for the story to be as clear for us as it was for them. As we know the farmers then did not have the equipment (motorized tractors with monster plows) that we have today. So they farmed a bit differently. They scattered their seed by hand pretty thick and as even as possible over the field that had been cleared of rocks and clutter. Then they plowed it under, usually with hand-held plows. Of course that meant there was a lot of wasted seed. I remember seeing my Daddy do what he called *broadcasting* his tender green seeds. (This was a mixture of turnip, mustard, and collard seed). I picture this as what those farmers in the story did. Daddy did it so that he could have a thicker crop. The thicker growth prevented the ground from drying so bad between the tiny plants. Plus this was a better use of the land. As the young greens were pulled, it left room for the turnips to grow their roots. When they were pulled, it made room for the collards to form big heads. I suspect that was some of the goals the farmers had back then too.

Another thing we need to think of while we listen to the story is that the seed itself was different then than today. We run down to the local Feed & Seed and buy the seed we need. And someone has figured a formula to tell us exactly how much is needed to produce the length of row wanted. And the seed we buy has been treated to be more productive and to resist bugs. In other words if we need ten seeds for the job, we buy ten seeds. Back then the only place the farmer got his seed was to save it from the crops of the year before. That meant that a portion of his crop had to be grown for the purpose of going to seed. And that meant that the seed he had was just what nature made it...no better...no less. From my gardening days of trying to save seed, I learned real quick that if I wanted ten plants, I probably needed fifty to one hundred seeds! I figured it was cheaper to buy the seed! To let that much of my crop go to seed and then try to store it over the winter took some effort! But the farmer then did not have that option. His seed was precious. So now, we can get back to Jesus and the story He was telling the crowd.

He told of the farmer that had prepared his land and began to scatter the seed on the field. As he tossed the seeds, of course, some of it went off to the edges of the field and fell on unprepared dirt. Then, as today, the birds seem to know when the seeds are being thrown out. They celebrated Spring with the readily available meal. They needed the easy food to raise their babies I guess. That is just a fact that goes with Spring planting. In fact my Daddy had a saying that went with planting his garden. As he tossed each handful of seed out, he counted:

"ONE FOR THE RABBIT; ONE FOR THE CROW; ONE FOR THE GOPHER, AND ONE TO GROW."

So as Jesus told this parable, I think He knew Daddy's saying. But He continued on with His story and told of the seed that fell on the rocky paths around the garden. Because the warm sunshine heated that bit of dirt on the stones faster, those seeds just seemed to jump out of the ground into tiny tender plants. But the very reason that made them sprout so quickly was the very reason they died off just as fast. There was not enough dirt to support the life they had started. They had sprouted so fast that they had not developed a root and there was no moisture in the bit of earth that covered the stones.

Then Jesus reminded us that some seeds would fall where the thorns were growing. Anyone that has ever tried to grow a garden knows the hardest part of its' survival is keeping the weeds out. The thorns and weeds that grow wild are the strongest plants in any geographic area. They have adapted to the soil and weather completely and you cannot kill them. You will loose some of your crop to them. And yet, in spite of all the difficulties planting and growing a garden, it is worth the effort. A few good seeds will fall where they should. A few seeds grow into the plants you want, and they are productive. Those few provide food for your family for the year and give seeds for the following year. Jesus tells us that some of that good seed produces up to thirty times its worth; and some sixty times, and some even up to one hundred times. That is good seed!' But at the end of this parable, Jesus says something a bit strong and maybe a bit harsh for this simple story. He warns all listening,

"HE WHO HAS EARS TO HEAR, LET HIM HEAR!"

At this point all three of the gospels indicate that the crowd broke up and left Jesus alone with the twelve. The disciples realized that the story was more than a simple story for the people and they began to question Jesus. They wondered aloud 'why' Jesus would speak in parables to the people and what could this parable mean, other than being a story about how to plant your crops successfully. They are confused and wondered why Jesus would tell a parable rather than speak in a manner that might be easier to understand. Jesus answered their questions in Matthew 13:10-17. I gave those verses earlier in our study and we discussed them then. Jesus knew that there would be some people in the crowd that would understand that His story was about things of a spiritual nature more than agriculture advice. And He knew there would be those in the crowd that would mock Him and anything He had to say, no matter what it was about. He chose to speak in parables so that those who heard the true meaning could grow in His truths but that those that would reject Him would not have the truth to mock. In other words, He did not cast His pearls before swine, which is one of His parables that we will study later (Parable #33 "Profaning the Holy"). But Jesus was concerned from the beginning of His Ministry that the disciples should understand every word. Since this was at the first of His ministry He carefully explained this parable to the twelve. He wanted them to have the depth of understanding they would need to be effective teachers that could spread the gospel after His time here was over.

He explained to them that the seed is the word of God. The seed is the gospel. When it is thrown out to the people some will hear and not understand it at all. That is the neighbor you invite to services with you Sunday morning; and he laughs and tells you he already has plans to sleep in that morning. The Word does not ever reach his heart before Satan comes and snatches it away. That is the seed that fell by the wayside and was eaten by the birds.

The seeds that fall on the warm rocky soil are those that hear the Word and are excited by the truths they hear. They are the people in today's time that attend a revival or a Sunday Worship on Easter morning and recognize the excitement that fellow Christians are celebrating. They feel the warmth and love of Christ from the Believers sitting around them. They want to be a part of that. They KNOW they need that fellowship in their life. And their heart is filled with the joy of Christian love! But after church that day, they go back to their life and get too busy to tend to the new plant that has sprouted in their heart. They have no *Root* to support them and they don't have time to go back to the Church to seek support. Like the plant that had no moisture, they don't seek the life-giving Word. They don't seek the nurturing the church family would have given them. They don't feel like they need any help. The first time anything or anybody questions their faith, it disappears. The joy is gone.

The person that hears the truth and welcomes it into his life and then takes that tender new plant out into the world and tries to live with it there, is bound to loose it to the cares and pleasures of the world. The things that tempt the new Christian in the world cannot live beside the will of God. This person cannot have both, the old ways he lived before, and the new life Jesus has offered. To live your life with Jesus has to be a complete commitment and this person, being choked by the thorns and temptations will not survive as a child of God without the strength and support of fellowship and love from other Christians.

And then, there are the few good seeds that fall on good soil and that manage to live in spite of the birds, no life giving moisture, and in spite of the thorns; they live and flourish. Those are the people that hear and understand God's Word and His Will. Those are the ones that learn and try to live God's will. They spread the gospel by telling others and by living in a way that shows God in their life. Those are the people that are proud to be God's children and do their best to lead others into the fold. Some of these folk will lead thirty fold to Jesus, some sixty; and some a hundred fold! Jesus is telling us here that He expects us to produce a crop according to our own ability. He did not set a certain amount as necessary. He did not say every seed would have to produce a hundred fold to be a 'good seed.' He wants each seed to do its best work, and that is 'good' enough! So do whatever is your best work!

Then there was the warning Matthew and Mark quoted. I am sure some people thought things like, "Of course I can hear Him" and others, "Why do I want to hear Him?" But Jesus was telling them and us, that He wanted us to hear not just the words He spoke. He wanted everyone to hear the spirit of the words. He was warning all of us that to hear the spirit is most important to our Christian life! The words are important but the spirit is essential to our Christian growth.

I like the wording Luke used to end this parable when he quoted Jesus:

> "...THOSE WHO HAVING HEARD THE WORD WITH A NOBLE AND GOOD HEART, KEEP IT AND BEAR FRUIT WITH PATIENCE."

Jesus sums up the meaning of His warning with this simple statement. Those that do hear the Spirit of the words in their heart will produce the crop He is looking for from them

2- WICKED TENANTS

MATTHEW 21: 33-46 (Confirmed)

Taught in Jerusalem to the multitude and the Pharisees

"Hear another parable: there was a certain landowner who planted a vineyard and set a hedge around it, dug a winepress in it and built a tower. And he leased it to vinedressers and went into a far country. Now when vintage-time drew near, he sent his servants to the vine-dressers, that they might receive its fruit. And the vinedressers took his servants, beat one, killed one, and stoned another. Again he sent other servants, more than the first, and they did likewise to them. Then last of all he sent his son to them, saying, 'They will respect my son.' But when the vinedressers saw the son, they said among themselves, 'This is the heir. Come let us kill him and seize his inheritance.' So they took him, and cast him out of the vineyard and killed him. Therefore, when the owner of the vineyard comes, what will he do to those vinedressers?" They said to Him, "He will destroy those wicked men miserably, and lease his vineyard to other vinedressers who will render to him the fruits in their seasons." Jesus said to them, *"Have you never read in the Scriptures:*

THE STONE WHICH THE BUILDERS REJECTED HAS BECOME THE CHIEF CORNERSTONE. THIS WAS THE LORD'S DOING. AND IT IS MARVELOUS IN OUR EYES' (Psalms 118: 22- 23)

Therefore I say to you, the kingdom of God will be taken from you and given to a nation bearing the fruits of it. And whoever falls on this stone will be broken; but on whomever it falls, it will grind him to powder." Now when the chief priests and Pharisees heard His parables, they perceived that He was speaking of them. But when they sought to lay hands on Him, they feared the multitudes, because they took Him for a prophet."

MARK12: 1-12 (Confirmed)

Taught in Jerusalem to the multitude and the Pharisees

"Then He began to speak to them in parables: *"A man planted a vineyard and set a hedge around it, dug a place for the wine vat and built a tower. And he leased it to vine dressers and went into a far country. Now at vintage-time he sent a servant to the vinedressers, that he might receive some of the fruit of the vineyard from the vinedressers. And they took him and beat him and sent him away empty-handed. Again he sent them another servant, and at him they threw stones, wounded him in the head, and sent him away shamefully treated. And again he sent another, and him they killed; and many others, beating some and killing some. Therefore still having one son, his beloved, he also sent him to them last, saying, They will respect my son.' But those vinedressers said among themselves, 'This is the heir. Come let us kill him, and the inheritance will be ours.' So they took him and killed him and cast him out of the vineyard. Therefore what will the owner of the vineyard do? He will come and destroy the vinedressers, and give the vineyard to others. Have you not even read this Scripture:*

'THE STONE WHICH THE BUILDERS REJECTED HAS BECOME THE CHIEF CORNERSTONE. THIS WAS THE LORD'S DOING. AND IT IS MARVELOUS IN OUR EYES' (PSALMS 118:22-23)

And they sought to lay hands on Him, but feared the multitude, for they knew He had spoken the parable against them. So they left Him and went away."

LUKE 20:9-19 (Confirmed)

Taught in the Temple in Jerusalem to all present there, some authorities think on Tuesday of the last week

"Then He began to tell the people this parable: *A certain man planted a vineyard, leased it to vinedressers, and went into a far country for a long time. Now at vintage-time he sent a servant to the vinedressers, that they might give him some of the fruit of the vineyard. But the vinedressers beat him and sent him away empty-handed. Again he sent another servant; and they beat him also, treated him shamefully, and sent him away empty-handed. And again he sent a third; and they wounded him also and cast him out. Then the owner of the vineyard said, 'What shall I do? I will send my beloved son. Probably they will respect him when they see him.' But when the vinedressers saw him, they reasoned among themselves, saying, 'This is the heir. Come, let us kill him, that the inheritance may be ours.' So they cast him out of the vineyard and killed him. Therefore what will the owner of the vineyard do to them? He will come and destroy those vinedressers and give the vineyard to others.*" And when they heard it they said, "Certainly not!" Then He looked at them and said, "*What then is this that is written:*

THE STONE WHICH THE BUILDERS REJECTED HAS BECOME THE CHIEF CORNERSTONE. ? (PSALMS 118: 22-23)

Whoever falls on that stone will be broken: but on whomever it falls, it will grind him to powder." And the chief priests and the scribes that very hour sought to lay hands on Him, but they feared the people – for they knew He had spoken this parable against them

EXTRA READING

I SAMUEL 12: 22	II CHRONICLES 36:16	ISAIAH 8: 14-15
DANIEL 2:44	LUKE 13:28	ACTS 2:23
HEBREW 1:1-2		

Jesus told this parable within the walls of Jerusalem, according to Luke (9:1) in the Temple. He was speaking to the crowds as well as to the Pharisees and His disciples. Sometimes knowing who He was speaking to gives you additional understanding of the parable. This is one of those cases. It was also taught during the Last Week, again, according to some authorities, on Tuesday of that week.

A wealthy man in the area acquired a good piece of land. He was a wise landowner and knew that for the land to be profitable, it needed working. So he tended it and prepared it. He then placed a hedge around it. That's sort of like us putting a fence around our property today. After that he planted grape vines and built the facilities needed to care for the crops. It then was his responsibility to find and hire the best vinedressers he could. He searched for experienced men. He wanted to trust those men so he looked for those that were familiar with the art of raising and processing grape products. Don't you imagine that men of that quality were the sons of men that had been vinedressers? He expected these men he hired to care for and produce a profitable crop from his investment. Satisfied that he had accomplished his goal, he went away and left the men he had hired in charge.

When harvest time came the landowner sent his servant to collect a small portion of the crop for his personal use. All three of the gospels tell us that at least one servant was sent and Matthew indicates that there were several servants sent that first trip. Either way, one or several, the vinedressers beat and stoned the servant(s) and sent them back empty-handed.

The landowner then sent stronger servants and their fate was the same as the first. They were killed or beaten and returned home with no sign of any profit from the vineyard for the landowner. According to the different gospels this was repeated a number of times. The landowner kept sending those to collect a bit of the crop. The scriptures never indicate at all that he was demanding all of the profit...only some of it for his own use. Finally he decided that in order to collect any of the profit he would send his son. Remember now, he had chosen carefully those that he had left in charge of his vineyard. He trusted them to care for it and make it profitable. He felt like they would respect his son as his representative and would treat him with the honor they would have given him if he had made the trip.

Unfortunately, the vinedressers did not treat this man's only son with respect and honor. Instead they thought that if he were dead then they could own the vineyard since the landowner had no more sons to inherit the land. So they killed the landowner's beloved son.

At this point Jesus asked those in the crowd to tell Him what the landowner should do. He wanted to know how the landowner should react to this horror that he had suffered at the hands of those he had thought he could trust.

All three gospels give the same response. The crowd (including Pharisees and the other elders) said that the landowner should come and destroy those vinedressers and give the vineyard to others. There was no doubt that those vinedressers needed to be destroyed. And there was no question but that the vineyard needed to be put in the care of other workers.

After the crowds had responded to Jesus' question, He then asked them had they not read the scripture concerning the rejected stone that became the cornerstone. He said that this was God's work and it was beautiful. He also gave them a very serious warning in reference to the stone. But before we study that, lets go back and try to understand the story He was telling that day.

As I understand this parable, the man or landowner was God. The vineyard was the kingdom of God. He carefully prepared and put things in order when He created it all. He then looked about and found the family that had been most faithful in their respect and love for Him. That family was the Hebrews, and the head of that family was Abraham. God told the Hebrews time and again that they were His Chosen Ones. He worked with them over and over showing them what He expected of them as His children. More times than I can say, they disappointed Him but He continued to love them and tried to explain to them the things He required.

As we study the Biblical history, we watch as God continued to try to show the kingdom to His Chosen family. He sent prophet after prophet to them. He forgave their disrespect over and over. Instead of honor for the prophets, many times they ignored and made fun of them. God forgave the Hebrews again. He blessed the people and sent another prophet. Finally God caused the family to be enslaved and to suffer much hardship at the hands of a pagan culture. But again, He proved that He had not forgotten that He had chose them and He had committed to them His love and protection. He freed them with all the rewards due a faithful people.

As they traveled away from the horrors of slavery, God told them how to set up a system of worship that would guide them and govern them. If they followed God's laws and behaved as He directed them all peoples of the world would see God in their lifestyle and God would be honored. There would be peace and respect for everyone

God got even more specific and gave the leadership of His law to the Levite tribe (one of the twelve tribes of the Hebrew nation). He gave the responsibility to them to teach and encourage and enforce His statues. The Levites were taught to study and teach the law to the others. A certain group within the tribe gained and demanded power and respect and called themselves the Pharisees (or the *separated* ones). The Pharisees are represented by the vinedressers in the parable that Jesus told that day. God trusted them with His kingdom (vineyard) and expected a profit from their hands. He wanted them to teach and lead others to Him. But they began to think of themselves as the only righteous persons around. They were selfish with their knowledge and tried to use the power of it to be of benefit to themselves. They were special in their own eyes and did not like their authority to be questioned at all. Instead of learning from and honoring the prophets God sent, the Pharisees at their best, ignored them; even at times stoning and killing those sent by God. They had no love or respect for one another, much less other peoples. They knew the words of the law in their head but it was not found in their heart.

So God sent His Son, His only Son. I won't say He, like the landowner in the parable, thought they might respect His Son: because God of course, knew better. He knew His Son would be rejected, and eventually killed. But He sent His Son offering them yet another chance to accept the spirit of His law as well as His love. God loves all His creation, not just the few that are born into the Israelite family. And He had chosen them to be teachers and leaders in this world, showing all peoples that God was the one and only Almighty Yahweh. Instead of showing the strength of character that He expected, they let the other cultures and religions influence them and divide them. God was very disappointed in their behavior.

He sent his Son to show His love to all the people now. No longer would God's Chosen have to be an Israelite. No longer would the knowledge of God have to come from the Pharisees. Gentiles were introduced to the True God through the Son. And now God's Chosen would be whoever accepted His Son as His Son and as their Savior.

The Pharisees listening to Jesus that day realized that He was speaking of them. They knew He was telling them that they had disappointed God again and had failed at the job God had meant for them to do. God had entrusted them as His Chosen vinedressers.

They realized that Jesus had asked that question, "What should the landowner do?" in such a way and at such a point in His story that even they had admitted that the vinedressers were wrong and needed replacing! Knowing a little about human nature, I suspect that a good bit of their anger that day was because they felt that they appeared foolish, even in their own eyes! They did not like Jesus showing all these people that they were failures.

And when Jesus warned them that He was there as the Cornerstone to God's Kingdom, they certainly were upset! All the power and self-imposed importance was being taken from them. Jesus, as the Son of God, was the basis of Salvation, not them and their empty quotations of the law. Jesus was telling them that they were not to be trusted with the growth of God's kingdom any longer. God was including other peoples (the Gentiles) in

His offer of salvation, forgiveness and love. Any person could be a part of the family of God's Chosen ones. The people no longer had to answer to the Pharisees. They no longer had to ask the Pharisees to intercede on their behalf with God. Each man could have a personal relationship with God through the love of Jesus Christ. God had chosen new vinedressers to spread the gospel: Jesus; His disciples; and others, such as Paul and Timothy, and eventually us.

The warning Jesus gave in the last verses of this parable was and is to be respected and not neglected. He very clearly tells the people that He is the foundation of God's kingdom. There is no doubt that He is speaking of Himself. He is the Stone that was rejected but was intended to be the Cornerstone. He is the Cornerstone on which salvation is built. He tells us that this was God's plan from the start and it was and is a good and beautiful plan.

There will be those that trip and fall on that foundation. No one's life is without some stumbling around. Believers are often bruised or injured by decisions made in their life. Those believers will be wounded. However, they will survive and have everlasting life with God and his Son.

But those that don't see or refuse to accept Jesus as that foundation until it falls on them will be condemned to be destroyed. They will spend eternity without any Presence of God or His love. Jesus does not mince His words in this warning.

PS. To this study:

If you will go back and re-read the quotation that Jesus used in this parable, you will find an Old Testament parable within this one!

3- THE FIG TREE

MATTHEW 24: 32-44 (Confirmed)

Teaching is from the discourse in the garden of Olivet. One of last teachings Jesus had for disciples. One of End Time teachings.

"Now learn this parable from the fig tree; When its branch has already become tender and puts forth leaves, you know that summer is near. So you also, when you see all these things, know that it is near – at the doors! Assuredly, I say to you, this generation will by no means pass away till all these things take place. Heaven and earth will pass away, but My words will by no means pass away. But of that day and hour no one knows, not even the angels of heaven, but My Father only. But as the days of Noah were, so also will the coming of the Son of Man be. For as in the days before the flood, they were eating and drinking, marrying and giving in marriage, until the day that Noah entered the ark, and did not know until the flood came and took them all away, so also will the coming of the Son of Man be. Then two men will be in the field: one will be taken and the other left. Two women will be grinding at the mill; one will be taken and the other left. Watch therefore, for you do not know what hour your Lord is coming. But know this, that if the master of the house had known what hour the thief would come, he would have watched and not allowed his house to be broken into. Therefore, you also be ready, for the Son of Man is coming at an hour you do not expect."

MARK 13:28-37 (Confirmed)

From the discourse in the garden of Olivet. One of last teachings Jesus had for the disciples.

"Now learn this parable from the fig tree: When its branch has already become tender, and puts forth leaves, you know that summer is near. So you also, when you see these things happening, know that it is near – at the doors! Assuredly, I say to you, this generation will by no means pass away till all these things take place. Heaven and earth

will pass away, but My words will by no means pass away. But of that day and hour, no one knows, not even the angels in heaven, nor the Son, but only the Father. Take heed, watch and pray; for you do not know when the time is. It is like a man going to a far country, who left his house and gave authority to his servants, and to each his work, and commanded the doorkeeper to watch. Watch, therefore, for you do not know when the master of the house is coming - in the evening, at midnight, at the crowing of the rooster, or in the morning - lest, coming suddenly, he find you sleeping. And what I say to you, I say to all; Watch!"

LUKE 21:29-36 (Confirmed)

From the discourse in the garden of Olivet. One of last teachings Jesus had for the disciples.

"Then He spoke to them a parable: *"Look at the fig tree, and all the trees. When they are already budding, you see and know for yourselves that summer is now near. So you also, when you see these things happening, know that the kingdom of God is near. Assuredly, I say to you, this generation will by no means pass away till all things take place. Heaven and earth will pass away, but My words will by no means pass away. But take heed to yourselves, lest your hearts be weighed down with carousing, drunkenness, and cares of this life, and that Day come on you unexpectedly. For it will come as a snare on all those who dwell on the face of the whole earth. Watch therefore, and pray always that you may be counted worthy to escape all these things that will come to pass, and to stand before the Son of Man."*

EXTRA READING

GENESIS 6: 3-6	MATTHEW 25:13	LUKE 9:27
LUKE 12:54-56	LUKE 17:34	ACTS 1:7
ACTS 7:52	I THESSALONIANS 5:1-6	JAMES 5:29
II PETER 3:8-18		

This is one parable of the Olivet Discourse or End-Time teachings. This parable, commonly called "The Fig Tree" is the third one that all three writers, Matthew, Mark, and Luke chose to include in their writings. As you see, Jesus, Himself, called this a parable.

This teaching takes place one afternoon just after the disciples and Jesus have attended worship. They have just left the temple where He spoke to all there, including the Pharisees. He warned them about false prophets. He told them to be aware of those preaching who say the right things but does not always behave as they should (Matthew 23:3.)He warned of hypocrites and blind leaders (Matthew 23:16.) He told them that some the teachers of the law were like whitewashed tombstones: beautiful on the outside but full of dead bones! (Matthew 23:27.)

According to most authorities, this was most likely Tuesday afternoon of the Last Week. They (Jesus and the disciples) had walked away from the crowds of the city and stopped on the Mount of Olivet (Olives). This late in the day any workers that might have been in the orchard would have left. There, Jesus could be alone with the twelve in the shade of the trees. In the quiet, Jesus continued to tell the disciples the things that were to happen in the future. He was very concerned that the twelve had all the understanding they would need to remain strong during the coming difficult days.

At this point the disciples seemed to understand that He was going to die on the cross. and that He would rise from the dead. They believed now that He was returning to God in heaven but would come back to claim His own. But like any human alive then or now, they were impatient. During this conversation the disciples asked Him how they would know that these times were here. They wanted to know when Jesus would come again. They wanted to know what the signs of those times would be.

So Jesus tried to make His teaching easy to understand. He again warned them of those that would try to deceive them by claiming to be Christ. Those false deceivers and false prophets would perform what would seem to be great miracles and signs. Some of the faithful would be fooled and follow them. He told them of wars, natural disasters, and struggles among people. He warned them of persecutions and hate, even among the faithful. Then He told them of the actual day of His second arrival. He will suddenly appear in the sky. The angels will blow the trumpet. And God's children will be gathered from all the corners of the earth into the sky with Him.

He reminded them that in the late spring, when the leaves began to bud on the fig trees, they knew summer was on its way shortly. Just as today I saw the pretty white flowers on the pear tree in my yard have begun to give way to the dainty green leaves. Each year I look for them. I know the hardest cold is nearly gone and spring is on the way. This has been a colder winter than usual, so spring is a very welcome thought. I think the men with Jesus that day were looking for the end times with the same hope. They loved Jesus and did not want to spend any time without Him here.

But in these verses Jesus is telling them (and us) that as we recognize the signs of spring: we should see the signs of His Second coming. He says when we see the signs He spoke of, we should <u>know</u> that the kingdom of God is at hand! Earlier Jesus had spoke of the end times to the multitudes and in those verses He was quite plain (and sounds a bit frustrated at their lack of understanding, Luke 12:54-56.)

The next few verses have confused me and I feel like they might have confused the disciples that day. I think the disciples understood that Jesus would return within their lifetime. I know, just from knowing human nature, that they hoped it would be a very short period of time. We know Paul thought He was returning during his lifetime. I think if I had sat and listened to these words of Jesus that precious afternoon, I would have believed it to be soon too.

I have finally realized that the when does not change anything very much for any believing individual. We say sometimes that we are waiting and eager for His return. That is really a bit wasteful of our time to act like that. We know that as our breath leaves our body, our spirit goes to God. So each us has only the short years of our live span to wait.

This morning I took a call from one of my husband's sisters telling me his oldest sister had died during the night. The fact that Jesus has waited two thousand years before His returns doesn't mean anything to her today. She is in His comforting arms NOW! Her eternity has begun! (One of my students pointed out to me that our eternity begins the day we accept Jesus as our Savior, not the day of our earthly death!) But truth that is, she is living her eternity today!

The when <u>does</u> matter to those that have not accepted Jesus as their Savior, so until He does come or until they die, they will have the chance to get ready. After either of those events there are no more opportunities. But the disciples were feeling grief at losing their personal relationship with Jesus, and they wanted Him to hurry back! Don't we all at one time or another wish with all our hearts that we could have that actual physical contact with Him? Don't we envy John when we read that he laid his head on Jesus' bosom?

I think sometimes we have very selfish reasons for that day to come now. Maybe we see a neighbor that sells drugs and beats his dog. We want God to come to end that activity in our neighborhood. Instead we should be singing the song I remember a bit of "Wait a little longer, dear Jesus. Just a few more days to get our loved ones in!" Now it is true, that drug selling neighbor is not our 'loved' one, but he is a child of someone's family; and more important, God wants him to be one of His children! And if we are to be found doing God's will, we will either be praying for or praying with this wayward child.

Each of the writers quoted Jesus when He assured us that "this generation would not pass away" before all these things have taken place. He also told us that heaven and earth would pass away but His words would never pass away. This is where I think the disciples came to believe they would live to see the Second coming. A generation is usually counted as 33 years; a second way of describing it is, birth of a man until the birth of his son, etc. Either way it would have been easy for the disciples to see this statement as prove of His coming soon. Now, as I have stated in the title of this work, *A Layman's (A Laywoman's) Study…* I am not formally educated in any Bible study. This is one of those times I truly wish I were. These words in this section of this parable have worried me for weeks now. I cannot be sure what Jesus meant. It just so happens that at this time, neither of my cohorts, my pastor nor my mom, are available to advise me. So here goes with what I think…if I can even put it into words that make any sense to anyone.

I know Jesus had just spent a good while telling His twelve followers about the events that were to take place at the End Times. He had given them warnings of what to expect and what to be prepared for. He had told of the horrors that were to be for his children during those final years and He had made it as plain as John did later in the *Book of Revelations*. He told them of the years of Tribulation and the trying problems that would face every Christian for a part of that time. Then He said those words about the generation that would not pass.

Since time has passed, (better than two thousand years) it is plain that He was not talking about the generation of the twelve. So who was He speaking of? I think He was telling us that WHEN we see the events He spoke of, (wars and rumors of war, earthquakes, other natural disasters, or the horrors that people can do to people) then that generation is the last to wait. That generation, if they are alert, should recognize the signs of the times. Each generation, at least as many of them that I have known, has thought those times were at hand. Each one thought that all the current events were true and prophecy had been completed. It is obvious that to this point everything has not come to pass yet. I have no doubt though that we should be watching carefully.

We must remember that when Jesus speaks of anything that involves time, He does not see it as we do, He thinks in terms of Eternity. We have no concept of eternity! If we think of time, we have a start and a stop, a beginning and an ending. There is no such truth with the word *eternity*. So what seems like an endless period of time to us could be an afternoon to Jesus. That's not an accurate description I'm sure; but it is the best I can do with my lack of understanding about eternity. I guess to explain what I am trying to say, I will again refer to the words of a song. "When we've been there ten thousand years, bright shining as the sun; we've no less days to sing God's praise, than when we'd first begun!" That's eternity. And that is the way Jesus sees time.

Now to tackle the words that says "heaven and earth will pass away." For understanding of this, I have turned to *Revelations*. I still don't understand exactly what Jesus meant but I do know John saw this in his visions (Revelations 21:1). And I know that Peter discussed it pretty extensively in II Peter 3:8-18. Peter tells us that the new heaven and new earth is one where righteousness exist, rather than the sinfulness we have now. So maybe that is what Jesus is telling us.

It is very interesting to me, since I have had such a difficult time with these few verses, that right after Peter tells us as best he can, what they mean; he then tells us that we should be very careful when we interpret Jesus' words! He tells us that some things are just hard to understand. So I'll hush at this point on this subject! Maybe someday I can ask Jesus to explain it to me; or at least I can discuss it with Peter for a few hundred years.

Jesus then explains to us that NO ONE knows when this time will be, except God, the Father. Jesus does not know. The angels do not know. Knowing this, I do not think any man can even claim that he can figure it out or predict it! Many, many have tried during my lifetime. They announced it on television. They encouraged people to pack and be ready. They climb on top of mountains so they can be the first to join Him. And they have done so many silly things that I cannot remember or list them all here. Needless to say, the next day after their predictions, they faded into the darkness where there were no camera lights. The sad part of this really is, not just that these so called prophets exist today but that there are people that believe in them. At this time there is one such prophesy floating around that the Last Day is to be in about 30 months from now (December 21, 2012). (Are you reading this past that date? If so, there you are…another group of folks will be hiding from the press and if that prediction does turn out to be true, so be it. We'll skip reading this and ask Jesus about the parables!

We know it will happen it is to be sometime, so we need to be prepared, but I don't think I need to pack anything. As Jesus told us in Mark, we need to watch and pray. In Matthew, Jesus reminded us of the days of Noah. The people were warned by Noah but they did not believe him, until the rain hit them in the head! This had to be a frightening experience! Up until that point all their moisture needs had been met by dew. They continued their life style right up until the water began to wash them away. It will be like that again. In spite of all our knowledge people will be surprised! Mankind will refuse to take heed and repent of their sin. I guess those activities are so much fun and eternity is so unreal, it just isn't worth making the change. Jesus is very specific. There will be two men working. The angels gathering God's children will claim one; one will be left. He tell us in Luke that people will be living carefree and carelessly and ignoring the warnings. Those will be caught in the snare or the trap of disbelief.

Jesus has warned us as completely as we can be warned with this parable and you can count on His words to be true and the lasting truth! Because His words here are filled with so much hope and joy, we (mankind), year after year, have believed *in my lifetime* and one day, in someone's lifetime, the Second coming will happen! We must have our hearts ready all the time.

4- THE MUSTARD SEED
(Kingdom of Heaven Parable)

MATTHEW 13:31-32 (Confirmed)
___

Taught by the sea to the multitudes

Another parable He put forth unto them, saying, " *The kingdom of heaven is like a mustard seed, which a man took and sowed in his field. Which indeed is the least of all the seeds; but when it is grown it is greater than the herbs and becomes a tree, so that the birds of the air come and nests in its branches.*"

MARK 4:30-32 (Confirmed)
___

Not told where this was taught but verse 10 tells it was for disciples

Then He said, "*To what shall we liken the kingdom of God? Or with what parable shall we picture it? It is like a mustard seed which, when it is sown on the ground, is smaller than all the seeds on earth: but when it is sown, it grows up and becomes greater than all herbs, and shoots out large branches, so that the birds of the air may nest under its shade.*"

LUKE 13:18-19
___

Luke indicates was taught in Temple in verse10

Then He said, "*What is the kingdom of God like? And to what shall I compare it? It is like a mustard seed, which a man took and put in his garden; and it grew and became a large tree, and the birds of the air nested in its branches.*"

EXTRA READING
___

EZEKIEL 17:22- 24

Each of the gospels gives a bit different information concerning the where and who of this parable. This parable was used by Jesus in His teachings at least twice, and more than likely three times. Once was in His sermon by the Sea of Galilee when He spoke from the boat on the edge of the shore, as we were told by Matthew. Luke told us of another time in the Temple. All those that were in the temple heard Jesus that time. In Mark it is indicated that this was a special time where only the disciples were with Jesus, but he does not tell us where they were. So that seems to show us Jesus thought this was a parable that needed our attention. He, Himself, made sure as many as possible heard it.

It is one of the many that is often listed as the "Kingdom of Heaven" parables. In them, Jesus is trying to show a true vision of the Kingdom of God. He understands that our human minds have a difficult time seeing such a sight: (such as trying to understand the word eternity.) So He compares the vision to very many different things we are familiar with. He patiently tries to help us understand. He often used plants and gardening scenes in His teachings. Those are subjects that are comfortable to most people.

This parable is one of two that Jesus used a mustard seed as the object to illustrate His teaching. We are very familiar here in this area and time period with the mustard plant. We plant it and it grows well. It is among the plants we enjoy as spring greens, fresh from the garden. By time winter has gone we are very ready to taste the freshness of mustard! And, oh, the smell of it cooking! Nothing can compare to it!

But this plant grows to approximately 6 inches tall before we gather it. If it grows to the eighteen inches it is capable of…well we call that run-up mustard and it can be eaten but usually that only happens when we are letting it go-to-seed. And that only happens at the end of the season because mustard greens do not do well in the heat of summer. So how does that knowledge help us to understand this parable?

The seed of our mustard is a tiny, tiny black spot. I won't say it is the size of a period because it is a bit larger than the font on this machine but it is smaller than I could draw if I were using a sharp-point magic marker. In fact the size might compare to this letter 'o'. Yes, it is pretty close, maybe a bit smaller. So that compares well to the story Jesus was telling. We have a start here to understanding, don't we? But not enough, so I had to go digging in *The Bible Almanac*. There I found information about a plant grown in that area of the world and in that time.

The plant was called black mustard and it grew wild on the banks of the Sea of Galilee. It was an herb that grew to six to eight feet high. It was called black mustard because the seeds, like ours were black and that was the part of the plant they used. The bush (or tree) was covered in yellow flowers, like our mustard is when it runs-up. The seeds were used for flavoring in many of the dishes they prepared then. They were also a favorite source of food for the birds. They could build their nests there and have an easily available food supply for their new babies.

Now, knowing the differences in our yellow' mustard (which is not an herb) and their black mustard; how does that help us to understand the lesson Jesus is sharing with us here? Well, to those of us born here in South Carolina, it explains a mustard plant that is big enough for nesting birds!

The man in the story took the smallest, most insignificant seed available and from it produced a plant that would supply his family with all of the flavoring they would need for a long, long time. At the same time the birds would benefit with a protected home and food for their families.

Is Jesus telling us that with the slightest effort on our part, the Kingdom of Heaven will be made available to us? With the least amount of trust and obedience, God will furnish for us a protected environment that meets all our needs as is done in the story for the birds. (Remember in another story He has told us that we are far more important than the birds!) And in this story, the seeds were not a necessity of life but a product that would make the farmer's life (and food) tastier. The seed enhanced his life. Jesus was telling us that the Kingdom of Heaven is a safe haven that meets the needs of shelter and the pangs of hunger. But in addition, the life there will be such an enhancement of what we know as the good life, that we can't even picture it now.

The Kingdom of Heaven is more than just a beautiful place. There we will be completely comfortable in our thoughts of safety. We will know all our needs will be met. The blessings there for us will make life more than pleasant but delightful! As the flavoring improved the taste of the food, heaven will enhance our life more that we can even imagine today. I think that David describes it as well in the following verse as it can be worded:

"YOU WILL SHOW ME THE PATH OF LIFE;
IN YOUR PRESENCE IS FULLNESS OF JOY;
AT YOUR RIGHT HAND ARE PLEASURES
FOREVERMORE."

(PSALM 16, VERSE 11, BY DAVID)

5- INTO / OUT OF MOUTHS

MATTHEW 15:10-20 (Confirmed)

At small town of Gennesaret on NW shore of Sea of Galilee. Spoken to multitudes and explained later to Peter and other disciples

"When He had called the multitude to Himself, He said to them, *"Hear and understand: Not what goes into the mouth defiles a man: but what comes out of the mouth, this defiles a man."* Then his disciples came and said to Him, "Do you know that the Pharisees were offended when they heard this saying?" But He answered and said, *"Every plant which My heavenly Father has not planted will be uprooted. Let them alone. They are blind leaders of the blind. And if the blind leads the blind, both will fall into a ditch."* Then Peter answered and said to Him, "Explain this parable to us." So Jesus said, *"Are you also still without understanding? Do you not yet understand that whatever enters the mouth goes into the stomach and is eliminated? But those things which proceed out of the mouth come from the heart, and they defile a man. For out of the heart proceed evil thoughts, murders, adulteries, fornications, thefts, false witness, blasphemies. These are the things which defile a man, but to eat with unwashed hands does not defile a man,"*

MARK 7:14-23 (Confirmed)

At small town of Gennesaret on NW shore of Sea of Galilee. Spoken to multitudes and explained later to Peter and other disciples

"When He had called all the multitude to Himself, He said to them, *"Hear Me, everyone and understand: There is nothing that enters a man from outside which can defile him: but the things which come out of him, those are the things that defile a man. If anyone has ears to hear, let him hear!"* When He had entered a house away from the crowd, His disciples asked Him concerning the parable. So He said to them, *"Are you thus without understanding also? Do you not perceive that whatever enters a man from outside cannot defile him, because it does not enter his heart but his stomach, and is eliminated, thus purifying all foods?"* And He said, *"What comes out of a man, that defiles a man. For from within, out of the heart of men, proceed evil thoughts, adulteries, fornications, murders; thefts, covetousness, wickedness, deceit, lewdness, an evil eye, blasphemy, pride, foolishness. All these evil things come from within and defile a man."*

EXTRA READING

GENESIS 6:5	JOB 15: 5-6	PSALMS 39:1	ISAIAH 59:3
MATTHEW 23:25	LUKE 11:37-40	JOHN 15:3	ACTS 10:14-15
ROMANS 1:24-25	GALATIANS 5:19-26	TITUS 1:15	JAMES 3:6

This parable is found in Matthew and Mark. Both writers confirm that it is a parable. (See Matthew 15:15 and Mark7:17.) It is also one of the parables that many lists I found had left out. I don't understand that but then I don't understand a lot concerning those lists. I cannot believe it should be left out since the writers both called it one! They were there. I will not dispute their word.

Matthew told us in 14:34 and Mark told us in 6:53 that the twelve with Jesus crossed over the Sea of Galilee. They docked near the town of Gennesaret. It was a small town on the northwest shore of the sea. There a crowd gathered as soon as the people found out that Jesus was there. By this time Jesus, because of His miracles, was well known throughout the countryside.

But this day there were others gathering to see Jesus, not just those seeking healing. Some of the Pharisees and other teachers of the law had come from Jerusalem to this place to confront Jesus. It was their goal to make Him appear foolish. They intended to prove He did not follow the Jewish law and that He encouraged His followers to disobey too. They asked Him why neither He nor His disciples followed the traditions such as washing their hands before every meal.

Jesus then asked them why did they allow traditions to overrule the actual law of God? He reminded them that God had told everyone to "honor your father and mother" (Exodus 20:12.) Money that should have been used to help support their parents during their old age, was dedicated, or set aside, to be given to the temple at some future date, (which really then would be given back to them as the Priests). If they made this promise of the funds, then they were released from the responsibility of helping their parents by the Jewish tradition. But that release went against God's commandment (Matthew 15: 1-7) (Mark 7: 9-13.) Then Jesus addressed the accusations the Pharisees had made concerning the hand washing. And to answer this, He spoke a parable to the crowd, the Jewish elders, and His disciples.

I think this is the clearest, easiest to understand parable He used. He said that nothing going into the mouth could defile a man. He explained that only what comes out of the man's mouth could defile him!

In later verses where Peter asked Him to explain the parable Jesus was astonished that they did not understand. He carefully gave them a lesson on physical anatomy. Whatever a man eats goes through the system, the needed nutrients are used and the waste leaves the body. Food products, of any kind, are treated the same way. The law had endless rules (and *some* of them were from God's word) of what man could eat and how it should be prepared. But, in most cases, if you read with your eyes open, you will realize that it was a matter of food spoiling if the rules were not followed. After all there were no refrigerators or freezers. And don't you suspect that God was protecting the people from problems such as high cholesterol? So even then it was not the food itself that was harmful. It was the fact that it was very likely to spoil and cause an illness. The food would not defile the man – poison him…maybe.

But the things that are in a man's heart; hate, wickedness, lewdness, any evil or disobedient thought; all these things that come out of a man's mouth do defile him. If a man hates his neighbor for any reason (be it envy, jealousy, prejudice, or any other reason) then he will say hurtful and mean things about or to that neighbor. That neighbor then will certainly question the *goodness* of the God that man claims to follow! That is defilement!

But in the verses between Jesus speaking the parable and explaining it to His disciples, He spoke another parable in Matthew. This too is one that other lists have left out or included in this one because it is part of the same conversation the disciples were having with Jesus that day. I chose to include it here for today. Some authorities have named it "Blind Leading Blind" . The disciples asked Jesus if He was aware of the anger the Pharisees had when He spoke the first parable. Added to the anger they must have had earlier when He told them they were letting their traditions over rule God's law, I imagine that by this time they were what we would call "fit to be tied!" Don't you? Anyway, back to the second parable:

Jesus told the twelve, in reference to the Pharisees, that every plant, which God had not planted, would be uprooted. And then He spoke of blind leaders leading the blind. That is an accident waiting to happen, isn't it?

Jesus said to the twelve that every man that tried to quote law and make up rules or traditions that did not have the call from God in his heart would not succeed in the long run. Their ministry would be short lived. That plant, or law would be destroyed or uprooted. The one law that I think of as an example is the Catholic tradition that they could eat only fish on Friday. That was not a Jewish 'law' but it is the kind of thing I am speaking of…and it has not lasted. Just as Jesus said it was uprooted and is no longer a law. The disciples should not fret nor worry about the Pharisees' anger or disapproval, just leave it be and go on with their own lives. I think we would be very neglectful to gloss over that statement. Jesus said "Let them alone."

Today we in this age tend to worry too much over other peoples sins or lawlessness. Jesus is clear here that we should leave judgment to the Judge. Pray for them, yes, we should. The rest is up to God.

Jesus then rewords the same message by saying that the Pharisees are blind leaders. They cannot and do not see the truth in the very words that they teach. They teach a group of people that just sit and listen to the words, and see no reason to even seek the truth of those words. I would ask our Pastor if he ever sees that behavior in his congregation? Logic alone says that if the blind leads the blind, with neither is capable of seeking to find the true way, they are going to fall in the ditch!

6- PATCHED GARMENTS / NEW WINESKINS

MATTHEW 9:14-17

Was visiting in Matthew's home. Taught to all guests, Pharisees, and disciples of John

"Then the disciples of John came to Him, saying, " Why do we and the Pharisees fast often, but your disciples do not fast?" And Jesus said to them, *"Can the friends of the bridegroom mourn as long as the bridegroom is with them? But the days will come when the bridegroom will be taken away from them, and then they will fast. No one puts a piece of unshrunk cloth on a old garment; for the patch pulls away from the garment, and the tear is made worse. Nor do they put new wine into old wineskins, or else the wineskins break, the wine is spilled, and the wineskins are ruined. But they put new wine into new wineskins, and they both are preserved."*

MARK 2:18-22

Was visiting in Matthew's home. Taught to all guests, Pharisees, and disciples of John

"The disciples of John and of the Pharisees were fasting. Then they came and said to Him, *"Why do the disciples of John and of the Pharisees fast, but Your disciples do not fast?" And Jesus said to them, "Can the friends of the bridegroom fast while the bridegroom is with them? As long as they have the bridegroom with them they cannot fast. But the days will come when the bridegroom will be taken away from them, and then they will fast in those days. No one sews a piece of unshrunk cloth on an old garment; or else the new piece pulls away from the old, and the tear is made worse. And no one puts new wine into old wineskins; or else the new wine bursts the wineskins, the wine is spilled, and the wineskins are ruined. But new wine must be put into new wineskins."*

LUKE 5:33-39 (Confirmed)

Was visiting in Matthew's home. Taught to all guests, Pharisees, and disciples of John

"Then they said to Him, "Why do the disciples of John fast often and make prayers, and likewise those of the Pharisees, but Yours eat and drink?" And He said to them, *"Can you make the friends of the bridegroom fast while the bridegroom is with them? But the days will come when the bridegroom will be taken away from them; then they will fast in those days."* Then He spoke a parable to them: *"No one puts a piece from a new garment on an old one; otherwise the new makes a tear, and also the piece that was taken out of the new does not match the old. And no one puts new wine into old wineskins, or else the new wine will burst the wineskins and be spilled, and the wineskins will be ruined. But new wine must be put into new wineskins, and both are preserved. And no one, having drunk old wine, immediately desires new; for he says, 'The old is better.'"*

EXTRA READING

DANIEL 7:13-14	JOHN 3: 26-29	ACTS 1:9-11

Matthew, Mark, and Luke indicate that this parable was taught while Jesus was visiting at Matthew Levi's home. This teaching was confirmed as a parable by Luke. The disciples of John approached Him there and began to question Him. Both Mark and Luke said some members of the Pharisees were there too.

It all began with Jesus and His disciples walking through the town of Capernaum. Jesus called Matthew as a disciple and he responded with an eager heart. He then gave a dinner in Jesus' honor and invited all his friends, which of course, would have included other tax collectors.

I don't know how, unless as a Jew, Matthew invited the local Pharisees, but somehow they became aware of who was at that dinner and they gathered around. They questioned Jesus pretty harshly about His choice of friends. To them, one should not associate with those that were sinners and wrongdoers. Jesus responded with a parable we will study later, (Matthew 9:12-13) but for now we will look at the short version. He did not come to save the righteous. He came to call the unrighteous to repentance and to renew their fellowship with God.

At that point they (the Pharisees and the disciples of John) began to ask Him why neither He nor His disciples followed the tradition of fasting. It seems in the story that the Pharisees were in a time of fasting when this conversation was taking place. The question sounds to me like the disciples of John and maybe even the Pharisees were jealous that Jesus did not require His disciples to fast. I don't see the question as concern for their salvation. I just see people that want to eat supper too. But they were so wrapped up in tradition and the show of righteousness that they were enslaved to the law. It had nothing to do with what they felt in their heart.

Jesus answered them with a parable: He asked them if it was proper for the friends of the bridegroom to mourn while the Groom was in their presence? He told those questioning Him that the day would come when the Groom would no longer be with His friends, then they could grieve and fast. He also told them that no one uses a new piece of material to patch an old garment. He gave the reasons for this truth. One was that the old material was no longer strong enough to hold the stitching of the patch. When the garment would be washed the patch of new material would shrink, thus pulling the hole bigger. Another reason Jesus mentioned is that the new material would not match the older faded material. He continued trying to make this conversation clearer to the people listening to Him and told them that putting new wine into old wineskins was a bad idea. New wine has yet to ferment so putting it into old brittle skins would be a disaster. The skins would burst and one would loose all of his wine. If new wine is put in new skins, the skins will expand as the wine ferments. The product will age with the skins. The wine will be safe. Luke quoted Jesus when He reminded the crowds that many do not like 'new' wine. Most people prefer the taste of old wine.

It is not difficult for us to understand what Jesus was saying when He talked about the bridegroom. We have the advantage of reading the whole story but those there that day may not have yet heard Him refer to Himself as the Groom and God's children as the bride. We understand that the disciples were only going to have His presence for a short three years. They did not share that knowledge with us at that point. After that Jesus would leave them to return to His Father's house (Acts 1:9.) So this part of the parable is easy for our hard heads to absorb. We would celebrate time with Him too, by feasting and song if we had that chance! When He left it would indeed be a time of sadness and mourning.

Now I will try to tell you what I understand about the new patches of material and the new wineskins. Jesus is at this point comparing the old ways of righteousness, the law, to the new plan of salvation God is introducing to His children through Jesus Christ. The old ways of the Pharisees could not contain the new plan. The new plan God has in mind will expand and grow to include others (the Gentiles and you and me) and the old Jewish law could not tolerate that idea. The new plan could not be simply attached to the old ways. If that had been tried it is likely that the old would have been destroyed and the new lost in the process. Never did He at any time say the old wineskins (or old ways) should be thrown out or eliminated. The old laws have their place in God's plan. Jesus wants us to see that both the old and new together makes the whole. (It is not an accident that our Holy Bible is made up of the Old and New Testaments... the old and new make the whole.) If one takes any part of God's plan and neglects the other part, it will not be a complete plan.

He did tell us in Luke that many prefer the old wine. The taste is better. He knew there were those in the crowd that day were unwilling to accept the new plan of salvation at that point. He spoke though, as if in time they might be more willing to listen. Even though Jesus expected the people to some day accept His new plan, it hasn't happened completely yet. There are members of every church I have ever attended that did not want new people.

Heaven forbid, is their attitude that a young child should come with his parents and be a bit rowdy. There is no patience to allow that parent or child to have a few weeks to learn how to behave in church!

Do we have people in our congregations today that like the old ways better? Do we have people that think unless you preach 'in the old-time way' you don't have the Spirit of God in your work? Are there those in our church that think some newer songs are unacceptable? I don't think that people have changed that much from the day Jesus spoke to them. What is 'old ways' then and 'old ways' now may be different, but the people aren't.

This parable was in the very early stages of Jesus' ministry and yet He was sharing with them that He had been sent to show the true plan of salvation to them. Needless to say there were many there that day not able to understand at all. There were more than likely those that chose not to understand. But He was teaching…and did that knowing that some would eventually understand it!

WE ARE NOT AN AFTER-THOUGHT!

I have noticed that in some of these parables now that if I were a non-believer or a doubter of any extent that I might think just reading them for the first time, and not the whole Bible, that God's invitation to the rest of the world (aside from the Jewish people) was an after thought in His mind. That is an absolute <u>not</u> <u>true</u> statement. God knew from the beginning how the Chosen Ones would behave and misbehave in the years to come. It was in His Plan from the very first that Jesus would come and offer salvation to all the world. It was never an after thought that God loved ALL His children and that ALL would be given the chance to accept His invitation through the forgiveness and repentance that Jesus made possible on the cross. If ever there was any doubt, read the Book of John. From the first verse you are assured that Jesus was a part of the picture from before the first minute of God's creation of this earth!

It is my intentions here to talk about only a certain teaching that Jesus gave us at one time in His ministry. But I do not attempt here to try to teach the entire Bible each Sunday. Those of you that might be new believers or curious non-believers Please! Please read considerably more of the Holy Bible before you make any grand assumptions concerning God's love or God's plan of salvation!

7-HOUSE DIVIDED

MATTHEW 12:24-32

Place unknown. Taught to Pharisees, and others in crowd

"Now when the Pharisees heard it, they said, "This fellow does not cast out demons except by Beelzebub, the ruler of the demons." But Jesus knew their thoughts, and said to them: *"Every kingdom divided against itself is brought to desolation, and every city or house divided against itself will not stand. If Satan casts out Satan, he is divided against himself. How then will his kingdom stand? And if I cast out demons by Beelzebub, by whom do your sons cast them out? Therefore they shall be your judges. But if I cast out demons by the Spirit of God, surely the kingdom of God has come upon you. Or how can one enter a strong man's house and plunder his goods, unless he first binds the strong man? And then he will plunder his house. He who is not with Me is against Me, and he who does not gather with Me scatters abroad. Therefore I say to you, every sin and blasphemy will be forgiven men, but the blasphemy against the Spirit will not be forgiven men. Anyone who speaks a word against the Son of man, it will be forgiven him; but whoever speaks against the Holy Spirit, it will not be forgiven him, either in this age or in the age to come."*

MARK 3:22-30 (Confirmed)

At a house, most likely in Capernaum. Taught to Pharisees, and others in crowd

"And the scribes who came down from Jerusalem said, "He has Beelzebub" and "By the ruler of the demons He casts out demons." So He called them to Himself and said to them in parables: *"How can Satan cast out Satan? If a kingdom is divided against itself, that kingdom cannot stand. And if a house is divided against itself, that house cannot stand. And if Satan has risen up against himself, and is divided, he cannot stand, but has an end. No one can enter a strong man's house and plunder his goods, unless he first binds the strong man. And then he will plunder his house. Assuredly, I say to you, all sins will be forgiven the sons of men, and what ever blasphemies they may utter: but he who blasphemes against the Holy Spirit never has forgiveness, but is subject to eternal condemnation –"* because they said, "He has an unclean spirit."

LUKE 11:14-23

Place unknown. Taught to Pharisees, and others in crowd

"And He was casting out a demon, and it was mute. So it was, when the demon had gone out, that the mute spoke; and the multitudes marveled. But some of them said, "He casts out demons by Beelzebub, the ruler of the demons." Others, testing Him, sought from Him a sign from heaven. But He, knowing their thoughts, said to them: *"Every kingdom divided against itself is brought to desolation, and a house divided against a house falls. If Satan also is divided against himself, how will his kingdom stand? Because you say I cast out demons by Beelzebub. And if I cast out demons by Beelzebub, by whom do your sons cast them out? Therefore they will be your judges. But if I cast out demons with the finger of God, surely the kingdom of God has come upon you. When a strong man, fully armed, guards his own palace, his goods are in peace. But when a stronger than he comes upon him and overcomes him, he takes from him all his armor in which he trusted, and divides his spoils. He who is not with Me is against Me, and he who does not gather with Me scatters."*

EXTRA READING

DANIEL 2:44	DANIEL 7:14	MATTHEW 9: 32-34
MATTHEW 10:25	MATTHEW 10:33	LUKE 12:10
JOHN 12:31	II CORTHINIANS 5:1	

This parable is among the ones I told you of earlier that was left out by many authorities. And among other scholars it was divided into two separate parables. According to the way I confirmed the parables, it must be included because Mark confirmed it. Since the entire thing is one conversation I left it intact and did not split it up. That makes it a bit difficult to understand but so be it. We never were promised it would be easy. Were we? The actual parable is much shorter than the material I have asked you to read. For example in Mark the verses 23-25 would be one and in verse 27 would be the second one that scholars accepted. I wanted to include the whole reading because it explains itself better with it all.

Neither Matthew nor Luke tells us where this discourse takes place. In the verses just before this teaching Jesus had just appointed the twelve to act as His disciples and teach the gospel. He had empowered them to heal and cast out demons in His name. After they returned from their mission trips they went into a house, most likely the home of one of the disciples, and most likely in Capernaum. Before they could rest or even eat a meal the crowd gathered to overflowing around them again.

There were a number of events that had just taken place and the Pharisees were watching Jesus pretty close. This day was on a Sabbath and the disciples had eaten some heads of grain as they walked through a field. (They were hungry!) But it was a sin to harvest crops on the Sabbath. While they were in Temple Jesus had healed a man's withered hand. Healing too, was a sin on the Sabbath. There was a lot that caused the Pharisees to be offended at Jesus.

As the Pharisees charged Jesus and his disciples with misconduct, He, in turn accused them of knowing the letter of the law but not having any idea of the spirit of it! He reminded them that even they would rescue the lamb that had fallen in the ditch on Sabbath. Yet they would allow a human being to suffer until a *proper* time to do a healing (Matthew 1-14.) All this was causing a lot of friction between Jesus and the religious leaders.

Then Jesus cast out a demon from a man in the crowd, and our story begins. This demon had caused the man to be mute. When the demon was gone the man could speak again. The crowd was very impressed. In fact this one act seems to have divided the opinions that people had of Jesus into a number of different groups, more than any other act had to this date.

(1) According to all three writers the Pharisees thought He was demon possessed.

(2) Mark tells us His family and friends thought He might be out of His mind or crazy (verse 21).

(3 And then there were those that saw Him as an absolute hero! They were amazed at His miracles. His authoritative speaking was a marvel to them. By this time in His ministry, no one was left 'untouched' by the personal contact they had with Jesus. One way or another everyone was totally influenced by Him. When the Pharisees began to accuse and charge Jesus with being possessed and casting out the demons by the authority of Beelzebub Jesus responded with the words of our lesson today.

He asked them how could Satan cast out Satan? He told them that a country that fights among it's own can not survive. Think about the horrors and division that was suffered in our own United States during the Civil War! It took place in 1860-1864 and today, 150 years later there is still residue and memories that are painful. There are people that are resentful and wounded from the thoughts of that time in our history. My husband is from the north and I, as you have properly already guessed, am a southerner. Sometimes he sees things that I overlook or am accustomed to seeing. He will ask me at those times why are southerners so bitter. The war is a long time over. My answer to him is, "We lost. If you loose you remember longer than if you win." Division causes weakness. Nothing that has ever been cut in two parts will ever be quite as strong again.

Jesus then told them (the Pharisees) that a house divided could not stand. The same thing that would divide a country would divide a home if the family members were at odds with one another. Have you ever known of, or been a part of a family feud? Has there ever been a time when two of your family members were not speaking to each other for some reason? If you have, then you know from experience that it did not stop with the two feuding. Everyone else in one way or another had to choose sides. The rift touched everyone!

Jesus used these examples to show those listening to Him that day how very silly it was to accuse Him of being under the power of Satan. Why would Satan allow anyone to use his name to cast out his own work? It would be his downfall to work against himself like that.

Then Jesus reminded the Pharisees that some of their own members often cast out demons in God's name. It was His statement that if only those that were under the power of Satan could cast out demons, as they had said of Him, then they had better look to their own before they judged

Him. He then assured them that He works with the authority of and in the Spirit of God.

Jesus uses a second parable to further explain His words. He tells of a strong man that protects his house and of one that is stronger that comes in to plunder his goods. In this Jesus is referring to Satan as the strong man that owns the house. The stronger One is Jesus, who binds that man and plunders the goods of the house. He takes all the defensive armor away and then divides the spoils of that man. Jesus is telling us here that He will raid the work of Satan and reclaim those that Satan had thought were his own treasures.

We are all familiar with the body being called our tabernacle or house. Jesus is using that familiar phrase here and saying that the strong man or Satan is guarding the demons or the temptations that have enslaved the person. Jesus is stronger, more powerful, and He will defeat the demons and free the believer that Satan has tried to claim.

Matthew and Luke quoted Jesus when He said that all those that are not with Him are against Him. Those that are against Him do not gather in any good but scatters it. I think that Jesus was saying here that those that accused Him and tried to lead others into thinking Him to be of the devil were offensive to God. This seems like a warning to them, that they were going to be held responsible for those they had mislead. We, too, will be held accountable for all we say to others.

At that point in the discourse Jesus gave a very direct warning to those accusing Him. He said in both Matthew and in Mark that the Pharisees were committing an unforgivable act when they falsely accused Jesus of being of the spirit of Satan. He explains that all sins are forgivable, with the exception of one. The hard-hearted attitude they had that resisted the Spirit of God was unacceptable. And by denying that the power of the Holy Spirit was what Jesus used to cast out the demon, they were denying that the Holy Spirit existed.

TO THOSE THAT QUESTION THE POWER OF THE
HOLY SPIRIT, IT WILL NOT BE FORGIVEN.

The unforgivable sin they were committing was not that they falsely accused Jesus. It was a sin to bear false witness against anyone, much less Jesus. But it could be forgiven with repentance and prayer. But they did not believe that He used the Spirit of God in His work. They were denying that power. Isn't it odd that they could easily believe and talk about and recognize the spirit of Satan, yet not acknowledge the Spirit of God?

As I teach a class or talk with people I have noticed the fastest way to loose their attention is to begin a serious conversation about the Holy Spirit. I am talking about people that think and want to be called Christians. I do not understand why it is so hard for some to accept the fact that He is real, as real as God the Father and Jesus Christ the Son. They do not seem to want to admit He lives within their own soul. Why? I'm completely confused on that one! He was a gift Jesus bestowed on us when He returned to the Father. Jesus knew we could not possibly maintain a faithful course in the Way without daily, even hourly assistance. Why do all these people think it is not 'cool' to mention or accept such a gift from God? (I think part of it is they are just plain afraid of ghosts.)

This warning to the righteous (or self-righteous) Pharisees told them that this sin could NOT be forgiven,

"...EITHER IN THIS AGE OR IN THE AGE TO COME."

That is today, friends! We must be made to see that Jesus was talking to us! We pretend we know that God and Jesus and the Holy Spirit make up the Trinity, but many stop at believing in only the Two.

Our Savior finds this to be totally offensive and completely unacceptable.

<u>By His own words, He will never forgive this sin.</u>

8- SPECK IN EYE

MATTHEW 7: 1-5

Taught during the Sermon on the Mount to the multitudes

"Judge not, that you be not be judged. For with what judgment you judge, you will be judged; and with the measure you use, it will be measured back to you. And why do you look at the speck in your brother's eye, but do not consider the plank in your own eye? Or how can you say to your brother, 'Let me remove the speck from your eye,' and look, a plank is in your own eye? Hypocrite! First remove the plank from your own eye, and then you will see clearly to remove the speck from your brother's eye."

LUKE 6:37-42 (Confirmed)

Taught during the Sermon on the Mount to the multitudes

"Judge not, and you shall not be judged. Condemn not, and you shall not be condemned. Forgive, and you will be forgiven. Give, and it will be given to you; good measure, pressed down, shaken together, and running over will be put into your bosom. For the same measure that you use, it will be measured back to you." And He spoke a parable to them: *"Can the blind lead the blind? Will they not both fall into the ditch? A disciple is not above his teacher, but everyone who is perfectly trained will be like his teacher. And why do you look at the speck in your brother's eye, but do not perceive the plank in your own eye? Or how can you say to your brother, 'Brother, let me remove the speck that is in your eye,' when you, yourself do not see the plank that is in your own eye? Hypocrite! First remove the plank from your own eye, and then you will see clearly to remove the speck that is in your brother's eye."*

EXTRA READING

MATTHEW 23;13-3	LUKE 6:27-36

This parable was taught in the discourse known by most Bible students as the Sermon on the Mount. It was taught to the many people that gathered there to hear this *new* prophet that was doing so many great miracles. It was early in Jesus' ministry but the crowds were already trying to follow Him wherever He went.

I think I have heard this parable taught in Church more than any other. And if you are one that attends church at all, or watched a pastor on television, you most likely have too. Today's pastors seem to think we all need a lesson in reference to our "judging" others. Jesus thought the same thing, enough so that this is one of His first teachings. One would assume we would have learned that lesson by now, wouldn't you? Luke quotes Jesus in his writings saying,

"JUDGE NOT, AND YOU SHALL NOT BE JUDGED...FORGIVE, AND YOU WILL BE FORGIVEN... FOR THE SAME MEASURE THAT YOU USE, IT WILL BE MEASURED BACK TO YOU."

Sounds so simple...The words about measuring, refer to actual measurements of things like the weight of grain you might be buying. For example if you are selling rice and weighing it out into a scale, you plan to put small rocks in it while you weigh it out. That is cheating the customer but it makes more money for you, right? But Jesus is telling you here that if you cheat others, count on others cheating you. But that is just a surface meaning for what Jesus is saying here. That's not nearly the whole story.

He has warned us that we should not put ourselves in the position of judging another. If we do then we will be judged. Jesus warned the Pharisees one day that they could not judge Him in reference to casting out demons. They had accused Him of doing it with the power of Satan (Matthew12:24-32.) He reminded them quickly that some of their members also cast out demons! By that, He was asking them did they believe that those members were working with Satan's power too? We know that none of us are perfect. We all are sinners. So can we decide that anyone else's sin is greater than our own? Or can we understand that by judging that person, we are committing a sin with that very act!

Jesus then offers a blessing to those of us that freely and completely learn to forgive those that do harm to us. He tells us that if we will forgive others, He will forgive us. By reversing that fact, beware that if you do not or cannot forgive the wrong done to you; Jesus will not, and cannot, forgive you. The reason I say cannot is because He is not a liar. He tells us we must forgive to be forgiven. We must take Jesus at His word and we must not assume He is a push over for those of us that are obviously (at least obvious in our own minds) His children. He will not make an exception because you study hard or attend church regularly. Think about it; those that we are not forgiving are His children too!

If I decided that it was a sin for my female students to wear red on Sunday then it would indeed be a sin for me too. Now that is ridiculous. I am not 'making up' sins for us to be concerned with; but I am saying that what ever I use to judge others is the same that Jesus will use to judge me. If I decide that some sin committed by someone is too much to forgive; maybe they killed their children; then my sins will be found to be too dishonorable to be forgiven. (In that last sentence I had written, "<u>may</u> be found." I had to change it to "<u>will</u> be found." But that is just an example of how we choose to gloss over our own sins!)

Now is all this to say that we should always condone or ignore that which is wrong? No, we should not close our heart to those sins we see in others (or our own), but we are to recognize the act as the sin, not the person. We should not have a fault-finding nature that is always trying to make ourselves better than our neighbor! In the verses just before these Jesus had just been telling us to love one another. If you will read Luke 6: 27-36 you will see how Jesus thinks we should treat others.

Jesus then began to speak in parables to explain His opinions about *judging*. He asked if the blind should lead the blind. He questioned if the disciples could ever be above their teacher. He said the blind would only lead the blind into the trouble; and the disciples could only be as good as they were taught. And then He asked how could one accuse another of having a speck in his eye if the one making the accusation had a plank in his own?

His question was really, how can you offer to assist your friend get over a small temptation that is plaguing him, when you have a larger problem eating away at you? It seems to be much easier to see the faults and sins of the friends you have than to see your own. We do judge and assess the activities of all those around us. If we don't know what they are doing, we assume they are up to mischief. If we see a bit of their carrying on, we make up a whole scenario to go with the part we do know. And what we make up is always to no good! We sit on our porches and have a story to tell about each trip our neighbor makes! Some how we find a form of entertainment in seeing others do wrong. And being the 'good person' that we think we are, we offer to help them get their life straightened out. We even offer to pray for them.

Jesus is telling the folks in that crowd that before they offer help in those cases, look to their selves. It is impossible to see the truth of the speck that your friend is suffering when you yourself have such a bigger problem! This goes back to what He said earlier. By the same standards that you set for others to meet, He will judge you. (And He expects you to judge yourself by that same set of rules.)

That is not saying that you can be no good to another person if you have sin in your life somewhere. If that were a hard fact, then none of us would have ever been lead into the fold. At least none of us since Jesus returned to heaven. There has been no perfect man on earth since then. There would be no one to teach and lead the others. But it does say that we cannot judge the other to be so imperfect that we appear to be near perfect, at least in our own mind. We must seek forgiveness each day for the specks and planks in our own eyes.

It is those planks that blind us to our own sin. If we are blinded by our own lack of control that gives in to sin, how can we possibly help some one else find the path that leads away from those temptations that bother them? Jesus wants us to love and help one another. He wants us to stay strong and be encouraging to each other. But there is a certain amount of effort that we must do for ourselves. I think that is what He is warning us about here in this parable. We should pray for our brother with the speck; but we desperately need to pray for the plank we have!

9- LEAVEN
(Kingdom of Heaven Parable)

MATTHEW 13:33 (Confirmed)

Taught in Sermon by the sea of Galilee to multitudes

"Another parable He spoke to them, *"The kingdom of Heaven is like leaven, which a woman took and hid in three measures of meal till it was all leavened."*

LUKE 13:20-21

Taught in a temple, it is unknown which temple but taught to all present at the time

"And again He said, *"To what shall I liken the kingdom of God? It is like leaven, which a woman took and hid in three measures of meal till it was all leavened."*

EXTRA READING

LUKE 12:1	I CORINTHIANS 5: 6

This parable is one of many of the 'Kingdom of Heaven' parables that Jesus told at various times trying to explain Heaven to the multitudes. The concept of Heaven is nearly impossible for the human mind to grasp.

The leaven mentioned in this story is what we call today yeast. Yeast is a substance that is put into flour or, as in this case, cornmeal, or more likely barley meal. When it is mixed with the flour and with a liquid, either water or milk, it causes the bread dough to rise. The baker can then divide it into many loaves or biscuits. It serves two purposes at that point in the bread. It makes a better tasting product. Have you ever baked a pan of biscuits using plain flour and no yeast? They are hard, flat and uneatable! Those biscuits appear to be very greasy. So that little bit of yeast has made the product taste better and useable and bigger. The yeast has allowed the flour to distribute the shortening and become fluffy.

Jesus is trying to tell us here about the future growth of the Kingdom. It is beginning as a small group (the twelve and Him.) Each day it grows with a few more understanding. Those few will spread the gospel to a few more. I remember when I was maybe six or seven and I was beginning to have friends outside the family circle, my younger sister was quite upset. She was concerned that if 'Sister' loved the neighbor girl, she could no longer love her too. But Mama told us that when you love one person, your heart grows big enough to love two. When you love two, your heart grows large enough to love four...and on and on and on...So we would always love each other, even when 'strangers' entered our world.

That was the same principal Jesus was sharing with this parable. Jesus is telling us to act as yeast and grow His Kingdom. As we spread the word to one and that one spreads the word to another... and on and on and on... It will be a blessing to those we show the gospel, and it will be a blessing to our own hearts! We all will 'grow' in God's word , like yeast causes the bread to rise!

***The Sunday I taught this lesson I took some biscuits baked with whole-wheat flour with no yeast or baking soda. It was a good visual prop for everyone to see a bit of what bread would have looked like then. It even served as a reminder of the bread cooked for Passover. And it was my intention that everyone would see how flat and unattractive the world would be if we did not help make God's kingdom grow. But I have to admit the strongest reaction from most members of the class was pity for my poor husband!

10- LOST SHEEP / LOST COIN

MATTHEW 18:10-14

Place unknown. Taught to disciples and others that were present

"Take heed that you do not despise one of these little ones, for I say to you that in heaven their angels always see the face of My Father who is in heaven. For the Son of man has come to save that which was lost. What do you think? If a man has a hundred sheep, and one of them goes astray, does he not leave the ninety-nine and go to the mountains to seek the one that is straying? And if he should find it, assuredly, I say to you, he rejoices more over that sheep than over the ninety-nine that did not go astray. Even so, it is not the will of your Father who is in heaven that one of these little ones should perish."

LUKE 15:1-10 (Confirmed)

Place unknown. Crowd included Disciples, Pharisees, scribes and others

*"*Then all the tax collectors and the sinners drew near to Him to hear Him. And the Pharisees and scribes complained, saying. "This Man receives sinners and eats with them." So He spoke this parable to them, saying, " *What man of you, having a hundred sheep, if he loses one of them, does not leave the ninety-nine in the wilderness, and go after the one which is lost until he finds it? And when he has found it, he lays it on his shoulders, rejoicing. And when he comes home, he calls together his friends and neighbors, saying to them, 'Rejoice with me, for I have found my sheep which was lost!' I say to you that likewise there will be more joy in heaven over one sinner who repents than over ninety-nine just persons who need no repentance. Or what woman, having ten silver coins, if she loses one coin, does not light a lamp, sweep the house, and search carefully until she finds it? And when she has found it, she calls her friends and neighbors together, saying, 'Rejoice with me, for I have found the piece which I lost!' Likewise, I say to you, there is joy in the presence of angels of God over one sinner who repents."*

EXTRA READING

| LUKE 9:56 | JOHN 6:39- 40 | JOHN 10:4- 5 |
| JOHN 10:25-30 | JOHN 17:12 | |

Neither of the two gospels that present this parable tells us where this lesson was taught but both indicates that the disciples were the intended audience that Jesus was addressing even though Luke did say there were others present. Matthew says that the disciples were questioning Jesus in reference to who would be the greatest in the kingdom of heaven. Jesus then called a child from those gathered around Him. He placed that child in the center of the group and told them that they all had to become as humble as that child to even enter the Kingdom of Heaven (Matt 18:1-4).

According to Luke's text the conversation began with the Pharisees making accusations against Jesus. They were not pleased with His association with the sinners (Luke15:1-2). In verse 3 Luke confirmed this to be a parable.

It is rare that the gospels are so very different in describing the surroundings concerning a parable. The differences lead me to believe that this must have been one of those times that Jesus used the same teaching in different discourses. It is understandable that He would do that since this is a very basic message as to why He came here to begin with! Any believer needs to understand this lesson before he can build and develop his faith. So it would have been one that Jesus would have wanted everyone to hear early in His ministry.

In Matthew Jesus began His parable with the answer to the disciples' question. He told them to beware that the little ones were protected. And He said that their angels could always see the face of God. He then told them that the Son of Man had come to save those that were lost. His teaching then goes into the parable we want to study. He talks of a man we would call a sheep farmer today. This farmer had one hundred sheep. One of his sheep strayed off from the flock. After the farmer had made sure the others were settled down to grazing in the wilderness, he left them to go off and search for the one that was gone. He would not stop looking until he found it. When the day was over and the lost lamb was safe with the others, can't you picture the farmer bragging about his good day? He was so happy and relieved that the lamb was returned that he forgot that the stray had been a problem to be dealt with earlier that morning!

In Luke Jesus began with the parable in answer to the accusations of the Pharisees. He told the same story He had told in Matthew concerning the lost sheep. The only difference in the story is that in Luke, the farmer invited his friends and family to celebrate with him over the return of his lamb. And then Jesus continued to try to show those listening that day the message He wanted them to understand. So He told them of a woman that had a limited amount of money, in this case only ten coins. Somehow she misplaced one coin. It is a big concern of anyone that might loose money. I know when I have one or two dollars in my pocket and if I reach to touch them, and I don't feel them there… well, the world stops until I recover that money. And this lady in Jesus' story was just like me, or I am just like her, since she came first. She stopped her chores, she lit a lamp, and she found her broom. Then she set about finding that coin!

When she found it she celebrated by inviting all her friends and neighbors over to share her joy! Now, I will admit I don't usually go to that extent to celebrate my two dollars but I am certainly glad when I do find them! (I usually end up remembering where I spent them.) And that lady was very happy to find her coin.

What is Jesus expressing in these verses of this parable? Some might think He was telling us how very protective we are of our possessions. Maybe He was trying to show us that we are too dependent on things. Either of those theories could be true. Either would be a good lesson for us to ponder; but in this instance, they are not what Jesus had on His mind that day.

In Matthew the first few verses give us a very clear message as to what is the opinion that Jesus has of new believers. (We need to remember that nearly all believers in that day were new converts) He is calling the new believers His *little ones*. The humble believers are those that are just beginning to trust and need the protection and guidance of those with a stronger and more developed faith. He also tells us that the angels that belong to those new children of God always see the face of God. There are two things of importance in that statement. First he is verifying the Jewish belief that people <u>do</u> have guardian angels. So we do have the comfort of that knowledge. There are angels watching over us! Jesus confirmed this in His own words! We don't have to wonder or question that fact anymore.

The second thing that one statement tells us is a warning. The angels of the new children always see God's face. OK, that means they always have access to God. They can always act as interceptor if the new child is in harm's way. And I am talking about danger from another person that might be misleading this child, or perhaps neglecting the needs of this new believer. As a child these new believers need to be nurtured. I am sure that all the warnings that were given to the multitudes by Jesus are serious business for us today too! This is a subject we have discussed as a class. Do we nurture those new members that come to us, as we should? We need to hear with our ears and our hearts! We must not forget they are called from the beginning the "children of God" .

Jesus then begins to teach the parable. The man represents God. The sheep are the believers in His fold. The lost sheep is the man (or woman) that goes astray. In the second part of the parable the woman represents God. (Boy! Won't that please some people in today's world? I hope no one would take that out of context and misquotes me on that one! I do believe God is male, with no doubt in my mind (I don't think there is any doubt) The only doubt that I would voice is one that NO ONE has gender as we know it today in heaven at all. But we as humans cannot picture that fact.

(Maybe I have stumbled on another truth that sometimes just seems to find us. Maybe God is telling us here that gender has nothing to do with His plan of salvation. None of us have ever really thought that it did. Maybe He is telling us that His gender (or ours) doesn't have any meaning in the story of life. We have known that men and women can be children of God. At the same time we insist God be male. Maybe He has no gender, as we know it today. I recently read a book, THE SHACK by Wm. Paul Young and in it, God was represented as a female. I absolutely loved the book. I saw many truths brought to light that I could not have put into words myself. But I sort of ignored the part about God being female. I just marked that up to the book being fiction. It seems now, that I might have been picking and choosing the truths I wanted to believe. Maybe, it is time for me to read it again.)

But it is for sure, time for me to stop wandering and to get back to the parable. Jesus told this parable. He, Himself, represented God as female in the second part. Again the coins were the believers and the tenth coin went astray.

Both of these stories, as well as the Prodigal Son, have the same messages. God loves all His children. Not one is unfit to be saved. And the joy He feels when one is brought into the fold is worthy of a great celebration. God and all the angels in heaven sing songs of joy when one child comes to salvation! It is His intention that all people will come to fellowship with Him. It is His desire that all peoples will seek forgiveness and attempt to follow His will. And I told you earlier that the farmer had forgotten about the anger, or disappointment he had felt when he discovered the lamb missing. I said that to remind you that when you seek forgiveness, God 'forgets' what a problem you have been previously! When He forgives your sins or your going astray, it is forgotten.

I truly believe that we as humans have a much harder time forgetting and forgiving ourselves. If you pinch me and later apologize, I will forgive you and go on with life. I doubt I'll ever think of it again. But I will never forget the name I called you when you did it! True, I apologized to you and you forgave me…but some night, maybe a year from now I will wake up with the horror of that on my mind and I am haunted about it again. And I wonder how could God forgive someone with the sins that I have committed in the record book. I have had counselors tell me that if a sin still pops up to haunt me, it is because it is one I have not asked forgiveness for…or my repentance was not sincere…This is not so simple…I wish it were. There are things I am so sorry for that I cannot wipe it out of my mind. I guess that is one way of being sure I have learned my lesson and won't do it again. But we don't have the ability to forget like God does. His love is so complete that He is able to wipe our sins away from existence if we have repented and asked for His forgiveness. It is no longer in the record book! But we don't have the ability to love that completely, especially for our own selves.

Matthew closes His version with these words:

> *"Even so, it is not the will of your Father who is in heaven that one of these little ones should perish."*

I cannot think of a better summary for this parable than those words, with the following ones. Luke 9:56 verifies the words of this parable when he quotes Jesus:

> *"For the Son of Man did not come to destroy lives but to save them."*

It is God's will that every soul will be brought to salvation. Each one is as important as the whole. There is none that God would leave behind if they would only seek Him.

There would never be a single lost sheep.

11- MARRIAGE FEAST / GREAT SUPPER
(Kingdom of Heaven Parable)

MATTHEW 22:1-14 (Confirmed)

Most likely taught in the Temple Court to multitude including Pharisees, disciples, and others

"And Jesus answered and spoke to them again by parables and said:

"The kingdom of heaven is like a certain king who arranged a marriage for his son, and sent out his servants to call those who were invited to the wedding; and they were not willing to come. Again, he sent out other servants, saying, " Tell those who are invited, 'See, I have prepared my dinner; my oxen and fatted cattle are killed, and all things are ready. Come to the wedding.' But they made light of it and went their ways, one to his own farm, another to his business. And the rest seized his servants, treated them spitefully, and killed them. But when the king heard about it, he was furious. And he sent out his armies, destroyed those murderers, and burned up their city. Then he said to his servants, 'The wedding is ready, but those who were invited were not worthy. Therefore go into the highways, and as many as you find, invite to the wedding.' So those servants went out into the highways and gathered together all whom they found, both bad and good. And the wedding hall was filled with guests. But when the king came in to see the guests, he saw a man there who did not have on a wedding garment. So he said to him, 'Friend, how did you come in here without a wedding garment?' And he was speechless. Then the king said to the servants, 'Bind him hand and foot, take him away, and cast him into outer darkness: there will be weeping and gnashing of teeth. For many are called, but few are chosen.'"

LUKE 14:15-24

Jesus was a guest of a Pharisee. Taught to all present at dinner. Including other Pharisees and leaders of community

"Now when one of those who sat at the table with Him heard these things, he said to Him, "Blessed is he who shall eat bread in the kingdom of God!" Then He said to him, *"A certain man gave a great supper and invited many, and sent his servant at supper time to say to those who were invited, 'Come for all things are now ready.' But they all with one accord began to make excuses. The first said to him, 'I have bought a piece of ground, and I must go and see it. I ask you to have me excused' And another said, 'I have bought five yoke of oxen, and I am going to test them. I ask you to have me excused.' Still another said, 'I have married a wife, and therefore, I can not come.' So that servant came and reported these things to his master. Then the master of the house, being angry, said to his servant, 'Go out quickly into the streets and lanes of the city, and bring in here the poor and the maimed and the lame and the blind.' And the servant said, 'Master, it is done as you commanded, and still there is room.' Then the master said to the servant, 'Go out into the highways and hedges, and compel them to come in, that my house may be filled. For I say to you that none of those men who were invited shall taste my supper.'"*

EXTRA READING

PROVERBS 9:2	PROVERBS 9:5	ISAIAH 55:1-2
MATTHEW 10:11-13	MATTHEW 20:16	JOHN 7:37-38
ROMANS 3:19-20	REVELATIONS 19:6 -10	

This is one of the Kingdom of Heaven parables where Jesus is trying to explain to those listening what can be expected in heaven. He realizes the difficulty humans have even accepting the concept of heaven; much less have any idea of what it will be like! Humans have many questions concerning heaven; Will we eat meals? Who will do the cooking? Wash the dishes? What will we wear? How do we get there? What will we do all day? Will we have special friends? Will each of us have our own apartment? Will we know our mama? Will she still be our mama? Will we remember anything from this life? Will our pets be there? Will they remember us as their owners? Will we be friends with those that we were feuding with here? How long will we be there? Will we know Paul and John? Will Matthew know I have written this paper and talked about him? It is clear I could fill this sheet with questions and never list all of them! That's just a few that come to my mind this few minutes! So if I put some thought behind it... WOW! And I have all inklings your list would be just as long and different! But in this parable Jesus has set out to answer one of those questions. Our purpose today is to find which question will be answered.

This parable is confirmed in Matthew. In Matthew it seems that Jesus might still be in one of the temple courts. He had been there in Chapter 21 and He had been teaching there. He had just cleaned house and tossed all the commercial businesses out of His Father's house. After that event He told the parables we call 'The Two Sons" and "The Wicked Tenants" and the next verses go into the parable we are studying today. That leads me to think that it was Matthew's opinion this was taught at the same time and in Temple.

In Luke, Jesus was a dinner guest at the home of an important Pharisee. Jesus sat at the table there He gave a teaching about healing on the Sabbath and told the parable called "The Ambitious Guest" and then He told the parable we are concerned with right now.

In Matthew the key character in the story was a king planning a wedding supper for his son. And in Luke it was a man planning a great supper for many chosen friends and acquaintances. My point is I think this is another case of Jesus using the same message at two separate times of His ministry; maybe even the same day. But at either teaching the audience would have been a mixture of people present: at the temple in Matthew's text the crowd would have included Jewish men, Pharisees and scribes, any official of the temple, disciples and various business men from the local area: at the home of the Pharisee as Luke described, the guest list would have been very nearly the same variety. There would have probably been more women present at the home in Luke's version. Both gospels indicate that this teaching took place on a Sabbath afternoon. Again according to some authorities, it would have been the Sunday before Easter Sunday.

The story Jesus told in Matthew says that the kingdom of heaven is like a king that planned a wedding feast for his son. He sent his servants out to invite the people he thought worthy to attend the celebration. They refused his offer to come. So he sent his servants to explain to them that the feast was prepared and waiting for them to come. And he told them of all the good things he had prepared, but they still refused. This time they even made fun of the king and abused the servants, killing some of them. The king became very angry and sent his armies out to avenge his servants and his honor. He had all those killed that had murdered his servants and burned their city.

Then the king sent other servants out to invite as many as they could find from the highways to the banquet. It did not matter to him whether they were good or bad as long as the wedding hall was full of people to celebrate with his son.

The hall was full and as the king walked about to admire the celebration, he saw a man without his Sunday best on. The king asked him how he got into the hall without special garments on and the man was without an answer. He was speechless. The king had his servants tie this man up and throw him out of the hall into the darkness. Jesus tells us then that there would be weeping and gnashing of teeth because many would be called, but only a few actually would be chosen.

The story Luke told in his text started with one of the guests sitting at table with Jesus . The guest seemed to recognize Jesus and made a comment that those that ate in the kingdom of God would be blessed. Then Jesus told the following story.

An important man planned and prepared a huge meal and sent his servants to the different homes to invite everyone. They all had one excuse or another and refused to attend the man's feast.

When the servant reported this to his master, he became very angry. He then sent his servant out into the streets to invite anyone and everyone to the party. The master had no care be the people poor or rich, maimed or whole, blind or sighted, it did not matter. He just wanted his hall to be full.

When the servant returned, the hall still had some room for more so the master sent him back out to compel others to attend this great supper. He wanted to be sure his home was filled so that there was no room for the first people he had invited. He told the servant that none of those originally invited should taste his food.

What does this parable tell us about the kingdom of heaven? Well, first lets see if we can understand what the marriage feast or great supper was like. From other books I have read, or movies I have watched, I understand that celebrations like the two mentioned here were very special occasions. Weddings, especially a king's son, were at least weeklong events. All kinds of things were planned for the guests: hunting events, dancing at night, all sorts of entertainment, and endless tables of food and drink. And as for the great supper the second man planned…that was pretty special too. He might not have had a particular reason for giving the dinner but he wanted to celebrate his friendships. The host of either event would have planned for his guests to stay and spend time at his home. It was a really big deal to have such a to do. And normally you would think the guests would have been honored to be invited.

The invited guests refused to attend, giving such flimsy excuses as to be unbelievable, such as tending to his stock or going to see a piece of land he had bought. (Why didn't he go see the land before he bought it?) Or one said to test out some oxen he had just bought, I'm sure he should have already tested them. And besides I doubt seriously that <u>he</u> would have tested them anyway. His servants would have done that! If I don't believe their excuses today, I'm sure the hosts didn't believe them then. They were insulted, as well they should have been. Those people they had chosen to be their guests did not seem to have the time to spare to even come to a dinner already prepared and waiting!

Considering the insults and disappointment the two hosts suffered, they both reacted in much the same way. They sent their servants to invite other people to the feast. Strangers off the street were more welcome in their homes than those they had thought were friends. These people were unknown to the host but they were treated as guests and in turn, showed honor to the hosts, except for one man that attended the wedding feast in Matthew's text. This man did not put on his best clothing to attend the dinner and the king took it as an insult. He was thrown out for his lack of respect.

Now, back to the question for which we are seeking an answer: what is this story telling us about the kingdom of heaven?

These affairs were in their time something to be considered a very special occasion. The people invited should have been excited and planning for it like a child today looks for Santa. Heaven is such a place that God has planned for His children. I can't sit here and tell you of the glories that will be there waiting for those that will be honored by going. I don't have that big an imagination! I have heard the songs and read the books and marked it all down in my heart…the cloudless skies…the streets of gold… the mansions with many rooms…the angels singing songs of praise…the crowns of jewels…the fellowship with Moses…the trees bearing twelve different fruits… and the throne of God…and the face of our precious Jesus Christ…

God has planned this event for His children. And at the time the children that He had invited were the Israelites, the Jewish nation, including the Pharisees. They were the Chosen Ones and they were offered all the blessings of this kingdom of heaven. But continuously they betrayed His love with disobedience and disrespect. Over and over they refused to honor God and accept His invitation. They had refused to tell others about their God and share His Love with the world. Finally God decided Himself to invite others to His Great Feast. He sent His Servant, His Son to invite them. He did not (and He does not) care if their reputations were good or bad. He did not care if they were rich or poor. He did not care if they were Jewish or pagan. He did not care if their bodies were wounded or whole. He wanted them to come and celebrate life with Him.

All the faults and things wrong would be repaired when these people loved God and repented of their sin. When they put on their best and showed God that they did indeed respect and honor Him, they would be plenty worthy to attend God's Great Feast. That is why the one man was asked to leave the king's feast. Remember? He was not in his best clothing. Jesus told us that many are called. Everyone has the invitation. But few are chosen. Those are the few that really understand we cannot take God's love for granted and just expect to slip into the feast without giving our best. We must respect and honor God and we must come as close to doing His will as we humanly can!

We teach God's endless love…and His love is greater than we <u>can</u> teach; but we must not assume all is forgiven and we can live as we choose, then we will all meet in heaven. That is not the word of God. Jesus warns us that there will be weeping and gnashing of teeth. In other words there will be some people calling themselves *Christian* (and truly believing it to be true) that are going to be very disappointed when the final invitations are extended.

I have heard many times a quote that I can't find today, and I'm not sure that it is actually in the Bible. In fact, in this case. I'm nearly positive that it is not. I think it is a "Grandma's idea" from somewhere. So many quotes that are accredited to the Bible are really Ben Franklin and such people. But regardless this one certainly fits here. It says:

GOD WILL HAVE HIS NUMBER, IF HE HAS TO TAKE
THE BABES FROM THE MOTHER'S ARMS.

This parable tells us who will be there. That is the question it answers. God will fill His heaven and He will do it with those that are worthy and deserving of this blessing, only those that put forth their very best effort. He does not judge us by our wealth, our health, our beauty, our nationality, or any other feature that we as humans use to distinguish one from another; but He will not accept second best! There will be no slackers allowed.

God does not need us, each individual, He has invited us to be a part of His plan; but His plan will be completed with or without us. He could, but He will not force the issue. It is our own choice to choose if we want to accept His gracious invitation.

12- THE TEN TALENTS
(Kingdom of Heaven Parable)

MATTHEW 25:14-30

Taught on Mount of Olivet (Olives) to the disciples. One of the End Time parables

"For the kingdom of heaven is like a man traveling to a far country, who called his own servants and delivered his goods to them. And to one he gave five talents, to another two, and to another one, to each according to his own ability; and immediately he went on a journey. Then he who had received the five talents went and traded them, and made another five talents. And likewise he who had received two gained two more also. But he who had received one went and dug in the ground, and hid his lord's money. After a long time the lord of those servants came and settled accounts with them. So he who had received five talents came and brought five other talents saying, 'Lord, you delivered to me five talents: look, I have gained five more talents besides them.' His lord said to him, 'Well done, good and faithful servant: you were faithful over a few things, I will make you ruler over many things. Enter into the joy of your lord.' He also who had received two talents came and said, 'Lord, you delivered to me two talents; look, I have gained two more talents besides them.' His lord said to him, 'Well done, good and faithful servant; you have been faithful over a few things. I will make you ruler over many things. Enter into the joy of your lord.' Then he who had received the one talent came and said, 'Lord, I knew you to be a hard man, reaping where you have not sown, and gathering where you have not scattered seed. And I was afraid, and went and hid your talent in the ground. Look, there you have what is yours.' But his lord answered and said to him, 'You wicked and lazy servant, you knew that I reap where I have not sown, and gather where I have not scattered seed. So you ought to have deposited my money with the bankers, and at my coming I would have received back my own with interest.' Therefore take the talent from

him, and give it to him who has ten talents. For unto everyone who has, more will be given, and he will have abundance; but from him who does not have, even what he has will be taken away. And cast the unprofitable servant into the outer darkness. There will be weeping and gnashing of teeth,"

LUKE 19:11-27 (Confirmed)

Taught during the trip to Jerusalem before the Last Week to the disciples, with others probably hearing Him

"Now as they heard these things, He spoke another parable, because He was near Jerusalem and because they thought the kingdom of God would appear immediately. Therefore He said, *"A certain nobleman went into a far country to receive for himself a kingdom and to return. So he called ten of his servants, delivered to them ten minas, and said to them, 'Do business till I come.' But his citizens hated him, and sent a delegation after him, saying; 'We will not have this man to reign over us.' And so it was that when he returned, having received the kingdom, he then commanded these servants, to whom he had given the money, to be called to him, That he might know how much every man had gained by trading. Then came the first saying, 'Master your mina has earned ten minas.' And he said to him, 'Well done, good servant; because you were faithful in a very little, have authority over ten cities.' And the second came saying, 'Master, your mina has earned five minas.' Likewise he said to him, 'You also be over five cities.' Then another came saying, 'Master, here is your mina, which I have kept away in a handkerchief. For I feared you, because you are an austere man. You collect what you did not deposit, and reap what you did not sow.' And he said to him, 'Out of your own mouth I will judge you, you wicked servant. You knew that I was an austere man, collecting what I did not deposit and reaping what I did not sow. Why then, did you not put my money in the bank, that at my coming I might have collected it with interest? And he said to those who stood by, 'Take the mina from him and give it to him who has ten minas.' (But they said to him, 'Master, he has ten minas.') For I say to you, that to everyone who has, will be given; and from him who does not have, even what he has will be taken away from him. But bring here those enemies of mine, who did not want me to reign over them, and slay them before me.'*

EXTRA READING

MATTHEW 13:12	MATTHEW 22:13	MATTHEW 24:45-47
LUKE 8:18	LUKE 22:29	JOHN 3:27
ROMANS 2:6-10	ROMANS 12:6	I CORINTHIANS 3:7-8
I CORINTHIANS 4:2	I CORINTHIANS 15:58	II CORINTHIANS 3:5
GALATIANS 6: 3-10		

Matthew places this parable in the discourse called the Sermon of Olivet. That means it was taught during the last week while Jesus was in Jerusalem for Passover celebrations and just before His crucifixion. Many call this set of teachings "The End Time" teachings. Jesus spent a good bit of that week trying to prepare His disciples for the coming events. Since it was taught on the Mount of Olivet (Olives), as Matthew reported, then it was only for the disciples. Do you remember we studied another parable earlier that was among those teachings that day? The twelve and Jesus had attended Temple and later went out from the city to rest in the olive garden near by. While they relaxed there Jesus told the twelve many parables and things He felt would help them cope with the days ahead.

Luke says this parable was taught while Jesus and the disciples traveled toward Jerusalem for Passover week. We have already studied some of His teachings from that time too. He most likely taught for most of the trip. His time with the disciples was now coming to an end, and like any good teacher He didn't want to leave them without as much knowledge as He had to give. Since this was a holiday for all Jews, there would have been others traveling on the same road with them.

This parable is one of the Kingdom of Heaven parables we have mentioned. Jesus is trying in every way to show His followers the beauty and glory of heaven. He wants them to know why it is the place that should be their lifetime goal. He wants them to understand that it is where His Father and He will be waiting for the children to come home. So He tells many of these kingdom parables. This parable is confirmed in the Book of Luke.

Matthew's text says that Jesus told the following story:

A man decided to go on a long trip so he called his servants to him and told them of the plans. He then divided his worldly goods among those servants to protect and guard while he was gone. He recognized that everyone has his own level of ability so he gave a different portion to each servant. Each servant would be held responsible for the portion he was given.

Let's stop a minute and learn what a talent was. A talent was a piece of money originally equal to the price of an ox. It was called an ox talent for a long time. Later as people became more sophisticated coins were shaped from metals: gold, silver, and copper. Unlike today, all money was made from precious metals. There were no paper versions.

NAME		WEIGHT
BEKAH	½ SHEKEL	.067 OZ
SHEKEL	20 GERAHS	.134 OZ.
MINA (MANEH)	50 SHEKELS	1 ¼ LBS
TALENT	3000 SHEKELS	75 LBS

It is very hard to place a dollar value on the coins then that we can compare to our money today. For one thing the references that I have give a good trace of coins and money but it goes back to well beyond the time that Jesus was here. It is hard to find the point of value during those particular years.

One of the biggest reason for having difficulty naming a value is that there were so many different coins; Roman, Egyptian, the Temple weights, Royal weights, common weights, and many more. It seems that each city or political entity had some form of its' own money.

We do have the weights required to make up the coins I have listed in the chart. And those are the Jewish temple weights for silver and for the common man. The weights for royalty were higher, for example a talent would have equaled a hundred-fifty pounds. The shekel was the standard of weight for the most used coin. (Joseph was sold to the traveling merchants for twenty pieces of silver or twenty shekels.) And Judas identified Jesus for thirty pieces of silver or thirty shekels. This was such a familiar coin that the writers did not always call these coins *shekels* (their proper name). They just called them pieces of silver.

If we compare the weight of a shekel with the weight of the talent the value of the talent is a lot of money! Seventy-five pounds compared to a little more than one tenth of an ounce. One other fact that we know is that the value of a gold coin was approximately fifteen percent higher than that of a silver coin of the same weight.

So you can see a talent was a good deal of money to leave with a servant. This man trusted one servant with five talents, a fortune in anybody's eyes! He left a second servant with two talents and the third servant with one.

The man chose well when he picked the first servant to take care of the five talents. The servant had no fear; he immediately re-invested the money and doubled the value! Smart, brave man! The second servant responded the same way. He, too, doubled his talents. Now the third man was frightened. His main goal was to protect the money entrusted to his care. So he did the only thing he could think of that would be totally safe. He hid the talent placed in his care.

When the man returned he called the servants to him and asked for an accounting of each one. The servant entrusted with five talents reported his investment and his gain of five more talents. The man was very pleased. He rewarded this servant by making him responsible over many more things. (He had told the servant he had done well with a few things. Can you imagine how rich this man must have been to call five talents a few things?!)

The second servant reported his investment to the man and he, too, was rewarded with more responsibility. But the third servant explained to the man that he was aware of the man's personality and character of being a hard man. The servant told him that he knew the man to be a man that took what he could where he found it; so, he, the servant, being a careful man himself, hid the talent he had been given and could now return it with no fear of losing any value of it through investments.

Needless to say, the man was not pleased at all. He used the servant's own words to explain his judgment of the servant. The servant knew him to be ruthless and greedy, yet he only returned the one talent. It should have been apparent to the servant that the man would always want his money to grow! The man would no longer trust anything to this servant. What he had, the one talent, would be taken from him and given to the man who had invested well and had ten talents. And this servant would be put away. The man told the others there that there would be weeping and unhappiness.

In Luke's text the man of the story Jesus told had to travel on a trip. He was about to receive a kingdom. He called ten of his servants to him and gave each one mina. They were to use this money while he was gone and carry out his business. After he left on his trip, others did not approve of his becoming a king, so they followed and tried to prevent this from happening. They were not successful in their goal so he acquired the kingship. When he returned, he called his servants to him for an accounting of his money.

The first servant had done exceedingly well! He now had ten minas to give his master. The king was very pleased and placed this servant in charge over ten cities within his new kingdom. The second servant had earned an additional four minas, giving him a total of five now. The king gave him the responsibility of five cities. The third servant had hidden the mina away tied in a handkerchief. He was proud now to return that mina to the master. He told the king he knew him to be man that would reap where he had not sown, so he had been afraid to take a chance on losing his money.

The king was very angry that that servant had not even deposited the money where it might have drawn interest while he was gone. He took the mina from him and gave it to the servant with ten minas, although others complained that that servant already had ten.

The king then explained that those that had would receive more. Those that did not have would loose what little they had thought they had. Then the king called for those that had protested his becoming a king and had them killed.

Both of these stories tell exactly the same message. It is a man in one, a king in the other. The money values are much different but for the sake of the story it does not matter at all. And the purpose Jesus had in either story was to continue to try to make His followers understand the kingdom of heaven. He is still hoping His disciples will see the glory of heaven through His parables. Luke even tells us the disciples were thinking that the kingdom would be coming very soon! Just like us today; and like every man that has lived between then and now! But it is yet to come, and we are yet to understand what it is going to be like! I hope through study of this parable we can get a bit more understanding from Jesus' words.

Matthew's wealthy man (in Luke, the king) was Jesus. He was to establish a kingdom. There were of course many that opposed that fact. They (some of them were the Pharisees) followed Him and continuously tried to prevent him from accomplishing it. But He succeeded in spite of all their efforts. He established His kingdom of the children of God. But that's the short version of what was going on in this story. That's sort of like telling the ending first. So let's go to the "in the meantime..."

When the story first started the man (God) called those that were His faithful servants and He gave out the talents or assignments that would help Him in the growth of His kingdom. Each person had a different number of talents. He expected each servant to do according to his own ability. And He trusted each one to carry out his responsibility. (Remember, our assignment, the only thing Jesus named for us to do, was and is. to spread the gospel.)

As we can see in the story, some did well. They invested carefully and as in the parable called "The Sower" some brought forth one hundred fold. And some were not productive at all. God told those that were productive that He would trust them with more assignments. He was '"Well pleased". This servant represents the worker in the church today; the woman that does the bookwork and handles the bank accounts well; the deacon that calls the widow and offers to help her find someone to build the ramp she needs at her doorsteps; and the pianist that practices for hours on end to be sure the music is pleasing to God's ears. Each person's ability falls in a different place and each person's job requires different commitments. But all are pleasing to God when done with the heart that does it to please God. Now those that do their jobs with the idea of how good it appears to the congregation...well, that is most likely covered in another parable.

The third servant, in both cases blamed the character of his master for his failure. That is the man that says because God is demanding and strict in His expectations, and the man is afraid of His displeasure, he would prefer to do nothing rather than risk doing something wrong. That is a pitiful excuse. Because the third man could have at least invested the money in a bank account that would have drawn some interest, and there was no risk in that. The servant would have had at bit of profit to show.

As the servant did it, the master got back only what He had given to the servant to begin with. This person in today's world doesn't mention God in any of his conversations. He's afraid he will offend someone. He doesn't bother to write a letter telling a friend about God's love. He is concerned that in today's world it is not politically correct to depend on God's grace. The servant was just plain lazy and that man in today's time is just as lazy!

Jesus is telling us in this parable that we all have been given a number of talents. And I found it very interesting to learn that the history of the meaning of that word *talent* came from this parable. It was originally used as a measurement of money, as we discussed at the start. But through time it became the word we use today that means a natural gift of some special ability, such as the ability to paint a picture, or the gift of gab (to talk to anyone about anything). And that new use of the word is traced back specifically to this parable and Jesus' use of it that day. Isn't that super?

Anyway, we all have according to Jesus some amount of talent. Each is different and I've heard so many people say, "I do not have any talent for anything." They say they can't sing. They can't play an instrument. They can't do this or that or the other… maybe that is true, but they can pray! They can sweep the floors. Or they can knit lap blankets for the elderly. They can call the sick and chat a minute. They can drive an elderly lady to church. They can cook a meal for the recent widower.

Talents come in as many varieties as people do! But then lazy people like the third servant seem to be in abundance too. In most churches today I think the most of the work that is accomplished is done by far less than half the members. In one church my husband and I attended for a while there were approximately three hundred members. About thirty to thirty-five came regularly. About half of those did most of the work to maintain the church services. Why?

Because Jesus tells us here that if one like the third servant that does not complete his assignment, then that busy piano player does it. The assignments are delegated to another if they are neglected by one. God's plan will be carried out. It would be better if all would assume their rightful chores, but if not, then God will ask someone that loves Him and chooses to do His work to carry it out. Those people that work with love for God always seem to have the time and ability (or talent) to accomplish the job at hand. I'm not sure but what any of us could claim any "talent" if we tried! Maybe having a talent is just simply attempting the project! (Maybe I COULD sing if I had the nerve!)

When Jesus does return, He will call for an accounting for all the talents He has placed in your care. Those that have used and improved the ones He originally gave you, or trusted you with, will have acquired more through your experiences and He will be pleased. Those that have been unfaithful and let their resentment destroy their love and loyalty to God will be held in contempt and will face the wrath of God's judgment. Those that through their own wickedness that they should try to shift the blame for their misbehavior to God will face eternal judgment. There is not, nor can there be, any excuse for not returning to God something of your life more than just that you were breathing for so many years. I think that when I read of the servant that only returned what had been given to him. Some people try to do with their life.

The kingdom of heaven will be made up of those that do use the talents that God has given them. Those that have taken the chances that sometimes did hurt or scar or batter their heart and body. But all those ills will be wiped away in God's love and His pleasure to spend time with those of you that did the best you could.

13- WHEAT AND TARES
(Kingdom of Heaven Parable)

MATTHEW 13:24-30 (Confirmed)

Taught in Sermon by the Sea to multitudes

"Another parable He put forth to them, saying, " *The kingdom of heaven is like a man who sowed good seed in his field: but while men slept, his enemy came and sowed tares among the wheat and went his way. But when the grain had sprouted and produced a crop, then the tares also appeared. So the servants of the owner came and said to him, 'Sir, did you not sow good seed in your field? How then does it have tares?' He said to them, 'An enemy has done this.' The servants said to him, 'Do you want us then to go and gather them up?' But he said, 'No, lest while you gather up the tares you also uproot the wheat with them. Let both grow together until the harvest, and at the time of harvest I will say to the reapers, 'First gather together the tares and bind them in bundles to burn them, but gather the wheat into my barn.'"*

The following verses are Jesus' own words of interpretation of this parable. Taught at a house thought to be Peter's to the disciples

Matthew 13: 36-43

"Then Jesus sent the multitude away and went into the house. And His disciples came to Him, saying, " Explain to us the parable of the tares of the field." He answered and said to them: *"He who sows the good seed is the Son of Man. The field is the world, the good seeds are the sons of the kingdom, but the tares are the sons of the wicked one. The enemy who sowed them is the devil, the harvest is the end of the age, and the reapers are the angels. Therefore as the tares are gathered and burned in the fire, so it will be at the end of this age. The Son of Man will send out His angels, and they will gather out of His kingdom all things that offend, and those who practice lawlessness, and will cast them into the furnace of fire. There will be wailing and gnashing of teeth. Then the righteous will shine forth as the sun in the kingdom of their Father. He who has ears to hear, let him hear!"*

EXTRA READING

EZEKIEL 20:38	MATTHEW 13: 36-43	MATTHEW 13: 49-50
MATTHEW 18:7	MATTHEW 25:32	MARK 9:42
LUKE 17:1-2	II CORINTHIANS 5:10	

This parable is one of the Sermon by the Sea teachings. Jesus and the disciples had been traveling about and returned to Capernaum and stopped by the sea to rest. As they sat there a crowd began to gather. Jesus then got on a small fishing vessel and sat down. He sat and taught from the ship while the crowd stood on the edge of the shore. This parable is one of the kingdom of heaven teachings, where Jesus is trying to make the concept of heaven an understandable message for humans. Matthew confirmed this as a parable.

Jesus told the crowd of a man that sowed his field with good seed, but later at night someone went into the field and sowed the seeds of weeds (tares). As the wheat sprouted the tares grew too. The servants of the man were diligent in their job of caring for the field and saw the weeds. They asked the man if his seed had been good seed. He assured them that the seed had been good but that someone evil had mixed the tares in his field. They then asked him if he wanted them to gather the tares out of the field. He told them he did not want them to disturb the plants. He knew that if they pulled the tares up then, the small wheat plants would be dislodged from their roots too. It was his plan that he would let them grow, undisturbed together and later when he harvested it would be easier to separate the plants without harming the wheat. The tares could be gathered before the wheat and burned. Then the wheat could be harvested and stored.

At this point in the story Matthew related, Jesus then sent the crowd away. He and the disciples went to a near-by house to rest. Most Bible students think that it was the house of Peter. While they were there the disciples gathered around Jesus and asked Him what was the meaning of that parable. His interpretation is as clear as can be said so I have very little to add to this study. The scriptures tell us exactly what Jesus intended His children to learn from this teaching.

The only thing I can add to clarify this parable is maybe to tell you the meaning of a few words: or at least one particular word…tare. So I will do that first. I have always heard that the word tare was speaking of a weed. That could be any number of plants. We have to deal with all kinds of weeds when we are planting a garden, or as in this case a field. One particular plant I remember that used to haunt me in my field of Dixie Lee peas was the cocklebur. It grew four or five feet tall and had nasty spurs on it that would attach itself to any thing around. It was horrible if it got tangled into the cat's fur! And poor puppy would have a tail full if he one time passed through the garden. Everyday I worked in the field I would sit on the porch afterwards and pick these spurs from the legs of my jeans and from the laces in my shoes, and at times even my hair!

But as for weeds; at times even grass can be a weed. In fact any plant that grows where you do not want it to be, is usually called a weed. But this weed Jesus spoke of that day was especially bad. The Greek name for this plant is *zizanion*. The seeds (or heads) are poisonous. They can cause dizziness and death if eaten. It is a grass like plant that is common to that area. Today it is called *bearded darnel*. It looks very much like wheat as it grows, so the servants had been very diligent to even notice it so early in the growth cycle. After it forms a head on the shaft it can be distinguished from wheat easier. Today when this plant mixes in the wheat fields, and it does, it is separated, while the wheat is winnowed. The heads of the tares are smaller so they blow away with the chaff of the wheat. The farmer then sifts the wheat with a sieve that allows the smaller tare heads to pass through and thus, the wheat is clean of all the bad seed.

To interpret this parable I need to nearly follow Jesus' words, word for word, as He told it to the disciples. I can think of no way to say it clearer!

The man that owns the field and sows the good seeds is Jesus. The field where He sows His seed is the whole world. The good seeds He sows are the children of God. The evil man that sows the tares in the field is Satan. The seeds of the tares are the children of Satan. The time of Harvest is the end time we all look forward to daily. The servants that will gather the crop are the angels.

As the crop is harvested on that Day of Judgment, the angels will separate the crop into the tares and wheat. Those (tares) that have been disobedient, lawless, unfaithful to God, and unrepentant will be cast into the furnace of fire. Those (wheat) that have been faithful, obedient, steadfast, and lived according to God's will, (even with forgiven sin); will be gathered by the angels into the grace of God in the kingdom of heaven. These will spend eternity with God with His love surrounding them.

Jesus then gives His warning for those with ears to hear what He is saying. This warning is serious. He means what He says! The threat of the furnace of fire is a literal promise, not a figure of speech. So many times I hear today people that try to weaken or gloss over the threat of hell by saying things like, "It's not a good place to be". Well, the doctor's office while you wait hours on end is not a good place to be! But eventually you will leave and go home, or like my husband and I do, go out to eat somewhere. That's our reward for being patient while we wait. (Sometimes our reward is not really earned!)

My point here is that hell is not a temporally placement. You will not leave and go home. That is home if that is your judgment. Now, I realize I am probably preaching to the choir. If you are reading this paper, more than likely you have made your peace with God and look forward to a much better future than I have described in that last paragraph.

My reason for stressing the truth about hell is to remind you, it is your responsibility to be sure those around you knows the whole truth too. Jesus did not mince words when He told those there that day (and He was talking to His disciples), that the fires of hell are real. He too, was preaching to the choir. Maybe the choir needs to hear it! It should be our goal that as many people as possible around us, hear this story.

The kingdom of heaven will be made up of the good seeds. There they will live and walk in God's sunshine and blessings daily. In fact Jesus told us that day, that the righteous will shine as the sun!

14-HIDDEN TREASURER
15-PEARL OF VALUE
16-DRAGNET
17-HOUSEHOLDER
(All Are Kingdom of Heaven Parables)

These parables were taught at one of the disciple's home one afternoon. The home is believed by most authorities to be Peter's.

14- HIDDEN TREASURE
MATTHEW 13:44 (Confirmed)

"Again, the kingdom of heaven is like treasure hidden in a field, which a man found and hid; and for joy over it, he goes and sells all that he has and buys that field."

EXTRA READING

ISAIAH 55:1	JOHN 4:14	JOHN 6:35	JOHN 7:37-38

15- PEARL OF VALUE
MATTHEW 13:45-46 (Confirmed)

"Again, the kingdom of heaven is like a merchant seeking beautiful pearls, who when he found one pearl of great price, went and sold all that he had and bought it."

EXTRA READING

PROVERBS 2:1-4	PROVERBS 3:13-18	PROVERBS 8:10-11

#16 DRAGNET
MATTHEW 13:47-50 (Confirmed)

"Again, the kingdom of Heaven is like a dragnet that was cast into the sea and gathered some of every kind, which when it was full, they drew to shore; and they sat down and gathered the good into vessels, but threw the bad away. So it will be at the end of the age. The angels will come forth, separate the wicked from among the just, and cast them into the furnace of fire. There will be wailing and gnashing of teeth."

EXTRA READING

MATTHEW 25: 31-46 (actual verse in reference is #32)

17- HOUSEHOLDER
MATTHEW 13:51-52 (Confirmed)

"Jesus said to them, *"Have you understood all these things?"* They said to Him, "Yes, Lord." Then He said to them, *"Therefore every scribe instructed concerning the kingdom of heaven is like a householder who brings out of his treasure things new and old."*

EXTRA READING

PHILIPPIANS 3:7-9

I am sort of combining these four teachings. Jesus taught them together to His disciples one afternoon. He was teaching them about the kingdom of heaven and used all four different allegories to explain the concept to them. Since the thought in each is the same as in the other it seemed sort of silly on my part to write and re-write the same commentary. At the same time I wanted to maintain the integrity of each parable, because they are four separate and different ones. I did find it interesting that Matthew, himself, combined them in one sense. He confirmed them all with one verse. The following verse is the one that confirms them as parables of Jesus Christ:

> "NOW, IT CAME TO PASS, WHEN JESUS HAD FINISHED THESE PARABLES, THAT HE DEPARTED FROM THERE." MATTHEW 13:53

Have you ever found a hundred dollar bill? Have you ever found a diamond ring? Have you ever just walked up on anything of great value? Could you believe your luck, or did you count it among your blessings? If you found it with no chance of finding the owner, did you feel guilty about keeping it? I did find a hundred dollar bill, but it was in the pants pocket of a customer at the dry cleaners where I worked. So I knew who it belonged to. I had to give it back, and funny thing about it, I never missed it out of my pocket. Easy enough to understand, it never was mine. Now my mama found a large diamond in a washing machine at a laundry matt once! A beautiful stone but there was no way to find the owner. She had it mounted on a pretty setting and still wears it today to the best of my knowledge.

The man in parable #14 found a treasure buried on a piece of land. It must have been of great value. He was extremely happy to know where this gift was buried; but he knew he did not own the land. In order to make this treasure his own, he needed to own the land where it was buried. So he sold everything else he had possessed and used the funds to buy that field.

Jesus told this parable to His disciples, trying to help them understand a bit more about the kingdom of heaven. So we need to look at the words from that perspective. It is easy to see heaven as a dear treasure. What little we do know about it is extraordinarily special. The entire earth, being a creation of God has more beauty than one can possibly see and enjoy in a lifetime. It would be impossible to honestly describe it to someone that had not seen any of its glory. And that is the earth I am still talking about!

The wondrous place that heaven is, I can't even find words to begin to describe! And Jesus told us here that the man sold all he had to buy that field. I think He is telling us this time, that those that give their all toward the goal of going to heaven are the ones that will be there. I think He has said that if a man would sell all his possesses for an earthly field of dirt with a bit of treasure on it, how much more is heaven worth? He is telling us that the glories of heaven are the only treasures we possibly need, and to give our all, (talents, devotion, love, time, money and obedience) to accomplish that reward. It is well worth the effort!

This is not the only time Jesus has taught that earthly riches can't compare to heavenly blessings. And its not the only time He suggested that one should sell all their treasures in order to enter the gates of heaven.

This is one case where "putting all your eggs into one basket" is a good thing to do. Jesus once told a young man that the only thing keeping him from being nearly perfect (Luke 18: 22) was that this young man loved his possessions! His preference was to keep his earthly goods rather than enter into fellowship with God.

What is most important in your life? Today's comfort? Or eternity with Jesus? I'm not sure those are easy questions for any of us to answer truthfully. And there is no need to answer at all unless we do it with an honest heart. In the second of these parables Jesus again spoke of a man that found an earthly treasure that was worth, to him, everything he had ever owned. This lesson was so important to Jesus that He repeated it exactly here for us to ponder. If our goal is to spend eternity in heaven with the company of God and Jesus; if the treasures of our heart include the wisdom we need to accomplish this goal; then we need to give it our all. We can not allow our devotion to be even a ' little' bit for our houses or fancy clothes and then say we are completely totally committed to God's will. We cannot have two absolute commitments. At some point, one or the other will take precedence as most important.

Jesus talks in the third section of this study of the residents of heaven as compared to a dragnet that the fishermen used. I watched my Daddy use a small net a few times. He and I would go to the intercoastal waterway to fish and after he got tired of throwing the line in, with no results, he would use his net. That way he at least had some fish to take home. Usually when he would pull the net back up it would be filled with what he and I called *junk*: small fish not big enough to use as bait, all kinds of other critters with too many arms and legs, and an occasional tire off somebody's vehicle! But there was usually a couple of nice pan-sized spots or croakers in the net too. (Did you know a croaker really does croak? Scared the mud out of me one day when I caught one!) After a few throws with the dragnet, Daddy usually had enough good fish to cook for supper.

Jesus explained this exact process is to happen at the days of End Time. The net will be cast and the Angels will separate the *junk* from the few *keepers* and toss the junk away into a fire pit. The few keepers will join into fellowship for all eternity with our Holy Father and His Son!

After He told these parables to the disciples He asked them if they understood what He was saying to them. They said "Yes, Lord." He then added to His teaching, that every *scribe or* teacher of the law that has been instructed about the kingdom of heaven is like the homeowner that brings out of storage all his treasures, both the old family heirlooms, and the new purchases. He gives his all. He holds nothing back. The wisdom to accomplish the kingdom of heaven is the only treasure that holds any value for this homeowner.

We, through this study, and all the lessons in other studies, and all the sermons we have heard the Pastors preach, and the life-learned lessons we have dealt with, are informed students concerning the kingdom of heaven. I am not saying that we do not have a lot more to learn, but I am saying we have been given the information we need to make a decision about where our treasures should/might be. Jesus is very positive about the choice we should make, and time may be running out for that answer from us.

If Jesus asked you today: *"Have you understood all these things?"*
How would you answer His question?

18- RICH FARMER

LUKE 12:13-21 (Confirmed)

Place unknown but taught to multitudes

"Then one from the crowd said to Him, "Teacher, tell my brother to divide the inheritance with me." But He said to him, *"Man, who made me a judge or an arbitrator over you?"* And He said to them, *"Take heed and beware of covetousness, for one's life does not consist in the abundance of the things he possesses."* Then He spoke a parable to them saying, *"The ground of a certain rich man yielded plentifully. And he thought within himself, saying, 'What shall I do, since I have no room to store my crops?' So he said, 'I will do this: I will pull down my barns and build greater, and there I will store all my crops and my goods. And I will say to my soul, 'Soul, you have many goods laid up for many years; take your ease; eat, drink and be merry.' But God said to him, 'Fool! This night your soul will be required of you; then whose will those things be which you have provided?' So is he who lays up treasure for himself, and is not rich toward God."*

EXTRA READING

PSALM 39:6	PSALM 52:7	PROVERBS 30:8-9
I TIMOTHY 6:6-10	HEBREWS 13:5	

This parable was told only in Luke and was confirmed in Luke as a parable. We are not told exactly where the crowds were that day when Jesus spoke to them; but we do know there were a variety of people. We also know that one of the men in the crowd asked Jesus a question that invoked the parable that Jesus shared at that time.

The man asked Jesus to tell his brother to divide the inheritance with him and give him his share. There were very strict laws concerning the ways that inheritances were divided and handled in those days. We are not told if this man was the oldest or youngest son but it makes sense that he was a younger son. If he had been the eldest he would have been in charge of the distribution of the wealth himself. Jewish civil law allotted a double portion of any inheritance to the oldest son. With it, he also inherited the responsibility to care for the mother and unmarried sisters of the family. The younger sons received a single portion.

For example if there were five sons, then the wealth would be divided by six with the eldest getting two parts. Apparently this man's brother was delaying the disbursement of the wealth and he was tired of waiting for his share. Jesus told him to take heed and think carefully about being greedy. He warned the man that life is not made up of just the things we own. Then He spoke the parable of today's lesson.

Jesus told the people of a rich farmer that had had an exceptionally good year. His crops had done very good. As pleased as the farmer was, he still had some concerns. What would he do with all the crops he now had? He didn't have enough space to store it. His solution was to build bigger barns. And then he could relax and enjoy the leisure time he had earned. He would have much stored to last him many years so he could just eat, drink, and be merry.

I am going to have to tell you that I read this and reread this thinking,

"That is exactly the goal we all have set for ourselves!" I am 63 years old. Believe you me, I have spent a good number of days, weeks, months, and years thinking about retirement! This is a thought that has been on my mind for a long while. It is a thought that is on the mind of every friend I have today! Those that have not quite reached the 'age' are planning for it. They are saving for it. They are deciding how to deal with it. Those that, like me have got there, are learning to live with the consequences of the planning (or lack of planning) that we have done through the years past.

But whatever the results of the financial part of retirement, we all are counting the hours until we can eat, sleep, and be merry. No more getting up at five o'clock am. No more working all day and coming home to cook and clean until eleven o'clock pm. And then starting over! And how many of those nights of rest were interrupted by a sick child or a problem that your mind couldn't solve in the daylight hours because you were too busy. Yes, if I were sitting down with Jesus, man to woman, right now, I'd ask Him what's wrong with this man enjoying the blessings of being financially able to retire?!

Now I hear those of you saying I am being disrespectful, but you must realize I KNOW I can't speak ugly to Jesus; but He has told us to ask for wisdom and it will be granted. That's all I'm doing, asking for the wisdom to understand. I know Jesus would not have taught this parable without some lesson being there for us. So I am asking Jesus to show me what it is that this man has done that we might learn from his mistakes.

I found some understanding in a lot of study in different scriptures and different writers, but it still presented some questions for me. The first thought that come to my mind was... nowhere did the scriptures mention the rich farmer thanking God for the blessings of his abundant crops... mistake number one...he seemed to be taking credit for the bounty... not a complete answer but a thought.

The second thing...at no time did he offer to share his crops with those that might not have been so blessed... I don't even see a thought of his tithing his crops. He is simply going to 'save' it all for his own benefit and pleasure. Again he is leaving God and God's will completely out of his retirement plans.

Nothing is said about his health going down and him needing to retire; in fact you get the idea that his physical being is fine; he is going to spend his energy making merry...again not a word about a mission trip or any other ministry planned.

Now I know I have really stretched my imagination with this rich farmer but he is so much like us today that I am having a hard time putting him back in the first century! I think I get my best understanding of this parable from Paul in I Timothy 6:6-10. Paul usually speaks with such a flourish that he is sometimes a bit difficult for me to understand but he speaks very simple and plain in these verses. At least the Holy Spirit allowed these words to be clear to me this time. (I should not be surprised. I did ask Him for understanding)

Paul tells us that we bring nothing into this world and we will take nothing out. Therefore to have clothing and food to last us while we are here (and the promise is for today only) is plenty sufficient. That is all we need and we should be content with that. Anything else is an excess that should be shared. But Paul goes on to explain that those of us that have the uncontrolled desire to own more are quite likely to fall into the traps that greed opens up. How many times have I asked God why can't I have even a portion of the money I see other people with? I think how peaceful it would feel to be able to walk in a dealership and leave with a new car without all the hassle of paperwork or to be able to buy a big house beside a lovely lake and to enjoy those things...not to have to worry about making payments. I've finally come to the conclusion that those things are not going to happen to or for me and I have an inkling as to why but I still question it sometimes. For example, if I had the money to travel about, would I have time for this project?... just a question...

Paul goes on to tell us that those temptations and the lusts for more can quickly become a snare that snatches our soul right out from under us. He then quotes the favorite saying of all poor men:

"FOR THE LOVE OF MONEY IS A ROOT OF ALL KINDS OF EVIL..." (I Timothy 6:10)

And he explains that if we are spending so much of ourselves trying to accomplish being rich, then we are neglecting the pursuit of God's will. We need to spend more of our time searching for righteousness and faith. It is really all we have time to accomplish in a day's time... to fulfill God's will for that day.

In other verses Paul as well as other writers remind us that we need to be content in our knowledge that God will take care of our needs (that's called faith.) We should not covet the things we see in this world. Those things are temporary at the best and will do nothing to improve our spiritual life or our relationship with God. (Those things can't really improve our human relationships either!) It is true that you can buy friends. And they will remain friendly as long as you pay the price. But when the money is gone, so will they be!

God is One who truly does not judge us on the basis of name-brand shoes or a big house filled with crystal do-dads! There is not the slightest reason for you to try to impress Him with riches. You cannot own a house big enough or furnished well enough to make Him take notice. After all, think about it, HE OWNS it all already! When you die and have a nice stately funeral; and all your friends are there to admire the suit you wear...

So be it, but the suit will stay right there in the casket…you alone will be facing Jesus in glory without any of your riches to cloak or comfort you or disguise the true you with finery. You will stand before God that day as you are…and all those things will be left behind for others to divide.

19- BARREN FIG TREE

LUKE 13:1-9 (Confirmed)

Taught to multitudes, place unknown

"There were present at that season some who told Him about the Galileans whose blood Pilate had mingled with their sacrifices. And Jesus answered and said to them, *"Do you suppose that these Galileans were worse sinners than all other Galileans, because they suffered such things? I tell you, no, but unless you repent you will all likewise perish. Or those eighteen on whom the tower in Siloam fell and killed them, do you think that they were worse sinners than all other men who dwelt in Jerusalem? I tell you, no, but unless you repent you will all likewise perish."* He also spoke this parable, *"A certain man had a fig tree planted in his vineyard, and he came seeking fruit on it and found none. Then he said to the keeper of his vineyard, 'Look, for three years I have come seeking fruit on this fig tree and find none. Cut it down; why does it use up the ground?' But he answered and said to him, ' Sir, let it alone this year also, until I dig around it and fertilize it. And if it bears fruit, well. But if not, after that you can cut it down.'"*

EXTRA READING

MATTHEW 21:18-20	MARK 11: 12-14

Luke confirms this parable but he does not indicate at all where they were when Jesus taught it. I do understand that there was a multitude of people around Him at the time. When I asked you to read the first verses as well as those that are the actual parable, it was so that you could see the kind of atmosphere Jesus was working in that day.

The crowd was concerned that there had been two tragedies in the recent weeks. Apparently Pontius Pilate had had some Galileans killed while they were performing their sacrifices during Passover Week. And a tower had fell at some point somewhere and killed eighteen others. The people there were just like we are when we hear of disasters around us. It seems like everyday we hear of another one. I know media coverage is better today than then but they too, heard of the bad news that occurred in the world and it concerned them. I guess we get the news faster than they did. We hear it each night on the six o'clock broadcast, and it most likely took a period of time for it to make it to the cities not involved back then. But when it was heard, it was still a horrid disaster to be borne for those that found out about it.

When those people expressed their concern for the folks that had died Jesus spoke to them. He denied their fears that these people that had died were any more sinful than the ones still living. He used the occasion to tell them of the need to repent while they could. He also used that time to warn them of their own fate if they did not seek forgiveness right then. I see this as a very strong alter call! He then taught the parable we are to study today.

Jesus told of a man that had an orchard of fig trees. It had probably been established for a while and the trees were mature and productive. That is, all but one tree. He had been checking this tree for three years now, expecting it to bear fruit. And again this year it was bare. He was frustrated and tired of waiting for fruit from this one tree.

He called the groundskeeper and told him to chop the tree down! It was wasting space and he could put a new tree in that spot. But the gardener begged forgiveness for the tree for one more year. It was his plan to work the ground around the barren tree and fertilize it very good. He felt like if this was done for the tree, it would probably be fruitful the following year. And if with the special effort it still did not bear, then it could be destroyed.

This parable was difficult for me even though it seemed at first reading to be a simple story. But as I studied on it and pondered the different roles of the landowner; his servant, the groundskeeper; and the tree; I see God in both of the human roles. But isn't life funny? As I wrote this one paragraph it just all fell into place in my mind as clear as it could be!

God, of course is the landowner. He has been checking on (we will call this young tree-man Joe) for years now. But Joe does not seem to be even trying to carry out God's will. God is a patient Lord but His Patience has run thin with this person. God decides it is time to bring him to justice. He calls his Servant to tell Him of His plan. But the Servant intercedes for Joe. He begs that God will allow Him to show some special attention to Joe and give him one more chance. Jesus will nurture and work with Joe carefully for a period of time. If he still does not respond, then God can perform His justice. Joe can be found in contempt; but Jesus, in His love and compassion, has begged God for Joe to have one more chance!

Jesus is running interference for us today! At different points in our lives we have very unproductive times: unless Jesus was there to block for us, judgment could be serious business! His love and comfort is there to guide us through those tough days (or years) and God's grace pulls us back into the fold!

Thank you, Jesus! But the warning is in the first verses... We do not know when the last alter call that we will hear is to occur...we must seek forgiveness today...Now!

Jesus has warned us!

20- AMBITIOUS GUEST

LUKE 14: 7-11 (Confirmed)

Taught at the home of a Pharisee. All the guests there heard His teaching

"So He told a parable to those who were invited, when He noted how they chose the best places, saying to them, *"When you are invited by anyone to a wedding feast, do not sit down in the best place, lest one more honorable than you be invited by him; and he who invited you and him come and say to you, 'Give place to this man,' and then you begin with shame to take the lowest place. But when you are invited, go and sit down in the lowest place, so that he who invited you comes he may say to you, 'Friend, go up higher.' Then you will have glory in the presence of those who sit at the table with you. For whoever exalts himself will be humbled, and he who humbles himself will be exalted."*

EXTRA READING

PROVERBS 25:6-7	MATTHEW 23:11-12	LUKE 18: 9-14

Jesus told this parable when He was a guest at a dinner party of one of the Pharisees. As the other guests arrived Jesus watched them always choose the best seats available at the table (meaning the seats that were nearest the guest of honor or the host). So He told to them this parable:

He reminded them that they should not choose the best seat when they are invited to a home as a guest. Suppose the host has invited someone of greater honor than you, like the mayor of the city? Then you would be asked to vacate your place and let this more honorable person have that good seat. At that point you would be embarrassed and have to move further away from the host.

But if when you entered you had chosen a lesser seat and then the host came and invited you to move up to a better place, you would be honored and proud. Jesus did not go further with the story but it is simply logical that if you choose the lower seat and are not asked to move forward, well, at least you were not shamed. Even that would be better than being made to move down.

But I guess this guest was not really the point of the story that Jesus was telling. (We do that…get wrapped in the actual words of the story and be concerned for the details of 'what if'.) When we do that we loose sight of the lesson Jesus is teaching.

Jesus then spoke the words that were the point of His story:

"FOR WHOEVER EXALTS HIMSELF WILL BE HUMBLED, AND HE WHO HUMBLES HIMSELF WILL BE EXALTED."

The word *humble,* according to the dictionary in my Bible, is used as a verb. There is nearly a whole paragraph describing the things it can mean. One of the meanings is *to be low,* such as actually being physically below some other object. It can mean *bringing down* as saying things about another that might decrease their value in other's eyes. This meaning was also used in Ezekiel when God 'humbled' a great tree. But the standard meaning is when someone is humiliated or debased by circumstances or another's words or as we say today, "Boy, did I put him in his place!"

The word *exalt* also has a variety of definitions. *To be high* refers to a location such as a throne or hill or maybe the top of a tree. It also might be translated as *to be raised* such as raising a hand in a show of power. This word has a positive meaning when it is used to praise someone (maybe a king or God). It was a custom in some societies to call some political leaders the *most Exalted Magistrate* or such. But it also has a very negative meaning when it is speaking of a sign of haughtiness in a person's attitude. We often speak of that person as having *a proud look* or as being too big for his britches.

Jesus used this sentence in various teachings throughout His ministry. He knew how very easy it was/is for one to become proud of their accomplishments and to forget that those could not have taken place without the assistance of the Holy Spirit. We like to think, "I did that all by myself!" and we most likely even brag about it in our prayers thanking God for this ability. Remember the Pharisee that was in temple the same time as the tax collector (Luke 18:9-14.) He was a braggart and we are quick to see it when we read about him. But how much different are we?

When we paint a lovely picture it is so normal to be proud and even strut a bit, and that is one thing; but to strut because we are so good we always follow all the laws God has given us…well that's another ballgame. Right off the git go we have managed to break a few hundred wrongs! Pride goes before the fall…how many times did I hear my grandma say that? (She must have known how prideful I could be!)

This parable has a personal warning for me at this stage of my life. Several people have been very encouraging when they read some of this project I am working on now. I couldn't do it without their encouragements but I have to admit, some days it does go to my head. Those days I feel that pride grandma tried to rid my soul of all those years ago. And it is a different feeling for me because usually I am one that thinks I'm not quite up to par with others. And I bask in that feeling like laying in the sun on a beautiful day.

Then I remember who really writes this… the Holy Spirit is the author and I am the typist. And I'm not a very good one at that! Every word has to come from Him…I'm a country girl (yeah I'm a girl alright…at my age?) and I don't have these words in me until I open up and let Him lead me. So when I keep that in mind I can be free to be happy in doing this! And I am pleased, just the actual act of doing it is a pleasure.

Solomon gave this advice in his writings as well (Proverbs 25:6-7);

> "DO NOT EXALT YOURSELF IN THE PRESENCE OF THE KING AND DO NOT STAND IN THE PLACE OF THE GREAT FOR IT IS BETTER THAT HE SAY TO YOU, "COME UP HERE" THAN THAT YOU SHOULD BE PUT LOWER IN THE PRESENCE OF THE PRINCE, WHOM YOUR EYES HAVE SEEN."

Jesus was warning those that carry that pride as part of their daily garments that they will be brought down, and they will be made to see they are not as good as they thought. On that same day those that have known all along that their strengths were in the hands of God, will be rewarded for their faithfulness.

This is one of those warnings that Jesus gave us that is also a promise, not necessarily a promise we look forward to being kept…but it will. We can be sure of that.

> *"FOR WHOEVER EXALTS HIMSELF WILL BE HUMBLED, AND HE WHO HUMBLES HIMSELF WILL BE EXALTED."*

21- WIDOW AND JUDGE

LUKE 18:1-8 (Confirmed)

Taught on the trip to Jerusalem to the disciples but with others listening

"Then He spoke a parable to them, that men always ought to pray and not lose heart, saying, " *There was in a certain city a judge who did not fear God nor regard man. Now there was a widow in that city, and she came to him saying, 'Get justice for me from my adversary'. And he would not for a while; but afterward he said within himself, ' Though I do not fear God nor regard man, yet because this widow troubles me I will avenge her, lest by her continual coming she weary me.'"Then the Lord said, "Hear what the unjust judge said. And shall God not avenge His own elect who cry out day and night to Him, though He bears long with them? I tell you that He will avenge them speedily. Nevertheless, when the Son of Man comes, will He really find faith on the earth?"*

EXTRA READING

REVELATIONS 6:10

Luke tells us that this parable was taught during the trip to Jerusalem at the beginning of the Last Week before the crucifixion of Jesus. As we have said in earlier studies there was a mixture of peoples traveling toward the city for Passover Week celebrations.

Jesus spoke of a city that had a judge that had no fear of God. In other words he did not believe that he would some day be held accountable for his life decisions. A man that would not respect God would certainly have no respect for man! It is sad that a man such as that had become a political leader in that he was a judge! But it happened then, as well as it still happens today.

In that city there was also a widow lady that had some sort of problem that compelled her to seek justice. Apparently the problem was serious enough that she felt she needed a court to decide the actions needed to pacify her and right the wrong done to her. She approached the judge and told him of her needs. And he, having no respect or compassion for her simply ignored her for a while.

Some time passed and he realized it was in his own best interest to deal with her problem, if he didn't she would just continue to come to him and nag him. He knew he could grow very tired of hearing her complaints.

Jesus then asked the crowd around Him if they had heard what the unjust judge had said. Because the widow troubled him, with her problems, he decided to address her complaint. Or else she would tire him out continuing to approach and asking for assistance.

Jesus assures the crowd then that God will avenge His children's problems. He will answer our petitions for assistance. And He will do it speedily. If even an uncaring judge sees fit to avenge the widow, certainly a loving God will be there for His children! We do have to remember the word 'speedily' might mean something different to the Lord than it does to us. That's why we nurture and develop our faith. We need the patience that faith gives us some days to deal with our version of "speedily".

We have the promise that God will indeed hear our prayers and answer our grievances, but in His time and in His way. We are to pray about all our concerns and never lose heart that God has heard. He has and He will answer.

In the last half of verse 8 I see what I think is a bit of the human in Jesus. I have heard all my life that He was/is all God and all Man. It makes sense to me that on occasion the man would show through. And I see it there. He asked,

> *"Nevertheless, when the Son of Man comes, will He really find faith on the earth?"*

Now we know there will be some people with some amount of faith here. And Jesus knows that too. But He seems to question how many will really have the faith to truly trust God to answer their prayers. He seems to be showing a little doubt here that anyone understands God's total and complete love. I may have misunderstood these few words but they sound so unhappy to me. It bothers me to think I might be the cause of this sadness in Jesus' heart that day!

I remember when I was at home with my Mama I could not bear for her to cry if I had done something I should not have. It was much easier on me if she yelled or even spanked me! That's the way this verse in God's Word makes me feel. I can deal with His warnings and His promises of discipline better than I can handle His broken heart!

That alone makes me pray that the Holy Ghost will show me how to strengthen my faith! I don't want a single day of my remaining days to pass that I don't think of this short, simple parable. I want Jesus when I go to Him, to find in me the strength of faith He is speaking of in these verses! I want to see Him smile...not look sad.

22- PHARISEES AND TAX COLLECTOR

LUKE 18: 9-14 (Confirmed)

Taught as they traveled the road to Jerusalem. Disciples and others heard the teaching.

"Also He spoke this parable to some who trusted in themselves that they were righteous, and despised others; *"Two men went up into the temple to pray, one a Pharisee and the other a tax collector. The Pharisee stood and prayed thus with himself, 'God, I thank You that I am not like other men, extortioners, unjust, adulterers, or even as this tax collector. I fast twice a week; I give tithes of all that I possess.' And the tax collector, standing afar off, would not so much as raise his eyes to heaven, but beat his breast saying, 'God be merciful to me a sinner!' I tell you this man went down to his house justified rather than the other; for everyone who exalts himself will be humbled, and he who humbles himself will be exalted."*

EXTRA READING

LUKE 14:11

This is one of the teachings Jesus gave as they walked along the road to Jerusalem. He was speaking to the disciples but the was a number of others that were within hearing distance. It was a special holiday crowd that walked the road that day. Passover week was one of the biggest celebrations that the Jewish people acknowledged. Luke confirmed this parable, and was the only gospel to relate it.

Jesus told of two men that went to temple to pray. One of the men was a Pharisee, a leader and elder of Jewish law. He was to be a protector and guide of all the traditions given to Moses by God. The second man was a tax collector. Tax collectors were the most hated men in all of Judea. The

Romans hated them because they were usually Jewish men; and Jews hated them because they were employed by the Romans. Besides, nobody likes a tax collector, then or today. (But we all appreciate the benefits we might reap from the taxes we pay...police protection...fire department...etc...)

The Pharisee stood and said his prayer. He thanked God that he was a righteous man. He was grateful that he did all the right things, like tithing and fasting. And he said these things so that even the tax collector could know how righteous he was! He was proud that he could tell God how good he had been.

The tax collector approached his prayer with a much different attitude. He told God how sad he was that he did not always do things as he should. He begged God's forgiveness and pled for God to be merciful. He never had the nerve to even raise his eyes toward heaven. He spoke with his head bowed, and beat his chest with his fists in distress.

Jesus told the crowd then that the tax collector left temple with his prayers heard and forgiveness his gift. The Pharisee left with the same self-righteousness that he had entered in with. Jesus said that the man that exalts himself has received his reward and will be humbled as time goes by. But the humble man, kind and gentle in his heart, knowing that he cannot survive without God's grace will be exalted.

The Pharisee trusted himself to do right. He had no need for God's Holy Spirit to lead him because he already knew all the answers. He had no problem with his relationship with God because he had it all under control. I am really kind of surprised that he bothered to thank God for his righteousness. It sounds like to me, that he thought he did that too by himself!

The tax collector knew he was a sinful man. We all are. He was shamed but hopeful that God could and would forgive his wickedness. Now, I truly doubt that this man was any more sinful than many of the men here in our church building today. But he recognized he could not arrange forgiveness for himself. He knew he could not *clean the slate* so to speak. Only with God's grace and compassion could he walk in fellowship with the Holy Yahweh. And that is what he wanted to be able to do.

I want to speak a bit more about a statement I made in the previous paragraph...we all are sinners, and we know it...with our head. We are intelligent enough to KNOW we cannot live in this world and walk completely free of sin. But what about in our secret heart? How do we really feel? I asked that question with no flowery cover on it in our class last Sunday and ONE man answered me with what I called an honest heart. He said, "Miss Mary, I still sin but its little sins now, not like it used to be before I was saved." Now before you jump all over that and laugh till you cry, stop! Look down inside your own Christian heart and see the same words concerning your own feelings! The only thing different about that man was his honesty with the class. There is not but very, very few that could really say different than he did if they spoke the true word they feel!

None of us in that class are murders, thieves, bank robbers, adulterers, drunkards, kidnappers, on and on with the list. Maybe in years gone by we had some of those faults, but not today. So down inside (where it really counts) we do not think in terms of calling ourselves sinners. Most of us don't mind saying, as a general, in the public statement, "We all are sinners." But how many of us are like the tax collector and will stand before our families and churches and say "Lord, I am A sinner?" Or how many are more like the Pharisee than we would ever care to admit? Don't more of us say" I said all my 'Thank You Lord Prayers this week' I read all the verses the teacher said I should read. (I didn't have time for that Extra reading she talked about.) I prayed for that sinful neighbor Tuesday. I gave a couple cans of turnip greens to the community food bank. They were on sale at the store. I drove by the old woman's house down the street and waved at her Thursday. She didn't wave back, I guess she couldn't see me real good from the porch."

I won't continue with that line of speaking to you. I'm sure you can see where I'm going with it now. And even to my own mind the list is getting more and more silly. But I'm so afraid it is so true! I am so concerned that many more of us are kin to the Pharisee than we want to admit!

Those that exalt themselves will be humbled. The humble will be exalted. But what about those that have read this parable so they show a humble face to the world?

"Humble" is not something a person can fake for long. Their pride will show up soon and wipe that humble away. The world will see the true man (woman.) And, oh, by the way...God reads the heart...He knows those that pretend to be humble and those that truly are humble…He sees the true you! You might confuse the pastor for a few weeks, but not God for one minute!

23- GOOD SHEPHERD

JOHN 10:1-18 (Confirmed)

Taught to a multitude of people but John does not say where they were at the time.

"Most assuredly, I say to you, he who does not enter the sheepfold by the door, but climbs up some other way, the same is a thief and a robber. But he who enters by the door is the shepherd of the sheep. To him the doorkeeper opens, and the sheep hear his voice, and he calls his own sheep by name and leads them out. And when he brings out his own sheep, he goes before them; and the sheep follow him, for they know his voice. Yet they will by no means follow a stranger, but will flee from him, for they do not know the voice of strangers.'

Jesus used this illustration (parable), but they did not understand the things which He spoke to them. Then Jesus said to them again: *"Most assuredly, I say to you, I am the door of the sheep. All who ever came before Me are thieves and robbers, but the sheep did not hear them. I am the door. If anyone enters by Me, he will be saved, and will go in and out and find pasture. The thief does not come except to steal, and to kill, and to destroy. I have come that they may have life, and they may have it more abundantly. I am the good shepherd. The good shepherd gives his life for the sheep. But a hireling, he who is not the shepherd, one who does not own the sheep, sees the wolf coming and leaves the sheep and flees; and the wolf catches the sheep and scatters them. The hireling flees because he is a hireling and does not care about the sheep. I am the good shepherd; and I know My sheep, and am known by My own. As the Father knows Me, even so I know the Father, and I lay down My life for the sheep. And other sheep I have which are not of this fold; them also I must bring, and they will hear My voice; and there will be one flock and one shepherd. Therefore My Father loves Me, because I lay down My life that I may take it again. No one takes it from Me, but I lay it down of Myself. I have power to lay it down, and I have power to take it again. This command I have received from My Father.'"*

EXTRA READING

ZECHARIAH 11:15-17	EZEKIEL 34	MATTHEW 11:27
JOHN 5:20	HEBREWS 2:9	

This parable is disputed by most of today's Biblical authorities as NOT a parable at all, in spite of the fact that John used the word within the teaching. In fact it is the use of that word that is in the argument. Supposedly the word was miss-translated back when King James had the original work done. It is my contention that if that word is wrong, then many others are most likely wrong too; so I had might as well take the original King James Version off my list of study. I am not going to do that!

I do not believe God would have allowed the translation to have continued this long unless it was right. I am one that thinks if it is right it is right but if one word is wrong, well, then beware of any word! There are *new* translations that I DO question a good bit of their work. There are a few that I will not read again because I am so sure in my heart that they are wrong. But I had to read a bit of them to make that decision. And King James Version (the original) is not a problem for me.

But back to the parable, with all the study I have done in relation to what it takes to make a parable, this set of verses meet the qualifications. And it has been accepted as a parable by nearly as many pastors as I have heard speak in my lifetime. So this authority (me) set a standard that I intended to use to determine how many parables we knew Jesus used, and these verses made the list. If you disagree, so be it, but still at the end of the day, this teaching is the words of our Precious Jesus and He wanted us to learn from them.

John did not tell us where Jesus was at the time He spoke this teaching. I understand there was a multitude of peoples there that included the Pharisees. There were a number of them that continuously followed Jesus. This is unlike some of the parables in that it does not have a *certain man* or someone else as the main character, to be interpreted as someone else.

From the beginning Jesus has spoke of a shepherd in this one, a shepherd and his sheep.

I am going to make some assumptions at the start here to try to explain some of what Jesus tells us. I am basing this knowledge that I have on a couples of movies that I have seen and a few books I have read. And it just 'feels' true. (I am not 'feeling' the theological teachings). I am talking about historical facts only, the ways that the people lived then.

Those people that lived in town still had to have their animals and garden areas to survive just as those that lived in the more rural areas. There were no local IGA or Piggly Wiggly grocery stores. In the daytime a shepherd would take the families' sheep out to graze. At night the sheep would be brought back into the safety of the town walls. The space within the walls was dear so the town had a special area where all the sheep were bedded together at night. Now this was very different for those that lived in the rural areas. But I think the verses we are studying today are about those sheep that were kept in the town.

Jesus says in the very start that if one enters the sheep pen by any way other than the door, then he is up to mischief and no good. The doorkeeper (man on watch duty) will open the door to the real shepherd and the sheep will recognize the voice of the right shepherd.

One day when my husband and I were stuck in traffic that was not moving I had a chance to witness this event for myself. I wondered then why traffic was so bad. I know now it was so that someday I could share this with you! We were on an interstate highway that had a side road next to it, as so many do. There was a big farm like area on the backside of the side road (in spite of the fact that we were very near a large city). There was a huge field full of animals, sheep, goats, and I believe a few cows. I watched a man, the farmer, I guess, go to a gate and open it and call out. Almost instantly the sheep started walking toward him. I thought he must do that daily when he feeds them. But no, he didn't do anything but stand just outside that gate and talk to them. When all the sheep were with him he closed the gate, turned his back to the animals, and walked down the side road. The sheep followed him as he talked to them. I don't know what he was saying but they followed him right into another fenced area and he left them there. Never did the cows or even the goats respond in any way to the man but the sheep came right to him. It just amazed me!

And that is what Jesus is telling us about in these first verses. When the shepherd comes in the morning to take his sheep out, only those that belong in his flock will follow him. All the others will wait for their own shepherd. As has become something we are accustomed to hearing, the peoples listening that day did not understand what Jesus was trying to tell them. So He explained His words to them (and us):

His first words here say *"...I am the door of the sheep..."* and He says it again in verse nine. He is the way to be saved, the only way. Unless they come by way of the door, their entry is no good. Only thieves or robbers and those up to mischief try to enter by a way other than the door. He tells that others that have come before Him were phony and the sheep had not listened to them. The sheep that have heard Him will find good pasture and protection. Those that are not the true shepherd can only mean harm for the sheep.

In verse eleven Jesus says, *"I am the good shepherd."* This verse is one of the "I AM" quotes that Jesus used and that John quoted. And it is the basis of this parable. The background for this parable is found in Ezekiel 34. In that chapter the people that were rulers over God's children were unfaithful. God promised the children then that He would send a true Shepherd to be their Savior. In this parable Jesus is identifying Himself as that Shepherd and as that Savior!

Jesus then tells the crowds that the man hired to care for the family's sheep would not do as good a job as a member of the family would do. The hireling or employee would not have the dedication to the sheep needed to protect them. He by no means would expose his own health and safety to the dangers that might come to the sheep. He could care less if he was threatened whether the sheep become scattered or even killed. Well, for him it was all in a day's work and not worth his life.

Again, in verse fourteen Jesus said, *"I am the good shepherd."* He tells us He knows His sheep and His sheep know Him. And He tells us that the Father in heaven knows Him and that He knows the Father. This tells us that God knows Jesus as the Good Shepherd and that He had sent Him, as He had promised. This verse confirms Jesus as the long awaited Messiah. Then He confirms the prophecies that told of His death by saying here, *"... and I lay down My life for the sheep..."*

As a good shepherd would fight to the death for his sheep, Jesus will give His life for the salvation of His sheep. And then Jesus tells us of 'other' sheep that He wants to bring into the flock. He wants it to be one flock with one shepherd that all will know His voice and follow Him.

Most all that study these words today are sure He was/is speaking of the Gentiles. They are sure He speaks of those that were considered pagan, and any non-Jew of that day. But I have very definitely heard a whole different scenario for that one statement of Jesus'.

I talked with some Mormon missionaries one afternoon and learned a lot about their beliefs and practices. But the most important thing I took from that experience was … #1 They believe that Jesus was speaking of the land that is America today when He talked about sheep in another fold; and #2: They believe that during those three days that He was in the tomb, He was visiting that other flock. While He was here in America He gave the golden tablets to that flock that the Mormon leader later found and translated into The Book of Mormon, just as God gave the tablets to Moses. The way I understood it, just about the whole basis of their faith is based on this one verse. Now I am not trying to teach one thing about the Mormon faith. I've done absolutely no study in that direction; I just remember what those young men tried to explain to me in one short afternoon. And I am not satisfied that what they said is accurate.

We know today, that there are 'many flocks' around the world. And it does not matter to which one you currently belong, Jesus tells you here that there will only be one. And there will be only one Shepherd. So call yourself what you will, you must believe that Jesus Christ is the Savior sent by God; that Jesus Christ is the Son of God; and that Jesus Christ died for the redemption of your sins and He lives again!

And as the last verses in this study tell us, He did this with love for each of us! No one nor any army could have made this happen without His choice. He had the power and ability (given to Him by God) to stop the whole thing any second that He had wanted to. But He knew without that event, we would have stood NO CHANCE of entering into any kind of fellowship with Him or His Father. His desire to do God's will and His love for every person in this world today and yesterday and tomorrow was and is so complete He gave His life that we might have an eternal life with Him…I bow my head and say. "Thank You Jesus".

IN REFERENCE TO REMAINING PARABLES

The following parables (#24 - #46) are not confirmed by the use of the word parable in the scripture. But they are accepted by most Bible scholars and students to be parables. When you list the qualifications according to a literal definition of the word, then these works meet that criteria.

I would like to say that all the differences that the authorities had were in the following parables, but that is not the truth. If that were true then there would be no problem (at least less problems) counting "How many parables did Jesus teach?" But truth be told, there were just as many of the parables with the word within it that was questioned by one or more of the references I found. That makes it very hard for one to be confident in doing what she set out to do. All I can do is tell you that I think all the following are parables. And I know that the Holy Spirit has laid it on my heart that these sets of scripture are the ones I needed to put in this work. And I do know all of the following are words of Jesus Christ and we need to understand them.

~~~

24- SALT

MATTHEW 5:13

Taught at the Sermon on the Mount. Multitudes were in attendance there.

"You are the salt of the earth; but if the salt loses its flavor, how shall it be seasoned? It is then good for nothing but to be thrown out and trampled underfoot by men."

MARK 9:49-50

The twelve were with Jesus at a home in Capernaum for this teaching

"For everyone will be seasoned with fire, and every sacrifice will be seasoned with salt. Salt is good, but if the salt loses its flavor, how will you season it? Have salt in yourselves, and have peace with one another."

LUKE 14:34-35

Place unknown but Luke indicated it was to multitudes of people.

> *"Salt is good; but if the salt has lost its flavor, how shall it be seasoned? It is neither fit for the land nor for the dunghill,* but men throw it out. He who has ears to hear, let him hear!

EXTRA READING

LEVITICUS 2:13	NUMBERS 18:19
ROMANS 14:19	COLOSSIANS 4:6

This parable was not confirmed by the word parable but it was told in three of the gospels. It has been accepted by most authorities as a parable and is often preached as such.

In Matthew the parable was taught as part of the Sermon on the Mount. At that venue there were a multitude of peoples including the disciples and many elders from Temple. Mark indicated in his book that Jesus was at a home in Capernaum with the disciples, and they alone heard this teaching. Luke does not tell us where they were when Jesus used this parable but he does indicate there was a multitude of people there. With the differences between the different versions, I am going to assume that Jesus taught this parable more than once during His ministry.

All three stories are very much the same: telling the folk that they were the "salt" of the earth and that everyone will be seasoned by fire. Then Jesus questions the value of salt that has lost its flavor. He tells us it is of no value at all. And then He tells us to have peace with one another. It is a short few verses but Jesus thought them important enough to be taught to more than one group of people.

To learn why Jesus would use the allegory *salt* we need to go back into the Old Testament teachings for a bit. Leviticus 2:13 explains to us the importance of salt to the Jewish people:

> "AND EVERY OFFERING OF YOUR GRAIN OFFERING
> YOU SHALL SEASON WITH SALT; YOU SHALL NOT
> ALLOW THE SALT OF THE COVENANT OF YOUR GOD
> TO BE LACKING FROM YOUR GRAIN OFFERING.
> WITH ALL YOUR OFFERINGS YOU SHALL OFFER
> SALT."

According to their law, all grain given to the temple in sacrifice should be seasoned with salt. Since this grain would be used by the priests, I suspect they appreciated the extra flavoring but I really think it was most likely a matter of preserving the grain from mites and weevils. It was a law that all sacrifices offered to the Lord should be pleasing to the taste. But whatever the actual reason, it was God's law that the salt be added for each offering. Numbers18:19 also gives us another reason that Jesus might have chosen salt as the object of this parable:

> "ALL THE HEAVE OFFERINGS OF THE HOLY THINGS,
> WHICH THE CHILDREN OF ISRAEL OFFER TO THE

LORD, I HAVE GIVEN TO YOU AND YOUR SONS
AND DAUGHTERS WITH YOU AS AN ORDINANCE
FOREVER; IT IS A COVENANT OF SALT FOREVER
BEFORE THE LORD WITH YOU AND YOUR
DESCENDANTS WITH YOU"

In this verse the 'covenant of salt' is describing the covenant that God has established with His chosen children as one that He will honor (or preserve, as salt preserves food products) forever. This reminder from Jesus is reason enough for Him to use 'salt' as the subject of the parable.

He told the Jewish audience He was speaking to that they were the salt of the earth. But apparently He was concerned that some of them were no longer doing the job of preserving or seasoning as they should.

Salt in that area and in that time was collected from the Dead Sea, among other places and I cannot explain to you the chemical difference in that and the salt we have today in the boxes with the little girl carrying an umbrella. The Dead Sea was an inland lake about fifty miles long and about eleven miles at its' widest point. Salt was dissolved from the land that the rivers ran through and deposited in the lake water. Since there was no outlet for the water and the temperature could reach to one hundred twenty-five degrees the lake became saturated with salt and minerals. It is the saltiest water in the world, up to nine times as salty as any ocean.

But there was a difference, and that salt then could lose its flavor over a period of time. It would 'go flat' and could no longer be used to preserve food or to season it. As Jesus tells us at that point it was only good for the dunghill, or local trash site on the edge of town.

Jesus was reminding those there that day that they too could loose their spirit and will for God's word. In fact it seems that He thought they had already become of no use to the growth of the kingdom of God. Those that were no longer helping to preserve the word of God and not aiding in the growth of His kingdom were worthless.

He tells them that each person would be seasoned by fire. I don't think He was speaking of burning the person nor was He speaking about hell at this time; but He was speaking as He spoke when He told us that precious metals were purified by fire. All of us now, as well as those then, face and deal with hardships and challenges daily that either defeat our spiritual life or strengthen it. That is the fire He was speaking of that day. And He was saying that we need the salt (or backbone) to stand strong or else be trampled under by those temptations that destroy our faith.

He wants us to use that strength to help one another, to be there for each other during the weak times that each of us face. In Romans14:19 Paul tells us to pursue the things that make peace for one another and for the things that edify your Christian Brother. In other words we should do things that bring glory and honor to others. This is one way we can contribute to the growth of God's kingdom daily.

We often describe someone today that we admire as the "salt of the earth". When we say that we are inferring that the person was a true friend and honorable citizen. I am more than sure that figure of speech could be traced back directly to Jesus' words in this parable.

The product 'salt' has come to be linked to the health, (including healthy teeth); the purity of the body; the preservation of numerous things; and binding obligations or promises. And Paul, in his letter to the Colossians 4:6, links salt to wisdom. I guess that is where we got the phrase, "Take it with a grain of salt." It is obvious that this parable is one that is imbedded deep in our daily life.

LET YOUR SPEECH ALWAYS BE WITH GRACE, SEASONED WITH SALT, THAT YOU MAY KNOW HOW YOU OUGHT TO ANSWER EACH ONE. (PAUL IN COLOSSIANS 4:6)

25- THE LAMP

MATTHEW 5:14-16

Taught at the Sermon on the mount to multitudes

"You are the light of the world. A city that is set on a hill cannot be hidden. Nor do they light a lamp and put it under a basket, but on a lamp stand, and it gives light to all who are in the house. Let your light so shine before men, that they may see your good works and glorify your Father in heaven."

MATTHEW 5:14-16

Taught at the Sermon on the mount to multitudes

"You are the light of the world. A city that is set on a hill cannot be hidden. Nor do they light a lamp and put it under a basket, but on a lamp stand, and it gives light to all who are in the house. Let your light so shine before men, that they may see your good works and glorify your Father in heaven."

LUKE 8:16-18

Place unknown but a great crowd including the disciples and many of the women that had been healed of various illnesses and demons

"No one, when he has lit a lamp, covers it with a vessel or puts it under a bed, but sets it on a lamp stand, that those who enter may see the light. For nothing is secret that will not be revealed, nor anything hidden that will not be known and come to light. Therefore take heed how you hear. For whoever has, to him more will be given; and whoever does not have, even what he seems to have will be taken from him."

EXTRA READING

MATTHEW 7:2	MATTHEW 10:26	MATTHEW 13:43
LUKE 9:14	LUKE 11:33	LUKE 12:2
JOHN 1:4	JOHN 1:9-11	JOHN 3:19-21
JOHN 8:12	JOHN 9:5	JOHN 12: 46
I CORINTHIANS 4:5	II CORINTHIANS 6:14	EPHESIANS 5:8-14
PHILIPPIANS 2:15	I THESSALONIANS 5:4-6	I PETER 2:12

This parable was taught according to Matthew during the Sermon on the Mount very early in Jesus' ministry. In fact, according to Matthew this was the first parable that Jesus taught. It is the first that is recorded in the Gospels. Mark included this discourse in the Sermon by the Sea. Luke did not tell us where Jesus was when He taught this parable but Luke did stress that there were many of the women named as followers of Jesus present at this teaching. It is my understanding that this parable is one that Jesus used more than once. Even though it was not confirmed by either writer it has been accepted as a parable by most of today's Bible scholars.

Jesus said in the very first of this story that *"You are the light of the world."* This tells us that He was speaking to the Jewish people. They were meant to be just that…the light that would show the world God's love. He simply stated in the next sentence that a city on a hill could not be hidden. If they would stand up for God the world could not help but see His glory. He goes on to explain one does not light a lamp and then put it under something to hide it, but one always places that lamp on a lamp stand, where the glow will shine bright for all to enjoy. (The basket He talks about in this verse is a small bowl used to extinguish the fire on oil lamps.) Jesus is telling the Hebrew children that day that He expected them to live in such a way that the world would see God in their lives. And He is telling them to live in such a way that God will be glorified (and not shamed) by their behavior.

In Mark and Luke Jesus goes on to say that nothing will be hidden that will not be revealed to those that listen and hear with their heart. He said that nothing that should be known would be kept secret. And as in the parable, "Ten Talents", Jesus again tells us here that those that hear the Spirit of the words will be given more understanding; and warns those that don't listen, will have what wisdom they thought they had taken away.

I see this parable as having two sides, so to speak. I see Jesus telling us about the behavior He expects of us, as children of God. And I see Him telling us what behavior we can expect from Him. Though the verses here are short and few, there seems to be more references in the Bible to this parable than any other I have studied thus far! All the writers in the New Testament seemed to be very impressed with the message Jesus gave in these verses.

The message Jesus is giving us concerning our behavior is clear. He expects us to act as a guide and as a light to those that have not yet accepted Jesus as their Savior. Just as a lamp sits on a high stand and emits light so that all around it is visible and not hidden in darkness, we should be that for the other people around us. Please take note that at this point I am saying "we" and not just the Jewish people. We, as children of God now share this responsibility as plainly as they ever did. If we see the truth of God's word, and we do if we have listened with ears that were willing to receive the truth; then would we take that knowledge and hide it under the bed? Or would we lift it up for the entire world to see? Would there be those that we disapprove of that we would hide the word of God from them?

As a Christian is there anyone we could possibly wish in Hell? I can answer those questions pretty easily…if we have heard with our heart the true message of God's love, we would do <u>nothing</u> to prevent anyone from having a loving relationship with God and His Son! We would put the lamp at the highest spot available and show in all our activities that we do love God's children because they are our sisters and brothers! Not one thing that we do or say should be hidden in the darkness of deceit.

Now for the other side of this message: Jesus is telling us here what we know: He is the light of New Jerusalem. He is confirming this fact for the Jewish nation. When He made this statement John had not yet written the book of Revelations, but John did later explain the words Jesus had used that day:

> REVELATIONS 21: 22-23 BUT I SAW NO TEMPLE IN IT, FOR THE LORD GOD ALMIGHTY AND THE LAMB ARE ITS TEMPLE. THE CITY HAD NO NEED OF THE SUN OR OF THE MOON TO SHINE IN IT, FOR THE GLORY OF GOD ILLUMINATED IT. THE LAMB IS ITS LIGHT.

Since we have this fact established, now, we can see what else is in this parable to encourage and comfort us. Jesus, with His words here, has answered a lot of questions that seem to float in and out of my mind sometimes. I know that many times I have read different sections of scripture without having any understanding; and then all of a sudden one day I re-read it and the meaning I should have seen earlier hits me like a brick beside the head! And I've heard many other people express the same thing.

And I've discovered that at times a meaning to some particular verses might not be the same as it was the last time I read it. Then there is the phenomena that happens when the preacher gives a sermon on one subject that he feels we need but I hear a different message altogether. And the message I heard was the answer to some problem I had been dealing with in my life during that period of time. Knowing that does occur, I have took comfort in teaching because I knew that what ever I taught, the students would hear what God wanted them to know. With all these inconsistencies in the meaning of some scriptures, I have always been so afraid I would not understand something that was critical to my salvation or to my fellowship with God. Then my relationship might be less than it should be! This parable has given me the answer to those doubts and worries. Jesus promises us here that as well as us acting as a good lamp; He will act as a lamp.

"For there is nothing hidden which will not be revealed, nor has anything been kept secret that it should not come to light."

He has promised as clear as day here that He will reveal anything I need to know to have a full and complete relationship with Him! Just as a lamp makes all the corners and nooks visible, God's word will be made clear and understandable to us. He will keep no secrets from us! As we have need, or as He thinks we CAN understand, He will reveal the meaning to any scripture for us. For each of us that time may be different. It might be ten years down the road before He shows me a message you understood a long time ago. But He promises that I will be given that gift when it will be appropriate for me to understand! He will not allow anything that I need to know to be kept from me!

For this promise to be kept, we must do our part; read, study, pray for the wisdom and assistance of the Holy Ghost, and listen. We need to listen

26- THE PHYSICIAN

Taught at Matthew Levi's home to all present

"Now it happened, as Jesus sat at the table in the house, that behold, many tax collectors and sinners came and sat down with Him and His disciples. And when the Pharisees saw it, they said to His disciples, "Why does your Teacher eat with the tax collectors and sinners?" When Jesus heard that, He said to them, *"Those who are well have no need of a physician, but those who are sick. But go and learn what this means: ' I desire mercy and not sacrifice*'. For I did not come to call the righteous, but sinners to repentance.* (Hosea 6:6)

MARK 2:15-17

Taught at Matthew Levi's home to all present

"Now it happened, as He was dining in Levi's house, that many tax collectors and sinner's also sat together with Jesus and His disciples; for there were many, and they followed Him. And when the scribes and Pharisees saw Him eating with the tax collectors and sinners, they said to His disciples, "How is it that He eats and drinks with tax collectors and sinners?" When Jesus heard it, He said to them, *"Those who are well have no need of a physician, but those who are sick. I did not come to call the righteous, but sinners, to repentance."*

LUKE 5:29-32

Taught at Matthew Levi's home to all present

"Then Levi gave Him a great feast in his own house. And there were a great number of tax collectors and others who sat down with them. And their scribes and the Pharisees complained against His disciples, saying, " Why do you eat and drink with tax collectors and sinners?" Jesus answered and said to them, *"Those who are well have no need of a physician, but those who are sick. I have not come to call the righteous, but sinners, to repentance."*

EXTRA READING

| MATTHEW 11:19 | MATTHEW 11:35 | LUKE 15:1-2 |

This parable was not confirmed by the use of the word *parable* in any of the gospels; but all the references I used accepted it as a parable. This parable is a part of the discourse Jesus presented at the home of Matthew when He was invited to dinner there. (See parable #6 "Patched Garments /New Wineskins") It is Jesus' response when the Pharisees accused Him of associating with sinners. His answer was to speak very clearly. (Do you see here in this teaching that Jesus was not bashful to speak His mind?)

He explained that a person that is healthy does not need to seek the services of a doctor. All of us that seem to spend an awful amount of time going to appointments with different physicians know we certainly don't want to go if we are well! He then explains the parable within the parable. He did not come for those that are righteous. He did come for the sinners. They are the ones He has come to call to repentance. The easiest way I know to truly explain this parable is to testify to you how I learned its' meaning:

A few years ago my son was just beginning to attend Church regular as an adult and on his own. I was very proud but fearful of his tenderness in this new relationship he was building with God. Like a mama bear I was very protective. And very shortly my fears seemed to come to life. He joined a biker group called CMA. To understand my fear, you need to know I lived near Myrtle Beach for a long time and those bikers that attended Biker Week there were famous for mischief. I did not have a lot of respect for 'Biker gangs'.

He quickly let me know that those letters stood for Christian Motorcycle Association. I had some peace of mind until I found out that each weekend they as a group went to a different nightspot or bar. I confronted him and ask couldn't they find some other place for fellowship and entertainment. He told me they were not going exactly for fun and definitely not to drink alcoholic beverages or pick up wild women. So being mama I wondered then why did they have to go there. I knew there were places to go that did not have the temptations and stresses for young men that was in those bars. Then he told me they wanted to show, by example that they could have fun without the drinking. And he said, "Mama, we have to go where the people are. Those people are not going to attend a social at Church or even a barbeque at our homes! If we are to witness to them, we have to be where they are!"

Here I had spent all this time, being 'good' and avoiding as much temptation as I could. I had shunned those people I knew to be living outside God's will. I had avoided those places I knew, or thought I knew, God would not want me to be. I had been acting just exactly like a Pharisee. By trying to avoid 'sinners', I was committing one myself! My son taught me what Jesus wanted us to know.

Life is out there, we need to get in it and be His children wherever we happen to be standing. How else can we be a true witness?

27- TREASURERS OF THE HEART

MATTHEW 6:19-21
_____

Taught at the Sermon on the Mount to multitudes

"Do not lay up for yourselves treasures on earth, where moth and rust destroy and where thieves break in and steal: but lay up for yourselves treasures in heaven, where neither moth nor rust destroys and where thieves do not break in and steal. For where your treasure is, there your heart will be also."

LUKE 12:33-34
_____

Place is unknown but it was spoke to multitudes

"Sell what you have and give alms: provide yourselves money bags which do not grow old, a treasure in the heavens that does not fail, where no thief approaches nor moth destroys. For where your treasure is, there your heart will be also."

EXTRA READING
_____

DEUTERONOMY 15:7-10	JOB 31:19-22	PROVERBS 23:4-8
ISAIAH 58:7-9	MATTHEW 5:42	MATTHEW 19:21

According to Matthew this parable was taught among the many teachings that Jesus used while giving the Sermon on the Mount. Luke does not tell us where Jesus was at the time He used this parable, however he does tell us that a multitude of people heard this lesson.

It seems to be a simple story, and easy to understand. But since it is referred to so many times throughout the scriptures, undoubtedly it is a very basic, bottom line learning that we all need to think of daily. And as I study it, I have come to believe that it very well might be hard to live up to! So let's get started for trying to understand what Jesus felt we needed to know from these words.

He told the crowd that day to not store treasures on earth. He gave a number of good reasons why that would be good advice. Here on earth things rust and rot. Things get stolen or misplaced. Things grow old or loose value. The things we collect and try to salvage simply become a problem to protect. A good bit of our time is devoted to this project and a whole lot of our concerns go toward dealing with these things, either earning them, or storing them, or showing them off, or hiding them

And for what purpose do we concentrate all our energy toward this behavior? So we can live in the largest house? So we can drive the fanciest car? So everyone can say "She wears a new dress each Sunday?" Have you ever heard (or said) "You know, she is always so pretty and dressed so fine, but she has the IQ of a peanut?" Do you increase your personal value by wearing diamonds and rubies?

After you have worked fourteen hours a day for a few months so you could buy that new car, is it worth the time you missed with your children in the afternoons? The old car was fine. It got you back and forth with no problems but you liked the new color they were using this year. And now you have to work these hours for another five years. Is the color that nice? By then the car will be lost most of its' value. It will have scratches and dings and the upholstery will be worn; and the color will be out of style and you might need another one, but is it worth it?

Jesus told them to lay up their treasures in heaven. He gave many good reasons for doing that. It seems there is no rust or rot in heaven. We know any thieves that might be there have long since recanted and repented of their behavior, or they wouldn't be there! Apparently any clothing we might collect here is fuddy-duds compared to what we will have there. (And we can't take that designer fashion with us anyway!)

Jesus promises there will no problems like "What's for supper?" All our physical needs, as we know them, will be taken care of then…wait, no, that is not exactly what the scripture says. Jesus says that now, today, God will provide for all our needs. He is perfectly aware of what we need and it is His pleasure to provide it! But first we must seek the kingdom. And we do that by following His will as best we can.

It seems to me from the additional reading I have done in studying for this parable that right now at this point I should remind everyone, including myself, of the Golden Rule

"THEREFORE WHATEVER YOU WANT MEN TO DO TO YOU, DO ALSO TO THEM, FOR THIS IS THE LAW AND PROPHETS." MATTHEW 6: 12

And in Luke Chapter 6 Jesus gives us a clear list of the Rules of the Kingdom. He does not tell us to seek the kingdom without telling us how. The verses, Luke 6:20-38 are exact and detailed on how to love and who to love and how to become one of the sons of the Father in the kingdom of heaven.

If you read the verses you will see that it will not be easy to follow all the rules. To do it you certainly would have to have your heart in it. Unless you are committed totally and have your whole being working and thinking about it, you will never succeed. But Jesus is not going to give you an assignment that can't be done. And He tells you to lay up your treasures in heaven. He knows that with the help of the Holy Spirit it is an altogether possibility to accomplish. Just ask for His help! Just accept His offer of love and guidance!

And He told them (and us) not to worry about tomorrow…today has enough problems to entertain you and keep you busy. God has the future in His hands; He is capable of controlling it. You are not, so why would you waste your energy. Spend your time and concerns helping and loving all of God's children. Study His word so you can tell everyone you see or meet about His love and grace. Those treasures won't rot away…even on earth!

Paul, in Romans, simplified what I have tried to say in this paper. And Jesus spoke extremely clear with His instructions. It is a fact of life that we must do things like cook supper daily, but we don't have to worry about having food next month. Worrying won't change whatever the facts may be in the future; but God has it in mind and knows what to do about it.

Whatever you spend the most of your effort toward, is whatever you hold in your heart! Because it is in your heart you work toward it; because you work toward it, it is in your heart.

"BE OF THE SAME MIND TOWARD ONE ANOTHER.
DO NOT SET YOUR MIND ON HIGH THINGS, BUT
ASSOCIATE WITH THE HUMBLE.DO NOT BE WISE
IN YOUR OWN OPINION." PAUL IN ROMANS 12: 6

28- GOOD FATHER

MATTHEW 7:7-11

Taught at the Sermon on the Mount to the multitudes

"Ask, and it will be given to you; seek, and you will find; knock, and it will be opened to you. For everyone who asks receives, and he who seeks, finds, and to him who knocks, it will be opened. Or what man is there among you, who if his son asks for bread, will give him a stone? Or if he asks for a fish, will he give him a serpent? If you then, being evil, know how to give good gifts to your children, how much more will your Father who is in heaven give good things to those who ask Him!"

LUKE 11:9-13

Place unknown but Luke indicated it was to the disciples only.

"So I say to you, ask, and it will be given to you; seek and you will find; knock, and it will be opened to you. For everyone who asks receives, and he who seeks finds, and to him who knocks, it will be opened. If a son asks for bread from any father among you, will he give him a stone? Or if he asks for a fish, will he give him a serpent instead of a fish? Or if he asks for an egg, will he offer him a scorpion? If you then, being evil, know how to give good gifts to your children, how much more will your heavenly Father give the Holy Spirit to those who ask Him!"

EXTRA READING

| NUMBERS 23:19 | PROVERBS 8:17 | MARK 11:24 |
| JOHN 14:21 | JAMES 1:5 | JAMES 1:17 |

This teaching is not listed as a parable in many references that I have studied. I, too, question that the form is exactly a parable. But it is such a hopeful, positive spirited teaching that I choose to include it rather than exclude it. Its just one more piece of paper in this project but it is a long list of good promises from God! Many of the parables have been dire warnings, which we need to hear; but this is nothing but good blessings from a loving God! And this teaching is supported by so many other verses throughout the scriptures.

Matthew tells us this teaching was part of the Sermon on the Mount, and thus very early in Jesus' ministry. At the sermon there were many, many people to hear this discourse. Luke does not tell us where the twelve and Jesus were but he does indicate it was just the twelve there.

Jesus starts this with a simple but profound statement… *"Ask…seek… knock…"* Any of those requests will be answered is His promise. And then He reminds those listening that if one of their own children were to make a request for bread or fish or egg, would they respond to the child with a stone or a snake or a scorpion? Jesus tells the fathers in the crowd that they know they are sinful men and yet they would give the best they could to their children. With that statement Jesus asked how much more good could they expect from a non-sinful Heavenly Father? How could they expect anything but good from Him?

Mark confirms this promise in Mark 11:24 when he quotes Jesus:

> *"THEREFORE I SAY TO YOU, WHATEVER THINGS YOU ASK WHEN YOU PRAY, BELIEVE THAT YOU WILL RECEIVE THEM, AND YOU WILL HAVE THEM."*

Such an absolute, no doubt about it statement! Simply ask and believe and receive! I remember when we studied the "Mustard Seed" parable, Jesus told us there that anything was possible if we simply had faith. He is restating that within this study. A few years back (2008) our pastor preached a sermon and used the one verse of Proverbs 8:17. That verse is simply another confirmation of Jesus' words that day:

> "I LOVE THOSE WHO LOVE ME, AND THOSE THAT SEEK ME DILIGENTLY WILL FIND ME."

The Book of James (my most favorite book of all) also agrees with the hope found in these verses I have quoted. In James 1:5 he states:

"IF ANY OF YOU LACKS WISDOM, LET HIM ASK OF GOD, WHO GIVES TO ALL LIBERALLY AND WITHOUT REPROACH, AND IT WILL BE GIVEN TO HIM."

In other words if you do seek more knowledge and you do ask God for that gift, He is not going to think you are stupid or some such idea you might have about being ashamed to ask! You do not have to worry if you ask a question or ask for clarification on some point. You do not have to be afraid God might look at you as asking a silly question. That's simply not the truth. I do not think God would consider any honest quest for knowledge to be out of line or frivolous.

James also tells us further into the chapter (1:17) that every good gift is from God the Father in whom there is no variation or shadow of turning. In other words, God does not behave in a fickle manner. His personality does not be good one day and wicked the next. We, as humans, do just that. Today I might be loving and kind in spirit. Tomorrow I might have not slept well and be quite the crouch. God is always in a good mood. And all His gifts are just exactly what we need, as well as most often exactly what we wanted!

God is a Good Father; just as these verses tells us. Jesus spent this time trying to show those listening that day that there was no denying God's grace and love for His children. I am still not convinced that these verses are a parable but I <u>know</u> they are Jesus' words and that He felt we needed to hear them. He is trying to show us the sincerity of God and the love He has for all His children.

I know the doubt or disbelief that people feel is their own lack of faith. There is no way one could read and study these words and still question, "If God would give me this..." Whatever you need or want that is within the boundaries of God's will, will be given to you! Now I saw on television one day a man suing another for the return of a car that he had taken from the first man and then wrecked it. It turns out that the first man had stolen the car from someone else so the Judge explained to the first man that he could not replace something that had been acquired by illegal means to start with.

That is sort of how we must look for gifts from God. He is not going to give us something that is not good for us or that would harm our walk with Him. He will of course preserve that relationship before anything else. But all we have to do is ask! My Daddy would have and did give me anything I wanted if he could...unless he thought it would harm me. And my Daddy was just a man. As the following verses remind us, God is so much more!

> "GOD IS NOT A MAN, THAT HE SHOULD LIE, NOR A SON OF MAN, THAT HE SHOULD REPENT. HAS HE SAID, AND WILL HE NOT DO? OR HAS HE SPOKEN, AND WILL HE NOT MAKE IT GOOD?" NUMBERS 23:19

29- GOOD FRUIT / BAD FRUIT

MATTHEW 7:15-20

Taught at the Sermon on the Mount to multitudes including Pharisees

"Beware of false prophets, who come to you in sheep's clothing, but inwardly they are ravenous wolves. You will know them by their fruits. Do men gather grapes from thorn bushes or figs from thistles? Even so, every good tree bears good fruit, but a bad tree bears bad fruit. A good tree cannot bear bad fruit, nor can a bad tree bear good fruit. Every tree that does not bear good fruit is cut down and thrown into the fire. Therefore by their fruits you will know them."

LUKE 6:43-45

Place where taught unknown but multitudes present including disciples

"For a good tree does not bear bad fruit, nor does a bad tree bear good fruit. For every tree is known by its own fruit. For men do not gather figs from thorns, nor do they gather grapes from a bramble bush. A good man out of the good treasure of his heart brings forth good; and an evil man out of the evil treasure of his heart brings forth evil. For out of the abundance of the heart his mouth speaks."

EXTRA READING

DEUTERONOMY 13:1-5	JEREMIAH 23:16	MICAH 3:5-7
EZEKIEL 13:1-9	MATTHEW 12:33-37	

    This parable was taught at the Sermon on the Mount according to Matthew. Luke does not tell us exactly where they were when Jesus spoke this parable. But both writers indicate there were multitudes of people present. Neither writer confirmed this work as a parable but that does not seem to detract from its' value as a teaching of Jesus Christ. I think I have most often heard it used at revival services because it is a bit stern. And each pastor I heard use it gave a bit different meaning to it. Yet most everyone instantly recognizes any part that they might hear quoted as a parable of Jesus. The fact that it has been used so often makes it one of the clearest in our minds. The actual words of the verses are simple enough to understand. If you take this one at pure face value you will have a perfectly good lesson. You do not have to dig deeper into the scriptures to find a lasting and impressive message.

Jesus warns in these words that there were, and are, false prophets. God had been warning the Hebrews since early time of that fact (Deuteronomy 13:1-5). There are those that will deliberately and purposely set out to mislead any Christian (especially the new converts) from the will of God. Jesus said in this parable that they were wolves dressed as sheep. In other words, looking and behaving like one of the most gentile, less aggressive creatures created by God; they are really sly, wicked, and dangerous to every other creature alive! Today is no different than when He said those words all those years ago.

In today's time, those wolf-men are usually dressed as successful pastors and pretend to be strong faithful servants of God. But usually they are only interested in what funds they can collect from those people that do have a sincere heart and care about the needs of others. I am sorry to say that true loving Christians make an easy mark for those men. I am bothered a lot when I see one of those men on television with his lovely wife; and they are both stressing how much good can come from just a few dollars each month. But if you look carefully you will notice she has on a fine designer dress and enough diamonds on her hands to sink a battleship. And don't let him off the hook either! His tie probably cost more than most pastors' pay for a suit! I can't help but wonder how much suffering could be eliminated with a portion of those jewels. That man, nor his wife, doesn't care a bit about your salvation or the hardships of others…but he has found an easy target with a soft heart.

And neither does he care about your financial welfare. It does not matter to him that you might send your last dollar to help the poor folk he has told you about, (knowing that the greatest percent of the money is going into his own bank account.) I heard one man on television ask everyone to send him their monthly mortgage payment. He then promised that God would not let them loose their home if they were doing good with the money. Do not misunderstand me; I know God helps us all with our finances. I've often said and I have always believed, that I write the checks; but God does the arithmetic. There is no way I could make the dollars go as far as He does! But I do not think He wants us to be silly either!

I have never heard that wolf-man make an alter call. I have never heard him teach (or preach) the plan of salvation. I have heard some very soft, sweet music played low behind his voice as he asked for more money. I may be wrong about him; but I don't listen to him any more to make that determination. Jesus warned us and His warning is still appropriate for today. And the wolves aren't always big television superstars; some of them are small church pastors that take their authority and leadership too literal. Most cult leaders have started their ministry in small churches.

Jesus told us in this parable about the natural manner of trees. Good, healthy trees bare good fruit. Bad, unhealthy trees bare bad fruit, or no fruit. It can be no other way. It is a natural fact. And the same is true for people. And the kind of fruit found on the tree tells us what kind of tree it must be. An apple tree bares some variety of apples, not oranges. If you see acorns on the ground beneath a tree, you can be pretty sure it is an oak. A sweet gum tree only bares sweet gum balls. And with that knowledge you can understand Jesus' words when He said: *"Therefore by their fruits you will know them."*

As I said earlier, this parable, on the surface, is easy to understand. The wisdom that Jesus expects us to glean from this is right there in front of us. Jesus was not speaking of trees and bushes at this time. He was explaining that people can and do recognize other people for who and what they are. Anyone can pretend to have an opinion or emotion or feeling about a certain matter for a while, but eventually the true feelings will surface and shine through. If your faith in God is sincere, that will shine too. If you are putting on a show to impress someone, one day the lights will go down and your true feelings will appear. Be sure of it. As true as the natural facts concerning the *good* fruit growing on the *bad* tree, you cannot hide the selfish you behind good behavior. Unfortunately, we all try at one point or another; but to think you might fool God is simply ludicrous. It is unbelievable to even try. He knows your very thoughts!

The final warning Jesus gives in this parable is where He gives the consequences for the bad tree in the garden that put forth bad fruit... or no fruit (as in the parable "The Barren Fig Tree") The tree is to be cut down and burned in the fire. Jesus is plainly explaining the consequences of false or phony behavior of any person. I think this might be a good time to remind everyone that hell is a fire that goes on for eternity.

There is one more concern presented in this parable according to one of the references I used. Though I don't see the words as they speak of it, I will tell you about it. (There may be a very selfish reason that I don't see it.) I guess you will understand after I give you the information. This source thinks that He was speaking about prophets and teachers specifically. I know He often spoke in reference to the Pharisees, so this makes some sense to me. But according to this source, He was telling the believers clearly to rid their lives of false teachers and prophets, the same as the farmer would rid his garden of that unhealthy tree. I know that there are those that purposely try to mislead others from Christ and Jesus was telling the stronger believers to protect the less knowledgeable new converts by being careful in choosing their teachers and leaders.

I know I would not say anything wrong on purpose for nothing in this world. I know I try to study enough that I know what I'm talking about when I stand before you in class. But I also know I am not formally educated in any of this so sometimes I question my own ability. I know there are little nuances that I might miss and they might change some things so completely as to mean something entirely different from what I thought. That is one reason I question you so hard in class and try to get your opinions on the floor. We must learn together! It is not a one-sided deal. And you have the responsibility to study your lessons too. How else would you know if I did say something wrong?

I sometimes feel like teaching is a blind career in the fact that it does not produce fruit. Like the wolf-man, there will be no souls that I lead to Christ. Usually my students are already good, strong Christians. Else they would not attend so regular. I can give out no diplomas as proof of 'Learning'. I do not give final exams to test your ability and my capability, in other words, my tree has no fruit.

So as I teach this parable before you, I plead my case. And I beg your forgiveness when I do make mistakes. God's word is what we have today to understand His will in our lives. And it has been translated and re-translated over and over before it ever reached our ears. All we can possibly do is rely on the Holy Spirit to help us and be our guide! And if you never believe anything else about me…then know I depend on Him!

Jesus tells us that we will be either justified or condemned by the words of our mouth. And everyone will be judged by the fruit of his labor. But while we must be aware of the wrongs others do; it is a thin line between being aware and judging. We are not qualified to act as judges. That is for Jesus alone to do. I heard one pastor say:

"We cannot act as judges, but we can be fruit inspectors."

So, dear students, when you inspect my fruit, please be kind. I'm doing the best I know how!

30- TWO HOUSES / ON ROCK AND SAND

MATTHEW 7:24-27

Taught at the Sermon on the Mount to many multitudes of people

"Therefore whoever hears these sayings of Mine, and does them, I will liken him to a wise man who built his house on the rock: and the rain descended, the floods came, and the winds blew and beat on that house; and it did not fall, for it was founded on rock. But everyone who hears these sayings of Mine, and does not do them, will be like a foolish man who built his house on the sand; and the rain descended, the floods came, and the winds blew and beat on that house; and it fell. And great was its fall."

LUKE 6:46-49

Place not known but multitudes including the disciples were present at this teaching

"But why do you call Me, 'Lord, Lord', and not do the things which I say? Whoever comes to Me and hears My sayings and does them, I will show you whom he is like: he is like a man building a house, who dug deep and laid the foundation on the rock. And when the flood arose, the stream beat vehemently against that house, and could not shake it, for it was founded on the rock. But he who heard and did nothing is like a man who built a house on the earth without a foundation, against which the stream beat vehemently; and immediately it fell. And the ruin of that house was great."

EXTRA READING

| EXODUS 20:1-12 | MALACHI 1:6 | JAMES 1:22-25 |

This parable was told at the Sermon on the Mount according to the text of Matthew. This was one of the first sermons that Jesus delivered to His followers. Though it was early in His ministry, many, many people were listening and following Him as He traveled from place to place. Luke does not tell us exactly where Jesus was when He taught this, but he does include the disciples as members of the crowd present that day. From the wording of this parable it is not possible for me to determine if this was used at two separate times or if it was taught only once, with each writer giving the story as he remembered it.

Luke begins with a question that Jesus asked those listening. He is concerned with why would those there call Him "Lord" and yet not do as He asked them. It puzzled Him that people would claim Him as "Lord" and give Him the title of honor without showing the honor implied in the title! I think this parable shows some of the confusion that might be in the mind of a man with the thought patterns of God. As God, Jesus simply and totally expects a person that gives honor to another by naming them "Lord" to have that thought of honor in their heart. There is no iota of deceit or misunderstanding in the mind and heart of Jesus (God). There is no way He could possibly consider calling one something that He did not believe. And if one does believe another to have honor... why would you disrespect that honor by not acting on it? Why, or how could you not behave as that honorable person asked you to do?

But Jesus in His compassion for our lives' told this parable to help us gain that understanding that came so natural to Him, as all-God and all-Man. He knew we needed a lot of help with things that were so clear to Him.

He told us of a man that dug a deep and solid foundation in the rock for his home. This home was sturdy and safe no matter what the weather could produce. The wind could blow, the water could rise, and this man's house would be safe for his family. This man had protected his family and his belongings by building with a good foundation.

Then Jesus told us of a second man that apparently was in a hurry to establish his home place. So he neglected to dig down into the rock, but built his house on the surface sand. (Or perhaps he wanted a house by the shore and built in the sand there) But if that was true, he had not been near the shore long! Else he would have been aware that sand shifts often. If the wind blows the sand moves with it. That's how sand dunes come into being. If the water rises and then draws back, the sand goes with it. Wherever it stops the sand has made another dune. But what about the house that had been sitting there? It's gone. Or damaged beyond repair. If this house was not on the shore it does not matter; inland or beachside, sand is the same. So this man did not make a good decision or good investment in his family home. And Jesus told us that the ruin of that house was great.

What was Jesus saying to us that day? I think it was a good bit more than a lesson on where to build our homes, though that is important too. Throughout the Bible and the teachings we have learned from Jesus, He has often called our body, our actual physical body, a house. In it dwells our soul, the Holy Spirit, our heart, and all knowledge that God has shared with us (or wisdom, as we like to think of it). He has carried this comparison so far as to say on occasion that He knocks on the door of our heart, asking to enter.

So I said all that to say this, He is again, in this parable using that allegory. To have a strong, solid faith, we must build a strong, solid foundation.

We need to listen to His teachings. We need to understand these words. And we do that with study and prayer. When we do have the understanding, we need to act on what we've learned. We show honor to God by trying with all our hearts to <u>do</u> His will. If you love your Mom, you, as an adult, do what she asks because you love her. Because you respect her age and wisdom, you try to please her. And that is why you will try to do what God has asked. "With all your heart" you love Him, and respect Him, and show Him honor. When you say "Lord" it comes from deep inside your being as well as your mouth.

If the words that you have studied or read without much thought going into it, just pass through your mind and don't latch onto your heart, you will not be able to do God's will. From the beginning you will not have any idea of what He wants you to do. Without the foundation of knowledge the love is surface only. You may call Him "Lord" but do you really understand what it means to totally turn your life over to Him? Are you still trying to hold on to a bit of the control for yourself? I think we all do that at some point in our lives. And I think that point comes more often than we care to admit. We need to remember the warning Jesus gave us in this parable when He was speaking of the house on the sand and we need to remember our heart on the sand would have the same result:

31- FAITH AS A MUSTARD SEED

MATTHEW 17:18-21

Place unknown. Taught to disciples

"And Jesus rebuked the demon, and it came out of him; and the child was cured from that very hour. Then the disciples came to Jesus privately and said, "Why could we not cast it out?" So Jesus said to them, *"Because of your unbelief; for assuredly, I say to you, if you have faith as a mustard seed, you will say to this mountain, 'Move from here to there,' and it will move; and nothing will be impossible for you. However, this kind does not go out except by prayer and fasting."*

LUKE 17:5-6

Taught while traveling to Jerusalem to disciples and others in crowd

"And the apostles said to the Lord, "Increase our faith." So the Lord said, *"If you have faith as a mustard seed you can say to this mulberry tree, 'Be pulled by the roots and be planted in the sea.' and it would obey you."*

EXTRA READING

MATTHEW 21:21	JOHN 11:21-27	ROMANS 10:8-9
ROMANS 10:17	I CORINTHIANS 16:13	COLOSSIANS 1:23
II TIMOTHY 1:12-13	HEBREWS 11:1-13	

This parable was taught to the disciples. Matthew does not tell us where they were at the time, but Luke tells us they were on the journey toward Jerusalem. This was the trip they made just before the Last Week. If you read the scriptures before the actual parable you will see enough differences in the teachings to support the theory that Jesus taught this parables at least two separate times. I know that if I were to teach the same lesson on two different occasions, I most certainly would not word it exactly the same. And that is what I see here in Jesus' words, the same lesson, the same ideas, just different examples and illustrations.

This parable is not confirmed by either gospel but it is certainly accepted by all the references that I found to be a classic example of a parable. Matthew seems to be the favorite version used for Sunday School classes or for sermons. So much so, that when I read Luke's text with the mulberry tree instead of the mountain, I was truly surprised.

Jesus was teaching His disciples in these verses. In Matthew the disciples had been sent out to teach and heal in Jesus' name. This was one of the first *mission trips* we are told about in the gospels. They had traveled in pairs and tried to represent Jesus as best they could. But as we try today, sometimes things just doesn't go as well as we would want it to do. And they too met with a few failures, in spite of a sincere effort.

A man had presented himself to the disciples and told them that his child was possessed of a demon. He begged for their help and for a healing for his child. But when they tried to cast the demon out, they failed. Later the man approached Jesus and asked for His help. Jesus became very frustrated and asked the disciples how long did they think He was going to be with them. He wanted to know when they would be able to get along without Him. He then had the man bring his child to Him and He cast the demon out. The scripture tells us that the child was healed within the hour.

Later the disciples asked Jesus why did they fail. Jesus did not mince words when He answered them. *"Because of your unbelief..."* then He explained to them that if they had the faith as a mustard seed they could tell a mountain to move, and it would! A mustard seed...remember we talked about it being the size of this "o" in another study. Does this seem like an exaggeration to you? He tells them then... *"nothing will be impossible for you"*. He seemed a bit aggravated at them at that point, or maybe He was disappointed. But in the very next sentence He showed His love and compassion for His disciples by explaining that the problem they had been trying to solve required fasting as well as prayer. Apparently that particular demon was a stubborn one.

In Luke the disciples have asked Jesus to show them how to have more faith. That is a request we all have had at one time or another, and that was their request that day. I can picture them walking along the dusty road together. The twelve, all of them trying to hear every word He uttered, surrounding Jesus as close as they could be in the crowds. There were probably children running in and out between them squealing as they played. (It is always exciting to children to be going on a trip.) The road would have been busy. There would have been all kinds of people walking, going to the Passover celebrations in Jerusalem. Everyone would have been looking forward to the week of holidays.

Except Jesus, He was aware of what the week would bring for Him. And most likely He was in a more thoughtful mood than most of the crowd that day. He was trying to teach His disciples some of the last things He would have a chance to tell them. Don't you imagine He was concerned that they had the strength to carry them through the days ahead, especially since they were now asking Him for more faith?

When they asked this question, He tried to tell them how little faith they really needed to accomplish what they wanted…if it was sincere. He wanted them to be confident and to know that they could do the things He had asked of them. With the faith as a mustard seed, a mulberry tree would uproot itself and re-plant itself in the ocean, if it was told to!

I am sure that anyone reading this would question his/ her own ability to have that power! But I can't understand why we think as we do. Not one person I have ever met, or heard of, or thought into existence would call Jesus a liar! Yet we don't seem to believe Him either! Jesus would not tell us anything but the whole truth. We all claim to have faith to trust our eternal life to His teachings, yet which one of us will say the words that will allow the Holy Spirit to move the tree? Transplanting a tree or even moving a mountain is small stuff when it comes to comparing that to where you will spend eternity! That's a long time! Few care where the tree is planted, and though I would like a mountain near by, I most certainly do not want to spend one single minute out of the presence of God! Hell is not where I want to be for all time!

He asks so little of us, faith as a mustard seed. He offers us so much in return! Nothing is impossible to us! That is what He told the disciples that day. And that is what we read in the Holy Word today! All my life I have been taught this parable and I have questioned my own faith; that surely I had enough to fill the space the size of a mustard seed. Yet I too, would not dare to say the words, "Move, mountain." There were prayers said with some doubt or questions, wondering if God would hear them and answer them. I am talking about prayers that I KNEW and still KNOW were in God's will such as the salvation of a loved one. We won't even discuss those prayers that are selfish; just the ones we know were appropriate and good. I know there are people with a more pure and perhaps less selfish faith, but to think my faith was so small was very discouraging. And I had no idea what to do about it.

But then I began to study for this part of this work and I wrote it; stressing to all how very lacking we are in our faith, and at the same time I was telling everyone how Jesus was trying to boost our confidence with this parable. And I finished this lesson somewhere around the previous paragraph as best I could.

I carefully taped a tiny mustard seed to small slips of paper with Jesus' response to the disciples concerning their unbelief typed on it for each student. And I considered myself prepared and done; I was ready for Sunday morning's class.

Saturday night I sat down to re-read everything and the Holy Spirit joined me in my studies. With His encouragement, I read and re-read the scriptures. Suddenly He revealed to me something I had not seen in all my previous studying. We, all of us, when we think of or discuss this parable, we say "faith of a mustard seed" . That <u>ain't</u> what it says, children! It says "faith as a mustard seed" There is a big difference in the meanings of those two phrases.

So what is "faith as a mustard seed" ? A seed is not an entity that we would normally associate with having faith; it is not a creature with knowledge, but if it was… what would it be about? That seed knows within it is the power to grow a tree, according to our earlier studies, that would grow to six to eight feet high. It would have branches strong enough to support homes to a number of different bird families. It could and would produce enough seed to populate the entire surface of the earth with mustard trees if left alone to its work. Each tiny seed would have that pure and simple knowledge of its' capabilities…faith. That seed has one single purpose; it would and does do exactly what it was intended to do by God when created. Nothing else misleads it or causes it to stray from that one purpose.

We were created with one purpose, to be in companionship with God. To be in that state of being, we need to continuously be in His will for our life. We have been given one assignment; to show the gospel and love of God to all those we come into contact with. We need to remember the steadfastness of the mustard seed and determine ourselves to walk that one path. If we have the determination and solid faith that the seed has, all things are possible to us! When we pray for the salvation of some loved one (or some enemy) we never have to doubt that God will answer that prayer!

I have an idea that to pray for the mountain to move might not be a good thing to do; for several reasons, but the main one is, I suspect you might not really care if the mountain moves but instead you might be testing God with a prayer like that. Jesus, Himself told Satan not to test his God. (The second reason is that God put that mountain where He wanted it to begin with. Who are you to change that?)

But I am trying to say I think if we live with the single-mindedness of the mustard seed, our faith will grow, just as the disciples asked Jesus that day. Faith, as a mustard seed… that's all we need!

32- FAITHFUL AND WISE STEWARD

MATTHEW 24:45-51

Taught as one of the End Times teachings at the Sermon on Mount Olivet (Olives) to the disciples

"Who then is a faithful and wise servant, whom his master made ruler over his household, to give them food in due season? Blessed is that servant whom his master, when he comes, will find so doing. Assuredly, I say to you that he will make him ruler over all his goods. But if that evil servant says in his heart, 'My master is delaying his coming,' and begins to beat his fellow servants, and to eat and drink with the drunkards, the master of the servant will come on a day when he is not looking for him and at an hour that he is not aware of, and will cut him in two and appoint him his portion with the hypocrites. There shall be weeping and gnashing of the teeth."

LUKE 12:35-40

Place unknown but taught to a huge crowd

"Let your waist be girded and your lamps burning: and you yourselves be like men who wait for their master, when he will return from the wedding, that when he comes and knocks they may open to him immediately. Blessed are those servants whom the master, when he comes, will find watching. Assuredly, I say to you that he will gird himself and have them sit down and eat, and will come and serve them. And if he should come in the second watch, or come in the third watch, and find them so, blessed are those servants. But know this, that if the master of the house had known what hour the thief would come, he would have watched and not allowed his house to be broken into. Therefore you also be ready, for the Son of Man is coming at an hour you do not expect."

LUKE 12:41-48 Jesus' Response to questions concerning this parable

Again place unknown but taught to disciples

"Then Peter said to Him, "Lord, do You speak this parable only to us, or to all people?" And the Lord said, *"Who then is that faithful and wise steward, whom his master will make ruler over his household, to give them their portions of food in due season? Blessed is that servant whom his master will find so doing when he comes. Truly, I say to you, that he will make him ruler over all that he has. But if that servant says in his heart, 'My master is delaying his coming.' and begins to beat the male and female servants, and to eat and drink and be drunk, the master of that servant will come on a day when he is not looking for him, and at an hour when he is not aware, and will cut him in two and appoint him his portion with the unbelievers. And that servant who knew his master's will, and did not prepare himself or do according to his will, shall be beaten with many stripes. But he who did not know, yet committed things deserving of stripes, shall be beaten with few. For everyone to whom much is given, from him much will be required; and to whom much has been committed, of him they will ask the more.*

EXTRA READING

MATTHEW 24:42-44	MATTHEW 25:13	MARK13: 32-33
MARK 13:35-37	I THESSALONIANS 5:1-6	JAMES 4:17
I PETER 1:13	II PETER 3:10	

This parable was one of the ones that caused a lot of confusion in my poor mind when I first started this project. Each list that I found it on listed different verses. Each list gave it a different title. So at some point I thought it might be five or six different parables. (You have to know that at that point the whole project looked mighty impossible to me!) Gradually I found some rhyme and reason to the whole thing. So now I will attempt to show you what I think I found; and someday someone will see this and say, "Oh! No, not a different version!"

The Bible that I use most often, *The Open Bible* (NKJV) uses sub-titles above each set of teachings. In Matthew the editors have called this set of verses "The Illustration of Two Servants" . Remember the word *illustration* means *parable*.

In Luke there are two sub-titles with the verses: "The Parable of the Expectant Steward" and "The Faithful Steward" . And the second set of verses in Luke is almost word for word the same as Matthew's teaching. That is what is in one source (version). Try to imagine what I found in the several different versions I have used, and I know that you will have used some of those in your study, or even others that I don't have available to me. Since I have learned to trust that inside voice (the Holy Spirit) I do hope you can combine this with whatever you have discovered in your resources and make some sense of this parable(s). The teachings that Jesus wanted us to take away from it are the same; regardless of what title we call it. He included the parable we call "Ten Virgins" in this set of teachings too. We will study it a bit later.

In the verses previous to these in Matthew Jesus had just told those around Him that the End Time days would be a complete surprise to the world. And He is continuing that thought in this parable. Jesus saw the lack of understanding in the crowds of people and He knew that they must comprehend the consequences of not accepting the truth of this parable.

He asked them about a faithful servant, one that had been trusted by his master to rule over the home place. He spoke of the rewards that servant would receive for being found performing his duties after the master had been gone for awhile. The master would be proud and would give that servant more responsibilities.

And then He spoke of the disgrace of that same servant if he was found acting false toward his responsibilities. Sometimes the temptations of time might allow that servant to think he could do as he wished and still have time to straighten things out before the master returned. That is like a teenager, left at home alone for a weekend while Mom and Dad went for a short holiday. You can almost be sure he will have some sort of party that Mom and Dad would not have approved of, had they been home. And you can be sure the teen had planned all along to spend Sunday cleaning house. However, he did not count on the fact that the special lamp that Grandma gave to Mom would get broken into a million pieces. Nor did he ever think that those friends would get into Dad's wine closet and drink only the best and oldest! He never thought that things would be so out of control and unfixable!

Jesus told the multitude that day that they needed to be prepared (to gird their loins) and to watch carefully. He warned them stoutly and sternly that they would not know when the Son of man would re-appear and demand an accounting of their behavior. To gird their loins refers to the custom of men to pull the back of their skirt tail through their legs and tuck it up into a belt-like tie at their waist. This gave them more freedom in the movement of their legs to work without the robes flopping in the way. I'm sure this was the precursor to pants, as we know them now. It was a way of preparing to work…sort of like today we might say, "Roll up your sleeves…"

And He told them to keep watch… that too, was most likely more familiar to them than it would be if said in our day. Remember we studied earlier about the night watchman at the sheep pens. And there were watchmen on the towers of the town walls too. The watchmen were assigned a certain time period to work, the same as our shift work. There were at least two different sets of shifts, the Roman watch and the Jewish watch. The Roman watch was broken into four shifts throughout the night. The Jewish watch was divided into only three.

ROMAN WATCH	JEWISH WATCH
6pm – 9pm	6pm – 10 pm
9pm – 12 midnight	10pm –2 am
12 midnight- 3 am	2am-6am
3am-6am	

At different times through the scriptures references have been made to the first watch or such, and it seldom tells us which system it is referring to, but sometimes we can figure out which system is being used. For example we know that when Jesus walked on the water toward the fishing boat during the fourth watch (Matthew 14:25.) We know this had to be a reference to Roman time schedules, because the Jewish watch did not have a fourth division of time.

These watches were very important to the protection of their families as well as their stock back then. So they understood Jesus when He warned them to be on Watch. He has taught this lesson in many of His parables. He has told us over and over again that NO ONE knows when He will return…not one but God, the Father knows. Therefore each moment we need to be ready.

Some years ago my friend and her daughter visited me at my home. The daughter was in those early years of teenage and as hardheaded as one can be. Even though this was true, I loved seeing my friend and tried to ignore the growing pains of a young person. After all, my friend had already suffered through those same pains with my children years earlier.

The girl was bored at her Mom's friend's house, with no other kids around and the adult women talking about things of absolutely no interest to her. So as a good Mom, my friend had allowed her to bring what she called 'a boom box' and a few of her CD's. That way she at least had the comfort of her music. She inserted a CD that she thought would please me because it was a country artist. It was one that I was very familiar with, and though he never was a favorite of mine, I was just glad it wasn't some of the other types of music I have heard young people play on their boom boxes. (That is one well-named product!)

But as I talked with my friend, (we were in the kitchen trying to cook a meal) and as that song blared out on the kitchen table, I was shocked at the words I heard coming from it! I turned to the girl-child and asked her what on earth was that I heard. She, as proud as punch, explained that she had a copy of the CD that was not meant for radio play. It contained language that I never dreamed one would put in a song. I didn't know they made different versions of the same song…x-rated and radio-play. But I told her to turn it off! She argued and I explained that if my husband walked in and heard it, he would destroy the whole CD, maybe even the boom box! She was very upset and pouted for a good while afterwards but she finally settled down and watched a bit of television.

As she pouted, my friend started to act a bit offended that I came down so hard on her baby. I tried to tell her my feelings on it but she, like her daughter was a bit hardheaded, and did not want to listen. Finally I got a touch angry and asked her, "What if Jesus came right now, and He found that noise coming out of a box sitting on MY KITCHEN TABLE?" Then I got my heart broke because her response was, "Mary, He hasn't come in two thousand years, I don't think we have to be concerned with the next five minutes!"

That is just what Jesus is warning us about in this parable. So many will carry that attitude through their whole life and will not be ready when they face Jesus in judgment. Thankfully, neither my friend nor her daughter still thinks like that. Both are living their lives, as best I know, in a way that will be pleasing to the Master when He returns but there are so many others that are not! It's so easy to slip into that "It ain't gonna happen today" thought pattern. But we cannot let our guard down. We seem to think that we will always have the second-chance option available. Jesus told us we <u>must</u> stay aware and alert!

PS. A lesson that Jesus teaches throughout nearly all of the parables is sort of lost, with our concern of the particular story we might be studying at the time...but it continuously appears in the words we are reading...

Do you remember earlier in this story, I said that the master of the house would reward the good servant with more responsibilities? Do you remember hearing that same quotation a number of times now? What about the parable called "The Ten Talents?" That's just one example. There have been several, and there will be more. The good, faithful servant of God's word will be rewarded with more responsibilities and the unfaithful will loose whatever talents he had thought he had.

But think it through. Work it around your mind and see what comes up. We, as humans, most often think of a reward from our employers in terms of more time off and more pay. Never do we consider the thought of more responsibilities and more accountability as a gift of honor! Human nature is apparently LAZY!

Jesus has told us over and over again that the true pleasures and earned rewards of living is found in doing the work of our Lord! Seems like we all might be due a slight attitude adjustment.

33- PROFANING THE HOLY

MATTHEW 7:6

From the Sermon on the Mount and spoken to the multitude

> *"Do not give what is holy to the dogs; nor cast your pearls*
> *before swine, lest they trample them under their feet, and*
> *turn and tear you to pieces."*

EXTRA READING

PSALMS 141:5	PROVERBS 9: 7-9	MATTHEW 13:12

This parable is part of the teachings Jesus spoke at the Sermon on the Mount. It is also one that He made reference to in another teaching later. Do not give what is "holy" to the dogs. Simple enough to understand... right? Do not cast your pearls in front of swine. Of course not! Or trampled they would be, for sure!

Jesus has told us in the verses before this one that we should beware of being critical of others. But by contrast here He is telling us that we do need to be aware there are persons that are evil. And these evil people would just mock and twist the precious Holy Words of God, if given any chance at all. As children of God that are trying to follow the great commission, we feel obligated to try to warn them that their actions have consequences. But Jesus is telling us here that if they do not respond and repent after continuously talking to them, there is no further reason to keep trying to show them their sinful ways. If they are not ready to admit they are sinners, they are certainly not ready to ask for forgiveness! And all you will do at this point is make them angry and combative.

Back off, you have planted the seed, let it grow. Allow the Holy Spirit to have time to work and always remember them in your prayers. And

KNOW that God is in control; He loves these hardheaded children even more than you can imagine.

34- UNMERCIFUL SERVANT (INSOLVENT DEBTOR)
(Kingdom of Heaven Parable)

MATTHEW 18:21-35

Taught somewhere in the city of Capernaum, perhaps at the house of Peter. Not sure if others besides disciples were present.

"Then Peter came to Him and said, "Lord, how often shall my brother sin against me, and I forgive him? Up to seven times?" Jesus said to him, "*I do not say to you, up to seven times, but up to seventy times seven. Therefore the kingdom of Heaven is like a certain king who wanted to settle accounts with his servants. And when he had begun to settle accounts, one was brought to him who owed him ten thousand talents. But as he was not able to pay, his master commanded that he be sold, with his wife and children, and all that he had, and that payment be made. The servant therefore fell down before him saying, 'Master, have patience with me, and I will pay you all.' Then the master of that servant was moved with compassion, released him and forgave him the debt. But that servant went out and found one of his fellow servants who owed him a hundred denarii; and he laid hands on him and took him by the throat, saying 'Pay me what you owe!' So his fellow servant fell down at his feet and begged him, saying, 'Have patience with me, and I will pay you all.' And he would not but went and threw him into prison till he should pay the debt. So when his fellow servants saw what had been done, they were very grieved, and came and told their master all that had been done. Then his master, after he had called him, said to him, 'You wicked servant! I forgave you all that debt because you begged me. Should you not also have had compassion on your fellow servant, just as I had pity on you?' And his master was angry, and delivered him to the torturers until he should pay all that was due to him.*

So My heavenly Father also will do to you if each of you, from his heart, does not forgive his brother his trespasses."

EXTRA READING

II KINGS 4:1-7	MATTHEW 6:12	MATTHEW 6:14-15
MARK 11:25-26	LUKE 7:41-43	COLOSSIANS 3:12-15
I PETER 4:8-9		

This parable was taught in the city of Capernaum according to Matthew, but it is one of the few that Matthew did not tell us exactly where Jesus was at the time. Most authorities are pretty sure that they were at Peter's home, and if that is true then most likely there were few there except the disciples alone with Jesus. This parable was one of the parables that were told only in Matthew. He told a number of teachings concerning money that the others did not mention. Some authorities suspect that because Matthew's way of earning a living involved money (tax collector) he would have been more inclined to remember those teachings; just as Luke (a physician) noticed the healing stories more often.

Peter asked Jesus for clarification on the act of forgiveness if a Christian brother had wronged him in some manner. And when he asked Jesus, he showed genuine Christian grace in the question as he asked it. He wanted to know if he should forgive this brother seven times over again and again for sins against himself. The Jewish law clearly states that one should forgive another four times over, only if the person has truly repented and apologized for his sin. Since Peter agreed to more than four times, and never mentioned repentance or an apology, he showed that the grace of God was working in his heart. He was being much more gracious than the Jewish law ever required. He was showing to all those present that the love of Christ was acting in his spirit.

However, when Jesus responded we realize that Jesus' love and compassion goes more than a bit further than the law. He told Peter that he must forgive this person seven times seventy…or an unlimited number of times. And He never mentioned the repentance either!

Have you ever heard, no, have you ever spoke the words of this quote? "FOOL ME THE FIRST TIME, SHAME ON YOU; FOOL ME THE SECOND TIME, SHAME ON ME!"

Doesn't that quote indicate that if you wrong me the first time, you should be ashamed for what you have done? But if I allow you to wrong me the second time, I should be the one shamed because I should not have trusted you again. Isn't that pretty much what we truly think in today's world? Do you believe that we are that much different than folks back then? No, I don't. And I think Peter was showing sincere kindness and love for his fellow man when he questioned Jesus. Can you imagine letting someone wrong you seven times (or even four) times and still trusting and loving that person? I think Jesus, the Man, understood this. So Jesus, the Lord, told this parable so that they (and us, today) might understand how it SHOULD be in our hearts.

Jesus told of a king that for some reason decided it was time to settle all accounts with his servants. As he did this, one was brought before him that owed ten thousand talents to the king. I have no idea how he could possibly owe that much. We recently studied in the parable called "Ten Talents" how very much money one talent was. I cannot imagine why the king would have allowed one servant to accumulate such a debt. But, however, it happened, and now the servant could not possibly pay it back.

The king made the decision that since the man could never raise such an amount, he as his owner, would sell the man, his wife, his children, and all his property. That was the only way the king could recoup even a small portion of the money. I doubt very seriously that the family would have remained together after such a sell. Most likely the same new owner would not have purchased them all. This was probably considered a fate worse than death to that servant. It would have felt like that to me, if I were in that position. You can't help but feel so sad for the situation the servant has brought upon himself and his family. Sometimes we do things like that and bring a total sadness on all of those around us. It is true when others say. "Well, he brought it on himself. It's all his fault." But truth, or not, the pain is still real and hurts the same as if someone else did the harmful deed…maybe the hurt is more.

The servant fell before the king, and begged his forgiveness and begged his patience. He promised with every breath in his body to re-pay every penny of the amount owed! The king, being more compassionate than most I think, forgave the servant the entire debt! The servant could continue his life, with his family in tact, and without any debt owed! Can you imagine a complete chance to start your life over, with all your possessions and no bills to pay for them? That was one servant that could really shout from the rooftops "God bless the king!"

The servant went on with his life, you would think with love filling his heart. But as Jesus told His story we see that humans aren't always as grateful for blessings as they might could be. That servant went out into the town and found another servant that owed to him one hundred denarii. Now, a denarius was worth approximately what a man could earn for one day's wages. Since this man was a servant in the house of the king, it is unlikely that he could ever pay this debt, and certainly not in a timely manner. The first, forgiven servant grabbed him and demanded his money right away!

The second servant fell before the first and begged the first to have patience with him. He promised with every breath of his body to re-pay every penny of the money owed. But as the other servants of the house watched, this man would not forgive his fellow worker; instead he had him put into prison until his family could re-pay the debt. The others that had seen both men approached about their debts were entirely saddened at the results of this event. They then went to the king and told him about the behavior of the first servant.

The king was furious! He called the servant back into his presence and reprimanded him severely. The king was shocked at the lack of compassion this servant had shown for his fellow servant! He sent him directly to jail and demanded that he be tortured until his entire debt was repaid! We can be fairly certain that this turned out to be a life-sentence for this first servant. And his family would also spend their lives with this debt as the focus of their daily activities.

Jesus closed this teaching with a very simple, clear statement. There is no need for any one to interpret or try to clarify what He has said:

"SO MY HEAVENLY FATHER ALSO WILL DO TO YOU IF EACH OF YOU, FROM HIS HEART, DOES NOT FORGIVE HIS BROTHER HIS TRESPASSES."

This by no means is the only time Jesus talked about our forgiveness being based on whether or not we forgive others. Remember the Lord's Prayer?

"AND FORGIVE US OUR DEBTS, AS WE FORGIVE OUR DEBTORS."

Please notice that little word "as". Again it gives a very definite meaning to a phrase that might otherwise mean something different. It is clear here that our own judgment will be based totally on how we love one another; and how we express that love. Sometimes it is extremely hard to forgive. Sometimes we think that to forgive is not even expected from us.

I have not had a family member or friend murdered or some such crime committed against me. But I did loose my dear friend to a wreck caused by a man that was trying to escape with a stolen vehicle. She was killed instantly when she was hit so hard right in the driver's side door that she flew through the windshield of her own car...in spite of the air bags inflating. No one around me ever said I should forgive this man. I don't think anyone thought it was possible. And now, today, nearly ten years later, when I think of the time he cheated me out of with her... when I think how proud she would have been to read this work with me...I almost hate him again; just like I did that day. I guess, as an adult, (knowing now what the word 'hate' really means) he is the only person I ever truly hated, even for a period of time!

But time has passed and the pain is down to a low boil, and I've finally come to know that the hate only hurts me. He could care less what he did that day. He didn't care then for anything except to get away with someone else's pick-up and he doesn't care today if I remember him with disgust. So hate in my heart just makes me look at God's beautiful world with tainted eyes. I can't live like that. And Jesus doesn't want me to behave like that. So I pray for this man, that he will know someday just what he did. And that he will seek God's wisdom in his life.

And I try very hard to remember that my own sins have hurt someone too. Maybe I didn't kill someone with a careless mistake. But I have to know: a sin is a sin. There are no big sins, and little sins. There are no little white lies and unforgivable lies. All things, according to Jesus are forgivable except denying the Holy Spirit...for me and the other person.

This man is a child of God and Jesus loves him! What right do I have to think I am a better person than he is? So while he prays for forgiveness for what he did that day, I need to pray for forgiveness for what I have done for years now.

"FORGIVE ME MY SINS, <u>AS</u> I FORGIVE OTHERS THAT
HAVE SINNED AGAINST ME."

Those that enter the kingdom of heaven will be those that have been able in their hearts, to forgive all those that hurt them in some way. We pray daily, (or should) that God will forgive us as we forgive someone else. But do we remember that if we do not forgive down in the bottom of our heart, the consequences are drastic?

35- LABORERS IN VINEYARD
(Kingdom of Heaven Parable)

MATTHEW 20:1-16

Taught somewhere in the countryside of Judea, in the previous verses He had been speaking to a multitude of people, including the disciples

"For the kingdom of heaven is like a landowner who went out early in the morning to hire laborers for his vineyard. Now when he had agreed with the laborers for a denarius a day, he sent them into his vineyard. And he went out about the third hour and saw others standing idle in the marketplace and said to them, 'You also go into the vineyard, and whatever is right I will give you.' So they went. And again he went out about the sixth and ninth hour, and did likewise. And about the eleventh hour he went out and found others standing idle, and said to them, 'Why have you been standing idle all day?' They said to him, 'Because no one hired us.' He said to them, ' You also go into the vineyard, and whatever is right you will receive.' So when evening had come, the owner of the vineyard said to his steward, 'Call the laborers and give them their wages, beginning with the last to the first. And when those came who were hired about the eleventh hour, they each received a denarius. But when the first came, they supposed that they would receive more; and they likewise received each a denarius. And when they had received it, they complained against the landowner, saying, 'These last men have worked only one hour, and you made them equal to us who have borne the burden and the heat of the day.' But he answered one of them and said, 'Friend, I am doing you no wrong. Did you not agree with me for a denarius? Take what is yours and go your way, I wish to give to this last man the same as to you. Is it not lawful for me to do what I wish with my own things? Or is your eye evil because I am good? ' So the last will be first, and the first last. For many are called, but few are chosen."

EXTRA READING:

DEUTERONOMY 15: 9-14	ISAIAH 29:16	ISAIAH 45:9
I THESSALONIANS 4:16-17	ROMANS 9:20-21	
REVELATIONS 6:9-11		

This parable was only related in Matthew, and as the last one we studied the story told a message that involved money. It does seem that Matthew was impressed with those messages and remembered them better than some of the others. But I think that Jesus told those messages because He knew that as men, humans understood the value of money easier than they might have understood the value of something less tangible. All men, today as well as then, know that a dollar is hard earned and there is no question that it means something to them if it is taken from them, or as in this case they feel cheated. But that is jumping a bit ahead of what I need to say.

Jesus told a story about a man that went out early in the morning (probably about six am.) to hire workers for his vineyard. Men gathered in the marketplace each day if they wanted to work and an employer would approach them there. He would then hire them much as we sometimes hire help for the day now. There is always a spot in town where men gather if they want work. Even in a small town like our rural area has such a place today. In this case, the farmer hired as many as were there and agreed that a denarius was a fair wage. The workers also agreed that it was indeed a fair amount for working that day.

Later in the morning (most likely around nine a.m.) the farmer went again to the marketplace and saw others there looking for work. He hired them too and agreed to pay them a fair wage for their labor. He repeated this procedure again about the noon hour; and again at about three p.m. At approximately five p.m. the farmer again went into the marketplace and saw men standing, waiting to be hired for work. So he hired them, promising to pay them what was fair.

At six p.m. he called his servant to come and pay all the workers for their day's labor. He told the servant to call the workers that started last to be paid first. And he gave each of those that started at five p.m. a denarius; the same for those that started at three p.m. and so on for each that had begun to work at noon and nine a.m. Those workers that had started at six a.m. watched this with a lot of interest. They just knew in their mind that because they had worked more hours than the others, and the farmer paid those workers a denarius, then they would get more. The farmer was being what seemed to them very generous and they expected that to continue in their favor.

When the steward of the farmer gave each of them that had started at six a.m. a denarius too, they were most unhappy. They complained to the farmer that it was not fair that they received the same pay as those men that had only worked one hour. The farmer reminded them that they had an agreement with him, a denarius for a day's labor. He had kept his promise and paid them what was agreed. And he also told them that it was his own money to give it to whom he pleased and they had no right to even be concerned with what he did with his own property. At no point had he cheated them. They got what was just and according to the agreement. So it was his suggestion to them that they take what was their own and leave.

In this, a kingdom of heaven parable, Jesus has told us a couple of different things that are important to our growth as a Christian. The first I will discuss is the one that seems to be in the actual words. The surface meaning, if that is easier to understand. It is honorable to remember a promise. If an agreement is made between two persons, then it should be kept. Sometimes it is not to your benefit to remember a promise made, but it is always to your benefit to keep that promise.

There are times that promises seem to sort of backfire and turn into something that hurts you, but your word as a man (or woman) is more important than much else you can name! A broken promise is a lie. This farmer kept his word to the workers. He first, early that morning, made the agreement with them, and then he did as he promised. He kept his word to them. But that is the *easy* interpretation and only part of what Jesus wants us to learn. If I can I will try to show you the rest of the lesson that is here.

In this parable, if we let the farmer represent God, and the workers represent the children of God, we might pull a lot more from this story. Throughout time, men have been working for God in His vineyard. We can name those people all the way back beyond Abraham. Some were children nearly from their birth. Some became children on their death beds. Some tried everyday of their adult lives to be what would be pleasing in God's eyes. Some refused to even think about God until it was almost too late.

God has promised us that with salvation, we receive eternal life with Him and Jesus in heaven's glory. He has given the same promise to all children accepting Jesus as their Savior. Those that have spent their lives doing God's will, will be blessed with that eternal promise. Those that received Salvation in the last few minutes of their time here on earth will be blessed with that eternal promise too. They won't be penalized as a football player with time-out for bad behavior. God's forgiveness for those sinners that repent is total, complete, and instant. That is His promise. And He cannot lie!

And the fact that those workers in this parable questioned the fairness of the farmer is important too. If you read some of the extra reading I suggested you will see what I am talking about here. It is perfectly all right for you to ask God questions. Things that trouble you or confuse you need answers. God does not mind at all for you to ask questions. He encourages that from us. He tells us to seek wisdom. James told us in his writings that if we don't learn the answers to anything, it is because we didn't ask! (James 1: 5-6) James also tells us how to ask a question of God...with faith that we will receive an answer!

God, as the potter (Isaiah 45:9), as the creator (Isaiah 45:10), cannot be contested as to why or how He has done something. When we try to challenge God's authority with our questions we are way out of line. The pot, if it had a voice, could not ask the potter why it was shaped as it was. The potter did not have to even make it to begin with. He certainly had the right as the potter to shape it in any way he chose.

I have moved into those intangibles that I spoke of earlier and it is hard to express what I am thinking in my mind. Sometimes words don't come with a thought as clearly as one wants it to. Isn't that funny? I had never considered the idea that I could have a thought without words! But I think I've met that place now.

As Jesus closed this teaching, He said that the first will be last and the last will be first. And He then repeated the words He had said before in other parables..."that many are called and few are chosen."

I understand that this is a reference to the actual End Times events. I may be completely wrong, but I understand from the text in chapter 6 of Revelations, verses 9-11 there will be a few Jewish souls saved during the time of Tribulation. These people of course will be horribly killed for their testimony to Christ. At a point in the hours of their horror they asked Jesus when their souls would be avenged. Jesus spoke to them and told them it would be a short time. But the point I have for telling you about this (I certainly don't want to get caught up in trying to teach Revelations!) is to show you the prophecy in I Thessalonians (4:16-17) and the words of this parable will be fulfilled, in reference to the promise of the last being first, and first being last. These Christian Jews will be among the last to find salvation in God's love, but they will be among the first of the dead to join Jesus in the sky. After the dead ascend then those still living will rise to be with Jesus. Like the laborers in the vineyard, those saved toward the end of time (or toward the end of their own lives) will have the gift of eternity, the same as those that were saved as small children.

We are aware that many are called. It is God's desire that all souls are saved. Everyone has or will have the call presented to them to become one of God's own, but everyone will not answer that call. Unless they respond to God's plan of salvation, they will not be chosen to join Him in glory.

36- TWO SONS

Unknown exactly where but Jesus was in temple somewhere, perhaps the city of Bethany, He was speaking to group of Pharisees. All present in temple would have heard Him

"But what do you think? A man had two sons, and he came to the first and said, 'Son, go work today in my vineyard.' He answered and said, 'I will not,' but afterward he regretted it and went. Then he came to the second and said likewise. And he answered and said, 'I go, sir.' But he did not go. Which of the two did the will of his father?" They said to him, *"The first."* Jesus said to them, *"Assuredly, I say unto you that tax collectors and harlots enter the kingdom of God before you. For John came to you in the way of righteousness, and you did not believe him; but tax collectors and harlots believed him; and when you saw it, you did not afterward relent and believe him."*

EXTRA READING

| MATTHEW 9:2 | MATTHEW 9:22 | MATTHEW 21:27 |
| LUKE 7:29-30 | LUKE 7:36-50 | I TIMOTHY 1:12-14 |

This parable was taught in temple, most likely in the city of Bethany. In the verses before, Matthew speaks of Jesus and the disciples traveling to that city (21:17) and he told us that in the morning Jesus returned to the city (21:18). Some authorities seem to think that means He returned to Jerusalem. However it really does not change anything He said no matter which temple it was, so I won't dwell on that fact. While He was teaching in temple, the elders approached Him and asked Him by what authority did He speak. As in His normal speaking style when confronted, He answered their questions with questions of His own.

He asked them by whose authority did they believe that John the Baptist had baptized his followers? He knew it was a question that they could not answer without serious consequences one-way or the other. If they answered, "by heavens authority" then they could not explain how they had doubted and disbelieved John. If they said by man's authority, then many people would be offended because most believed John the Baptist to be a true Prophet of God, the first in nearly 400 years.

When the Pharisees could not give Him an answer, He refused to answer their question. Instead He spoke a parable to them. This parable was not confirmed by the standard that I set when I began this project; however, if you will read in verse #33, you will see Matthew quotes Jesus as He speaks, *"Hear another parable"*. That tells me that He had just spoken one. That makes these verses a parable too. Another detail, not worth confusion; Jesus was teaching a message He wanted us to understand.

He told them a story of a farmer with two sons. The farmer approached the first son and told him to go work in a certain vineyard for the day. The son told his father that he was not going to do it. I suppose he had plans for the day that were more important to him than doing as his dad asked. Later, after the son had time to reconsider the way he had spoken to his dad, he was remorseful and decided to go do the work asked of him.

In the meanwhile, the farmer had approached his second son and told him of the work that needed his attention. The second son quickly agreed to go do the work for his father. But he lied. He went on about his day and just simply ignored his dad's request.

After Jesus told this story, He turned to those listening and asked them, *"Which of the two did the will of his father?"* All those listening answered with one accord, "The first son."

As He heard their answer, He responded that tax collectors and harlots would enter the kingdom of God before any of them (the Pharisees). I wonder if they thought at first that He spoke as He did because they might have answered the question wrong. That's not what He was saying at all, but humans with human thoughts think things like that. His answer was such an insult to their minds, confusion almost had to be the result!

Tax collectors in heaven?! That was not possible! And harlots? Well, everyone knows there will be no harlots in heaven! That place of God's glory will be filled with the elders, their honorable wives, and the children that would follow in the footprints of their smart and well-behaved dads! But here this Man, Jesus, (by now some were saying He was the Messiah), was saying that they, the Pharisees as the religious leaders of all God's children were not going to be found in heaven! Why would He say such a thing?

To understand why He said these things, we need to read some of the extra reading verses I listed and add a bit of background to the story. When John began baptizing his followers, there were a great many that accepted his authority as that of any of the great prophets throughout history. But of course there were those that did not believe any thing John said or did as being from the Holy Spirit.

Those people considered John to be 'wild' and 'crazy'. Yet as many common men and women (meaning those that were not necessarily public leaders or such) trusted and believed in John, they were baptized; but the Pharisees and other leaders of the Jewish faith rejected and denied that it was the will of God to be baptized, especially by this man from the wilderness. They refused to admit that John was speaking with the blessings of God. So in these verses Jesus was reminding them that they had rejected the truth of John's teaching. Yet the 'less educated', the sinners in the world, the harlots and tax collectors, saw the plan of salvation taught with God's love clearly.

They understood that with repentance, their sins would be forgiven. And they recognized that by being baptized they were acknowledging in a public way that they were God's Children with the desire to do God's will. The act of being baptized was a public announcement to all that knew the now, forgiven sinner. He was making a promise to God, his friends, his family, and his acquaintances that it was his plan to try to walk in God's will from that day forward. He had made a public commitment with this act to show his love for God.

But this new plan and new way of expressing a fellowship with God completely ousted the need of people to depend on the Pharisees. Their role in religion was never going to be the same as it had been. John was offering each man a personal one-on-one relationship with God that did not require him to go through the Pharisees to ask for God's forgiveness.

In this new plan a man could believe and have God's love. God was not just the Almighty Lord. He was the Father, a loving and personal Deity.

It is the same today for those that accept Jesus as the Son of God. It is the same for those that believe Jesus died and was resurrected from the dead to pay the price we cannot pay for our sins. And it is the same for those that make the public commitment of being baptized in the name of Jesus Christ.

But after all this I have written, I still have not mentioned the reason that Jesus refused to answer the Pharisees to begin with when they asked Him by whose authority did He teach in the temple. The answer to that question is almost a separate message within the first.

The Pharisees (not all, but most), in spite of all their education and knowledge of the law of Moses have lived their lives in rejection to God. Somewhere in time passing they have forgotten that their job was to teach and guide others toward a relationship with the Father. They have come to the point that they, trusting in their own authority and believing in their own perfection, think that they have no need of God's guidance any longer. And with their having no need of God's guidance, they cannot possibly teach others to accept that assistance from God!

So Jesus, when He refused to give an answer to their question, was telling all of us, that those people that have willfully and deliberately denied God and refused to follow His will (in this case, they refused to see the need to be baptized) cannot be helped by more information. If they do not accept what they have been told, they are not ready to learn more. Remember all the times Jesus has told us that those that seek more wisdom, will be blessed with more wisdom. But those that think they already know it all…well, what they do know will be taken from them. There is no point in telling them anything else…yet. All we can do is pray for them to wake up before it is too late. But to tell them more of the story of Jesus at this point is a waste of time!

Plant the seed, give the Holy Spirit time to work, and let it grow.

37- TEN VIRGINS
(Kingdom of Heaven Parable)

MATTHEW 25:1-13

Taught in the End Time discourse on the Mount of Olivet (Olives) to the disciples

"Then the kingdom of heaven shall be likened to ten virgins who took their lamps and went out to meet the bridegroom. Now five of them were wise, and five were foolish. Those who were foolish took their lamps, and took no oil with them, but the wise took oil in their vessels with their lamps. But while the bridegroom was delayed, they all slumbered and slept. And at midnight a cry was heard: 'Behold, the bridegroom is coming, go out to meet him!' Then all the virgins arose and trimmed their lamps. And the foolish said to the wise, 'Give us some of your oil, for our lamps are going out.' But the wise answered, 'No, lest there should not be enough for us and you; but go rather to those who sell, and buy for yourselves.' And while they went to buy, the bridegroom came, and those who were ready went in with him to the wedding; and the door was shut. Afterwards the other virgins came also, saying, 'Lord, Lord, open to us!' But he answered and said, 'Assuredly, I say to you, I do not know you.' Watch, therefore, for you know neither the day nor the hour in which the Son of Man is coming."

EXTRA READING

MATTHEW 24:36/42	MARK 13:35	LUKE 12:35
LUKE 13:25	ROMANS 13:11	I THESSALONIANS 4:16
I THESSALONIANS 5:6		

This parable is one of the End Time teachings that Jesus taught during the afternoon He and the twelve spent time resting in the garden on Mount Olivet (Olives). This afternoon was one of the last times that Jesus had time alone with the disciples. Some sources think that this took place on Tuesday before the last Friday and the crucifixion of Christ. He is trying to explain to the disciples that they must be prepared at all times for His Second Coming.

Jesus told the disciples that the kingdom of heaven will be as ten virgins that took their lamps and went out to meet the bridegroom. The bridegroom was not quite ready to receive the virgins so they napped while they waited. Five of these girls were wise, in that they brought with them vessels of oil for their lamps just in case the groom was delayed. Five of the girls (Jesus called them foolish) did not bring any oil other than what was in their lamps, not preparing for any delay.

Around midnight a servant announced that the bridegroom was about to appear and they should prepare for him. All the girls rose and began to *trim* their lamps. The five without extra oil could not refill their lamps and they were about to go out. They begged oil from the other five girls but they refused to share. If they had then they, too, would not have sufficient oil for the occasion. They told the foolish girls to go find the venders that sold oil and purchase their own. So that is what they did. But by time they returned the groom had already come and claimed his bride and closed the door on the bridal chamber. The five foolish girls knocked loudly but the groom refused them entry. In fact he denied even knowing them at all.

This story is full of little facts, each important to the message that Jesus intended for us to understand. It needs to be taken apart and studied as carefully as we can. There are a number of customs and such mentioned that we are not familiar with in this day, so if I can explain them, the true meaning of the message becomes more clear.

First, the ten virgins represented purity. These girls have not been tainted by the worldly affairs around them. They have most likely been raised in a very protected home where their fathers and older brothers kept all other men away from them. It was not likely that any 'flirting' with the neighbor's boys ever occurred. They were most likely dressed with their faces covered with veils, not allowing anyone outside the females of their own family to even see their faces. Their mothers had most likely been very careful to whom they even spoke and for sure she monitored what they talked about. It is doubtful that these girls had the worldly experiences that our six year olds have today. They were the perfect example of innocence and purity. It is plain that at least five of them were accustomed to others taking care of them. The foolish five did not even think to prepare for darkness!

The second thing I want to try to show you is the importance of lamps. Lamps of those days were made of various materials. Often the well to do had lamps made of bronze or other metals. The less fortunate made their lamps of clay. The wicks were made of either a cotton twine like-product or of flax, twisted into a tight string or braided into a tight web-like material. It was a Jewish tradition that the elders of the temple made wicks for the temple from their old linen garments.

The oil used could have been olive oil, or pitch from different plants and trees, or even wax, such as a candle. Lamps were allowed to burn all night. It seems most Israelites were afraid of the dark. One source I used in this study said that a family would buy oil before food if they had to make a choice. A dark house meant that it had been deserted and robbers or the homeless would try to enter. There are references throughout the scriptures that indicate darkness is a symbol for wickedness or disaster . And in Proverbs 31:18 a prudent wife is described as one that does not allow her lamp to go out at night.. So, as we learn about the actual physical use of the lamp, we learn how very important it was to those that lived then. There were no night-lights burning in the bathroom. (There was no bathroom.) There were no streetlights illuminating their homes, outside and inside. There just were no lights at night at all except whatever the moon and stars provided.

Knowing that information, we can see how very important it was that the girls provide oil and wicks for their own lamps. To trim the lamp, they needed some tool to cut the edge from the wick because the hard, charred end would not re-light after it had burned awhile. And we can understand how very foolish those five girls were by not being prepared for the long night ahead of them. According to Proverbs, they would not have made 'good' wives anyway. They did not have the maturity to manage a lamp at night; they certainly didn't have the maturity to be a bride.

Normally in the stories we study in scripture uses the phrase *they were sleeping* to indicate *they were unprepared*. And that is somewhat true here. The story does tell us that all the girls were napping. But five of the girls were completely unprepared for the night. The only fact I can draw from this is that all the girls were a bit slack in being ready for the groom to appear. His coming was a surprise for all of them, even though the five were expecting him, and ready to prepare. I guess I can explain what I am trying to say by this example. Suppose I am expecting company for dinner; but they are traveling a great distance, and I am not sure what time they will arrive. I need to have dinner ready, but I don't want it to be cold and re-heated like leftovers. So I cook it to a point that it can be finished within a short time and when they arrive, I can complete it easily. I'm not totally prepared but I am ready to prepare. Does that make any sense at all?

And then the groom came. Those girls that had trimmed their lamps and poured their oil into their lamps were ready to present themselves in the bridal chamber. The girls that had oil with them were not willing to share it with the others. Those girls that had to go out and buy oil were completely surprised that he appeared when he did. When they returned and tried to present themselves, he had already closed the door and refused them entry. He told them, "I don't know you!" They were not there at the time to be presented to him. They were not ready. And he had no desire to meet them now. So Jesus ended this parable with the warning to watch. And He reminds us that we have no idea of the hour or day that He will return.

Now comes the time I will try to put all these bits of information into an understandable, coherent lesson that Jesus would approve.

Of course there is the overall message that Jesus has carried throughout His teachings. That message is that He has all along compared Himself to a Bridegroom that takes the children of God as His Bride. There are numerous references to this idea in scripture. There are various times the Bible speaks of the Marriage Supper that we all, as children of God, will share and enjoy. This is a continuous thought throughout the Old and New Testament. And in this parable it is of course the main theme we understand.

The groom is Jesus. The ten virgins are the children of God. The wise five are those that are prepared to join God when the time comes that they are called. The fact that they refused to share with the others shows us that our spiritual beings cannot be shared. It is a personal thing that cannot be done for one another. Because my sister is a 'Good' Christian does not make me one. My husband's faith and trust in God does not rub off on me. It is something that each person must do himself. The foolish five are those that have simply not yet accepted that they might be called any time. They know it will happen. They look forward to that time. But they do not expect it to be today…or any time in the near future. They are living for this time in the present and not prepared to face the future hours of darkness that might come their way. They were not watching, and they were not even prepared to watch.

When Jesus did come, in this story, and they finally realized the consequences of their foolishness, they knocked and He refused to open for them. This point in the story reminds me of the thousands of times I've seen the painting of Jesus knocking on the door of our heart. In that picture Jesus is doing the knocking, asking us to let Him enter. In this story, He has made His final judgment and it is the girls knocking. And so sadly, He says He does not know them. Apparently, they did not let Him in when He called on them. Now He does not know who they are and cannot let them enter.

Jesus is trying in everyway He can to explain to the disciples that they must be prepared at all times for His second coming. He has told them in other teachings that NO ONE knows when that time will be except God, the Father. This time could be next week or the next instant. Or it could be another thousand years (I seriously doubt that). But like all His disciples, and many others during those days just after His Ascension to heaven, we today look toward the eastern sky on a regular basis, sometimes with eagerness, and sometimes with wishful thinking, and sometimes begging a bit more of a delay.

We know that everyone is not watching for Him and we know that many are not prepared. This is a heartbreaking thought in our minds, but it is a fact we live with. All we can do is to continue to pray for the time these people will seek their salvation, and continue to keep our own spirits and hearts walking with forgiveness. Jesus has warned us with every parable we have studied to date and I suspect if He delays long enough for us to study the rest of them…He will have warned us in them too. He is coming, that is a promise. We must keep our spirit watchful and be prepared!

38- GROWING SEED
(Kingdom of Heaven Parable)

MARK 4: 26-29

Place taught is unknown, but Mark indicates that only the disciples were present

"And He said, "The kingdom of God is as if a man should scatter seed on the ground, and should sleep by night and rise by day, and the seed should sprout and grow, he himself does not know how. For the earth yields crops by itself; first the blade, then the head, after that the full grain in the head. But when the grain ripens, immediately he puts in the sickle, because the harvest has come."

EXTRA READING

MARK 8:35	JOHN 12:23-25	I CORINTHIANS 15:36-38
II PETER 3:18	REVELATIONS 14:15	

This parable is the only parable I found that was told by Mark only. Neither of the other gospels related this teaching in their work. Mark did not include nearly as many parables as the other writers; it was his intention to show the action side of Jesus' ministry. But in this case this parable seems to have impressed him as important. And nearly every word of it can be verified with scripture that supports its' message.

In this Jesus is continuing His lesson for the disciples in reference to the kingdom of heaven. He tells them that a man will scatter seed on the ground. And as he sleeps the seed sprouts and grows. This happens and even yet today, no man can quite understand how. And He says that the earth grows crops by itself. Weeds are a perfect example of that truth! First the blade appears, then the head, and then the full grain or seed. Man knows when that ripen head appears it is time for harvest. A short simple story and I understand this might be one reason why Mark was affected by it. He was always more concise with his words than the others, so this using few words but relating a full of message, would have been impressive to him. And perhaps for some reason he saw a complete story in these few words, where as for the others, they may have only seen another parable about a seed.

A man scatters seed. And in God's creation of that seed it has the ability to bring forth a new life some way. We know that when the seed is covered by the sun warmed earth and touched with a bit of dampness, it will sprout. But how many of you have gone into the garden and dug up one of the seeds to check on the progress? I have. I always was so eager for the squash or beans or whatever I had planted to break ground. And do any of you know what I found? I found a seed that was nearly rotten. At least that is what it looked like to me. As I became more experienced in gardening I learned the truth of this parable or at least the words of John 12:24. That seed must die before it can live. But after it dies and is re-born into a new plant it produces many individual heads! But if that seed remains alone, without the warmth of the earth and dampness of life-giving water, it will remain as one grain and nothing more will ever happen. It will never go through the miracle of life and growth and the multiplication that is possible.

So in a few words I, too, have given you the meaning of this parable. Like the seed that has sprouted and grew and made many more seeds; so like the gospel word will sprout and grow and make many more souls ready for the kingdom of heaven. We don't always understand how the Holy Spirit works through our words to influence someone to hear the truth of God's word, but we do know it does happen. And we know that even if we don't see the results of what we have tried to say to this person, that word is planted and it might take a while for it to grow. As the growing seed produces the crop we look for at harvest, the growing word will produce the harvest God is looking for from us.

But as I thought and prayed on this parable, and as I thought about Mark, the intelligent, quick moving young man that related this story for us, I knew there had to be more to this parable than just another story about a seed. Isn't it odd that Jesus would speak of one seed in this story?

Usually when we talk about seeds, it is not just one. But even the sub-title in my Bible names this story "The Growing Seed" . Jesus talks of "the" grain and "the" head and "the" seed. This seems very plain to me that Jesus for some reason is speaking of one certain seed.

Somehow, we do not know how, that seed will sprout and grow and grow to become a crop worthy of harvest. But first that seed has to die. This is just a known fact that we cannot explain the why of, just a truth we know. Did we ever think that Jesus might be telling those listening that He was like that seed? He was a strong, well-spoken person represented by the fully developed head of grain. And He was doing well in the world showing people who He was and what He stood for. But nothing in the natural world continues to live or continues to grow or produces a harvest without dying first.

I am telling you here, that I think perhaps this was one of the first times Jesus told His disciples of the things that were to take place on down the road. I think this was a very gentle way He began their education so they could be prepared for His death. But truthfully I'm not sure they understood this enough to have the memory stay in their minds. (Only Mark related this parable for us.) Jesus told us here that the harvest comes only after the death of the seed.

We know now, (and I doubt that they could have understood then) that the harvest that Jesus spoke of would only made worthy of the kingdom of heaven by His death. If it could have happened that there was a harvest just from His living, they still could not have entered the kingdom with the sin stained garments they wore. The sacrifices of the animals and the law could not clean their spirits sufficiently to enter heaven! So like the seed that dies to produce life, Jesus died that we might have life.

I think that somehow Mark saw this message and understood it, perhaps better than the others did at that point. Or maybe it was an after-the fact memory that brought this message to light for him. But however we decide that it came to be, we can thank Mark when we meet him for remembering this parable for us.

39- TWO DEBTORS

LUKE 7:36-50

Taught at home of Pharisee named Simon to all guests present

"Then one of the Pharisees asked Him to eat with him. And He went to the Pharisee's house, and sat down to eat. And behold, a woman in the city who was a sinner, when she knew that Jesus sat at the table in the Pharisee's house, brought an alabaster flask of fragrant oil, and stood at His feet behind Him weeping; and she began to wash His feet with her tears, and wiped them with the hair of her head; and she kissed His feet and anointed them with the fragrant oil. Now when the Pharisee who had invited Him saw this, he spoke to himself, saying, " This Man, if He were a prophet, would know who and what manner of woman this is who is touching Him, for she is a sinner." And Jesus answered and said to him, *"Simon, I have something to say to you."* So he said, "Teacher, say it." *"There was a certain creditor who had two debtors. One owed five hundred denarii, and the other fifty. And when they had nothing with which to repay, he freely forgave them both. Tell Me, therefore which of them will love him more?"* Simon answered and said, "I suppose the one whom he forgave more." And He said to him, *"You have rightly judged."* Then He turned to the woman and said to Simon, *"Do you see this woman? I entered your house; you gave Me no water for My feet, but she washed my feet with her tears and wiped them with the hair of her head. You gave Me no kiss, but this woman has not ceased to kiss my feet since the time I came in. You did not anoint My head with oil, but this woman has anointed My feet with fragrant oil. Therefore I say to you, her sins, which are many, are forgiven, for she loved much. But to whom little is forgiven, the same loves little."* Then He said to her, *"Your sins are forgiven."* And those who sat at the table with Him began to say to themselves, "Who is this who even forgives sins?" Then He said to the woman, *"Your faith has saved you. Go in peace."*

EXTRA READING

GENESIS 18:4/19:2/24:32/43:24	MATTHEW 9:2/9:4-7/ 9:22/18:28/25:35	PSALMS 23:5
PSALMS 92:10	ISAIAH 43:25	MARK 2:6-12
LUKE 5:21	JOHN 11:2	ROMANS 16:15-16
HEBREWS 13:2		

This parable was taught at the home of a Pharisee named Simon. Jesus was a guest for the evening meal. I am assuming this was the evening meal because most of the sources I have studied say the Jewish people normally ate only two meals a day. Usually the first meal (Breakfast) was eaten between nine o'clock and noon (and often it was called 'dinner') Then after the heat of the day passed they would eat a more relaxed meal called supper. There of course were other guests present for the meal, and most likely at least some of the disciples were there. The only women that were usually at a meal like this were the women of the house, and they were there to serve the guests. They did not join the men at the table.

The guests lounged around a low table. They sat in a leaning position with their left elbow propped on the table and ate with their right hand. The tables were long and more narrow than the ones we use today. And often at these suppers with guests, they had more than one table prepared for the meal.

As Jesus sat at the table with some of the other guests, a woman heard that He was there. She came into the room and stood just behind Him and near His feet. She was softly crying as she stood there. A few minutes passed and she began to wash His feet with her tears. And then she began to wipe His feet dry with her hair. After this she broke a bottle of oil and anointed His feet, kissing them as she worked.

Simon, the host, saw this and thought to himself that if Jesus was a prophet at all He would know that this was a sinner woman touching His feet. I get the idea that Simon thought Jesus should not allow this woman to touch His person at all. But Jesus, because He was who He was, knew what Simon was thinking. Jesus told Simon that He had something to tell him and Simon invited Him to speak. So Jesus spoke this parable:

Jesus told of two men that owed a third man a sum of money. One owed five hundred denarii. The other owed fifty denarii. But neither had the ability to repay the man that had loaned them the money. In his kindness, he forgave both men their complete debt. At this point of His story Jesus asked Simon which of the two debtors would love the man that had forgiven their debt the most? He answered that the one forgiven the most money would love him the most. Jesus assured him that he was correct. And then He turned to the woman and still speaking to Simon chastised him severely.

He reminded Simon that when he had entered Simon's home, he had not given Him water for His feet. Simon had not kissed Him, nor had he anointed His head. Yet this woman had done much more, even though she was considered the sinner, and she certainly was not the host in this home. Then Jesus turned to the woman and told her that her sins were forgiven. The others at the table with Him began to mumble among themselves asking who this person was, that thought He could forgive sins. And then He spoke to the woman again and told her that her faith had saved her and she should go in peace.

To understand much of these verses we need to look at the traditions of hospitality in that time and place. There were so many things completely different for those living then that we nearly need to make our mind a blank of all of today's life and try to picture what it was like.

To travel anywhere, from house to house, from your home to town, from town to town, wherever you went, you walked. And your shoes were not nice built up Nike' walking shoes. They were pieces of leather soles tied to your feet with leather straps. Sometimes some sort of cloth might be wrapped around your legs and feet, but that was not normal. The path or road you were walking on was not paved nor smoothed by big equipment. It was rocky, beaten down only by other walkers and time. At the very best, it was sand in dry weather; and it was mud in wet weather. Those of you that has walked any distance in sandals knows that the make of the shoe itself throws dirt up on your feet and legs. Anyone that has ever been to the beach in July knows that sand can be VERY hot to walk on! It will burn your feet in just a few steps. And anyone that has ever watched a western movie knows that leather when it gets wet, as it dries out it shrinks and binds. Walking in those days was very hard on the feet. So to be a good host in those days, any guest, one that was just traveling through or one that was invited to your home, was provided with fresh cool water to soak their poor bruised and burning feet. All the scripture in the extra reading from Genesis has to do with a good host and the washing of the guests' feet. In fact, the good host usually washed the feet of the guest, especially if the guest was invited, as Jesus was that day. But Simon had neglected this custom.

Second, when a guest entered your home, (and I am speaking of men) he was greeted with a kiss, usually to each cheek. This tradition is still honored in many of the eastern countries today. We often see this at big meetings held with the leaders of these places when it is covered by television. In Romans 16:16 Paul reminded the brothers in Christ to greet one another with a holy kiss. Apparently this was one Jewish custom that Paul thought should be continued. I think today, in our part of the world, it has been changed to what we call a "bear hug." But Simon did not give Jesus a kiss…nor a hug that day.

It was also considered an honor to a guest that when they entered the doors of your home, the man of the house would pray for blessings on the guest. It was part of the traditional greeting to participate in this ceremony of ' blessing' the honored guest. And a part of that ceremony was to dab a bit of special oil on the forehead with the finger. It was not a long or drawn out procedure but it was simply part of the greeting for a welcomed guest. The American Lakota Indian had similar customs for greeting their guests. For a period of time after the guests was seated around the fire pit in the tents, prayers and blessings were exchanged between the host and guests before the visit officially began. Today we do what we call 'small talk'." How's the weather in Tulsa? How are you doing? I'm fine, been working too hard. But I'm doing all right. Glad to have the work." But Simon did not anoint Jesus when He entered his home that day.

SIMON FAILED ON ALL THREE CUSTOMS TO GREET JESUS AS AN HONORED GUEST IN HIS HOME THAT DAY.

This woman first broke tradition by going into the home during a supper where she was not invited. But for her to see Jesus was worth the risk she felt. So she went. (John11:1-2 identified this woman as Mary, the sister of Martha and Lazarus. As we know from other scriptures, Lazarus and Jesus were good friends.) I don't understand this reference, because nowhere else that I can find does the Bible indicate that Mary was a woman of sinful nature. But unless this event happened more than once in the time while Jesus was here, this was indeed the woman in this story according to John, and he was there!

But she entered and stood near the feet of Jesus. It was so important to her to be near Him she had risked being expelled and publicly embarrassed to be there. It does not say she tried to gain His attention in any way. She stood behind Him in a humble stance and the Bible says she was ' weeping'. That word indicates a soft, probably nearly silent cry. Her tears fell on His feet, as He lounged there at the table. And she wiped them off with her hair. It is so obvious that her heart was either broken or she was so filled with love for Him that she could not control her emotions. Perhaps she was remorseful for her lifestyle. Perhaps she knew only He could offer any form of forgiveness. Perhaps she recognized the true form of love that came from His heart for those that were sinners. But for some reason this woman loved and honored Jesus enough to wash His feet with her tears.

When she had come into the room, she had come prepared to honor Jesus. She brought with her an alabaster flask of fragrant oil. Alabaster was a sort of natural material that was familiar to that area. There are two separate kinds. One was fine, white powder gypsum like material. It looked and acted somewhat like our sheetrock today. It could be formed and shaped somewhat like clay. But it was not stable. It broke very easily. The second kind was often found in the stalactites and stalagmites of the local caves. It was also white with grey markings like marble and often priceless pottery was made from it. Usually a piece made with this material had a translucent appearance that was admired. Fragrant oils that were stored inside the bowls and flask made from this would emit their odors through the walls of the pottery for years to come. This was considered a very valuable piece to own.

The fragrant oils that were stored inside were mixture of olive oils and other things that would add a favorite scent to the oil. Some people used frankincense, some used pressed flower oils to mix, some used aloes, and some used cinnamon. Any pleasant scent that the person might favor could be mixed with the oil and stored in the flask. Often women used the perfumed oils just as the women today use scents to make themselves smell good. This fragrant oil was precious and added to the value of the alabaster flask that woman had that day. When she anointed the feet of

Jesus with this oil, she showed great honor to Him. She used the oil that might have lasted her years to come for normal use.

Jesus recognized her need for forgiveness and He saw the honor she gave to Him. He knew her remorse for her sins against God was sincere and He gave her what she was seeking. He forgave her many sins, and He pointed out to Simon that her love was great. He then turned to her and told her that her faith had saved her, and blessed her with the wish for her to go and live in peace.

Those listening murmured and talked among themselves wondering who this Man was that claimed He could forgive sin. To everything they could think of this was a blasphemy of the first degree. No one could forgive sin except God, and only then with the prayers and sacrifices offered by a priest. So who was this Man that would speak 'forgiveness'?

The Pharisee Simon recognized in the story Jesus told that the debtor with the largest debt would love the man owed the most as the truth. But he did not seem to recognize that the woman with all the sins would love God more than he did…however he did not recognize himself as a sinner at all. So there is no way he could ever understand the whole point of Jesus' story that day.

I think, no I'm sure, that if we would recognize all the sins that we are guilty of, and the frequency of those sins, we might be more humbled. And we might, after realizing that only Jesus can offer forgiveness for those sins, learn to love Him more. And we might try a bit harder to be sure that every thing we do (or don't do) is in His will! And we might find more ways to honor Him. Would we break our alabaster flasks of expensive oils to anoint Jesus' feet?

40- GOOD SAMARITAN

LUKE 10:25-37

Place unknown but taught just after disciples (plus 70 others) returned from mission trip. All were rejoicing success of trip.

"And behold, a certain lawyer stood up and tested Him, saying, " Teacher, what shall I do to inherit eternal life?" He said to him, *"What is written in the law? What is your reading of it?"* So he answered and said, "You shall love the Lord your God with all your heart, with all your soul, with all your strength, and with all your mind, and your neighbor as yourself." And He said to him, *"You have answered rightly; do this and you will live."* But he, wanting to justify himself, said to Jesus, "And who is my neighbor?" Then Jesus answered and said, *"A certain man went down from Jerusalem to Jericho, and fell among thieves who stripped him of his clothing, wounded him, and departed, leaving him half dead. Now by chance a certain priest came down that road. And when he saw him, he passed by on the other side. Likewise a Levite, when he arrived at the place, came and looked, and passed by on the other side. But a certain Samaritan, as he journeyed, came where he was. And when he saw him, he had compassion. So he went to him and bandaged his wounds, pouring oil and wine, and he set him on his own animal, brought him to an inn, and took care of him. On the next day, when he departed, he took out two denarii, and gave them to the innkeeper, and said to him, 'Take care of him, and whatever more you spend, when I come again, I will repay you'. So which of these three do you think was neighbor to him who fell among the thieves?"* And he said, "He who showed mercy on him." Then Jesus said to him, *"Go and do likewise."*

EXTRA READING

PSALMS 31:11	PSALMS 38:11	PSALMS 88:18
PSALMS 112:9	PROVERBS 14:20-21	PROVERBS 19:7
MATTHEW 7:12	MATTHEW 22:37-40	LUKE 6:41
LUKE 6:46	JOHN 4:9	GALATIANS 5:14-15

Luke related this parable in his gospel. He did not tell us where Jesus was when He taught it. He did tell us that the Seventy had just returned from a mission trip. Jesus had sent them out with the authority to teach and heal in His Name. They were to travel to the places that Jesus was going to travel at a later time and prepare the folks to receive Jesus. The travelers were rejoicing over their success and even still astonished that the demons had responded to their use of Jesus' name! Jesus appeared to be very proud of the missionaries and their work. The Bible says He rejoiced "in the Spirit" and thanked God for the wisdom the men had. Scripture goes on to tell us that when He was alone with the disciples later, He told them, *"Blessed are the eyes which see the things you see."* He went on to explain to them that even prophets and other great men had wanted to understand what they already knew. This is one of a very few times I see true joy in Jesus' words and voice. I just enjoy reading this passage (Luke10:17-24) and seeing the happiness in Christ. So often we see a sadness that seems almost overwhelming. When we get to heaven I wonder if Jesus will be expressing this joy…or will He be thinking of those that did not repent and accept His gift of life? I know we are promised no more tears or sadness…but does that apply to Jesus too? We will be blessed with 'no memory' but will He?

But during this celebration Jesus is approached by a certain lawyer and asked the question that every man that ever lived has asked at one time, "Teacher, what shall I do to inherit eternal life?" Again, Jesus answered this question with one of His own. He asked the lawyer what was his reading of the law? How did he understand the law? The man answered that one should love God with all your being and love your neighbor as you love yourself. Jesus told him he had answered correctly, and that if he would do these things he would have eternal life. But the lawyer was not quite satisfied with the conversation: he asked Jesus then" And who is my neighbor?" and Jesus told him this parable:

A certain Jewish traveler went from Jerusalem to Jericho. He was attacked by robbers and beaten severely. All his clothing and possessions were stolen and he was left naked in the road to die. During the passing of the day a priest traveled the same road and saw the man lying there. He did not offer any help; instead he moved to the far edge of the road and kept on his journey. Another traveler, a Levite also passed by this wounded man and continued his trip without offering any assistance to this poor man. Later in the day a Samaritan was traveling the road and saw the Jewish man, wounded and nearly dead. He immediately approached the man and bandaged his wounds, anointing them with oil. Then he offered the man a bit of wine and put him on his burro. He took the man to a local inn and stayed there with him during the night and cared for him. The following day when he had to continue his journey, he paid the innkeeper generously and promised to pay more if it was needed to care for this man.

Jesus then asked the lawyer which of the three travelers was a neighbor to the beaten man? When the lawyer answered that the one who showed mercy on the man was the neighbor, Jesus agreed and gave the lawyer the advice to go and do likewise.

When I am working on one of the parables I usually put it into the computer and then I go away to think on it a while, sometimes a few hours, sometimes a few days. But it never fails that during that time things will happen that brings it back to my mind. This one had a particularly interesting event.

I was watching the old television series of "Sanford and Son" . Lamont (the son) was trying to load some junk from their yard into the back of the pick-up. He asked his "Pop" to help him with an old bathtub. Suddenly they saw a hobo sleeping in the tub. After Pop started to throw the old man off his property Lamont asked his dad to let the man stay a while and at least eat a meal with them. When Mr. Sanford argued with him, Lamont asked his dad if he remembered the Good Samaritan. Pop replied, "Ah, you know I never liked those old Japanese movies!"

On the surface this little story of mine has nothing to do with the study of the parable that Jesus told that day, or does it? Do we really understand what Jesus was saying or is it like watching a foreign movie with a language we do not speak? I should hope that most of us would have more respect for the words of our God than Mr. Sanford seemed to express. But an awful lot of us might not have much more understanding! I think we might have to dig deep to really pull out all He said in this teaching.

First I want to discuss the characters presented to us here:

1) the traveler… actually we know the least about him of all the characters. About the only thing we do know for sure is that he was a Jewish man. His journey began in Jerusalem and his destination was Jericho. According to the map of Palestine in my Bible during that time frame, it was a bit less than twenty miles. There seems to be a small mountain range there and Jerusalem is on one side, and Jericho is on the other. It could have been a difficult walk but apparently many people traveled that road daily.

2) the lawyer… Matthew 22:34-35 tells us that Pharisees were sometimes lawyers. But Luke 7:30 makes it clear that all Pharisees, even though they were trained in religious law, were not called lawyers. I suspect that the lawyers were taught to read civil law as well as religious law. Jesus was not always pleased with the lawyers. In fact He was very upset with them in general. He chastised them severely in Luke 11:45-52. In this parable it seems that this particular lawyer might be somewhat interested in the teachings of Jesus so like today, maybe they weren't all bad…

3) the priest and the Levite… I put both of these two together because in our minds today we do think of them as the same. We assume that all of the Levite tribe were priests in the temple. But that is not exactly true. The Levite tribe was chosen by God to do the work of and for the temple, but not necessarily the work of a priest. Some of them were responsible for things like taking care of the buildings and grounds, sort of like what we call today ' maintenance men'. Their work could have included everything from carpentry to sweeping or cleaning the altars after sacrifices were performed. So to be a priest, one had to be a Levite, but a Levite might not be a priest. But since both of these men worked at the temple and

both were headed toward Jerusalem, they might have been going to work.

4)the Samaritan...we need to go back into the Old Testament (II Kings17:24-41) to see where the Jewish-Samaritan relationship started. After the Israelite children were rescued from their captivity in Egypt and settled in the Promised Land, they began over a period of time to worship secretly the other gods of the peoples that had previously occupied the land. That indeed is making a long story short but God was extremely unhappy with their activities and allowed the people to be defeated in wars that led to their again being held captive in a foreign country. When they were removed from this land the king of Assyria shifted different peoples around to different national lands to prevent more troubles. With different nationalities and different religious beliefs living side by side there was less chance they would unite to resist his leadership. At that point many other people with many totally different beliefs and traditions were placed in Samaria. As the Israelites returned to the area and over many years, they married and mixed the bloodlines. They also lost some of their devotion to God and began to worship other gods. So by time Jesus was walking with men, the Samaritans had the name of "half-breed." No true Jew was suppose to have ANY dealings with a Samaritan. As we are told in Luke 17:11-19, one was not even to pass through the territory where the Samaritans lived. In Luke 9:52-55 Jesus did try to reach these people with His love, however they rejected Him at the point. He did again try to reach out to them in John 4:5-42 and this time He was received better. In fact a woman of Samaria recognized Him as the Messiah (which was something the Jews had certainly resisted!). And in Acts8:5-25 one of the missionaries, Phillip, traveled through Samaria and witnessed to many people there. Needless to say, there was much hard feelings and distrust between the Israelites and the Samaritans in those days. To be called "half-breeds" was an insult to their very being. They were treated as if they were nasty to touch or even look upon. And they, of course resented that much!

Now knowing who we are studying, it will be easier to understand the story and the importance of the message that Jesus told that day. First the original traveler was a Jew. The priest and Levite were almost obligated by their station in life to assist this traveler. But they didn't at all! Could we excuse them because he was naked and perhaps they could not tell if he was a Jew or some other nationality? Perhaps he was bloody and they could not get their own clothing messed since they were most likely going to temple? Or perhaps they thought him already dead and they did not want to go through the ceremonies necessary to cleanse themselves if they touched a dead man. See, even I can find all sorts of good reasons for their behavior. So I know, whatever crossed their minds that day, they had a perfectly acceptable reason for walking away from that wounded man, at least acceptable in their heart.

But what about the behavior of the Samaritan? With the treatment they had received for hundreds of years, and with the antagonistic emotions that still existed, he had no reason to stop. The only reason he would ever have to spend his time and his money to help the traveler was his love for mankind. You can be sure that the innkeeper charged him dearly to take care of the man. And you can be sure that when he made the promise to pay, he knew that would be the result of that statement. But he did not hesitate to accept the responsibility for the injured man. He shared everything he had with this stranger that he knew no more about than the priest had! But he didn't try to find any reason to walk away.

When Jesus finished telling this parable to the lawyer, He asked him which among all the characters was the good neighbor. The lawyer answered the man that showed mercy was indeed the good neighbor. Jesus confirmed his opinion by telling him to go, and do likewise with his life. Jesus has expressed in this teaching that anyone with a need that we can meet is our neighbor. It has nothing to do with who lives next door to you. It could, of course, include the person next door, but it is anyone that needs you. Color, race, age, nationality, gender, sinner or saved, none of that matters. Your neighbor is one of God's children that is in trouble and you have the ability and means to be of assistance. This child may or may not be of your social standing. This child may not be of your faith. This child may not be from your neck of the woods, (as we often say about strangers) but this child is loved by God! And to please Him, you need to recognize that fact. You need to do what you can for him.

As Jesus pointed out to the lawyer at the beginning, he could quote law and knew what the words meant. We too know what is right the majority of the time. Seldom does a problem cross our paths that we aren't aware of what we SHOULD do. The problem is do we do what we know to be right? A lot of times, no. We can find even more excuses for our failure than I found for the Levite in the story. We don't have time. We don't see any point in helping them because they will just get into trouble again. It is their own fault they have problems, let them learn from it. We don't have gas in the car. We don't have enough to do for ourselves. No one ever helped me out of a bind. On and on and on.

Do we choose to walk in God's will, or do we choose to follow our own pathway? It might appear to be more comfortable for a while, but is it really? I learned early into my teen years that it was just simply easier to follow Mama's route. I got caught EVERYTIME I tried to lie to her or to pull some stunt she disapproved of. Since those facts were true, it was just easier to deal with what ever came and tell her the truth. Then it was dealt with and over. It didn't hang over my head and torment me wondering when she would discover the error of my ways.

With God all that is true on a much grander scale. To do God's will from the beginning saves a lot of heartbreak later. He's much better at catching us than Mama was me! And I think at 63 years old, I can honestly say, Mama knows all my past mischievous activities. But He knows even while our mischief is in the planning stages! And He always holds us responsible for knowing right from wrong. Sometimes I could convince Mama that I didn't know any better (not real often); but we cannot lie to God.

He said, "*GO AND DO LIKEWISE.*"

It was not advice or a suggestion; it was a commandment. Jesus approved the heart of the Samaritan. It is His wish that we all were more like him.

41- MIDNIGHT FRIEND

LUKE 11:5-8

Luke told us that Jesus was in 'a certain place' when teaching this, but he does indicate that only the disciples were there

"And He said to them, *"Which of you shall have a friend, and go to him at midnight and say to him, 'Friend, lend me three loaves; for a friend of mine has come to me on his journey, and I have nothing to set before him.' and he will answer from within and say, 'Do not trouble me, the door is now shut, and my children are with me in bed; I cannot rise and give to you'? I say to you, though he will not rise and give to him because he is his friend, yet because of his persistence he will rise and give him as many as he needs."*

EXTRA READING

LUKE 11: 9-10	LUKE 18:1-5

This parable is told only in Luke and he does not tell us where the twelve and Jesus were, just "a certain place." I suppose those of that day might have known where that place was, but that knowledge is lost to history now. We do know in the verses just previous He had been teaching the disciples how to pray. And we know that in Matthew, when Jesus taught them the prayer we now call the Lord's Prayer, it was during the Sermon on the Mount. But at that place and time there were multitudes of people there. Luke indicates here, that only the disciples were present for this teaching.

In this parable Jesus asked them which of them had a friend that he could go to his home in the middle of the night and beg some food because another friend had suddenly, unexpectedly appeared at his door and he had nothing prepared to feed him? This sounds odd to us for a number of reasons. First we don't worry about feeding a guest or traveler like they did then. There were no all-night diners or Hardee's on the corners. The only place a traveler could find any provisions was to depend on the houses and homes along the way. And second, if we were concerned with feeding a guest at midnight, we would go to the local convenience store to purchase something. Again, this was not an option for the man in the story that Jesus told. Plus we have freezers and canned goods and many other means of storing food at home now, so normally we could prepare an emergency meal if we needed it.

But this man was caught without anything to fix and his traveling friend was hungry and tired. It was his obligation to try to offer comfort and food to this traveler. So he went to the home of his neighbor friend. He banged on the door and shouted loud enough that the friend inside could hear him. He explained his problem and begged just three loaves of bread from the neighbor.

The neighbor, being a friend, obviously comfortable enough that he could speak his mind, told him that he was in bed. His children were asleep. And he was not getting up to open the door at that time of night. He knew his friendship with the needy neighbor was firm enough to withstand his absolute refusal. And at midnight he wasn't real concerned about that anyway.

But a minute or two passed as he really woke up and he thought about the friend turning to him for assistance. Because he was a friend, and he recognized the persistence (one of the sources I studied translated that word as *boldness*) and the sincere need of his friend, he did rise and open the door. He gave his neighbor "as many loves of bread as he needed."

In the two verses following this story, (you will find listed as extra reading) Jesus tells us that if we ask, it will be given, if we seek, we will find it, and if we knock, it will be opened. These two verses easily belong to this parable, as well as the next one told in Luke. The two parables are telling us very plainly that God, as our Father, cares about our needs and desires! If a neighbor loves us enough to get up at midnight and give us what we need from his own kitchen, not for our own use but for the comfort of another friend of ours, then certainly we can understand that God, our Father, will provide whatever we need!

Surely we can know and expect God to always be there when we have a problem to suddenly appear like problems do. There is absolutely no doubt in my mind that I could knock at the door of any one of my closest neighbors and get help in the middle of the night if I needed it. And any one of them could seek assistance at my door too. If I have that total trust in a human neighbor, (and remembering humans can be moody) why would I ever doubt God?

Faith and trust in God should be just as basic as breathing; and just as accepted as a part of life. So many of us have problems accepting the love that comes to us from our kin and our friends. We often don't trust the fact that we are worthy of love from others...and I think that often, our lack of faith in God comes from that fact. We do not know how to forgive ourselves for some wickedness that has been in our past, so we don't think we are worthy of God's love; so then we don't trust Him to provide for us as He has promised. One of the strongest facts that come through to me from our studies is just that. We don't have faith in our Faith! We don't believe in our forgiveness. We don't consider ourselves worthy. And we are not remembering that God has and completely has forgiven all sins we repented of! That sin no longer even exists!

God does not break His promises! He cannot break His promises. By the very nature of His being, it is not possible for Him to lie or forget His commitments to us. God is <u>always</u> a friend, in any darkness of our lives.

42- COST OF TOWER (Cost of War)

LUKE 14:25-33

Place unknown, Had previously been at Pharisee's house for supper but as verses say, He had left and multitudes followed Him

"Now great multitudes went with Him. And He turned and said to them, *"If anyone comes to Me and does not hate his father and mother, wife and children, brothers and sisters, yes, and his own life also, he cannot be My disciple. And whoever does not bear his cross and come after Me cannot be My disciple. For which of you, intending to build a tower, does not sit down first and count the cost, whether he has enough to finish it – lest, after he has laid the foundation, and is not able to finish, all who see it begin to mock him, saying, 'This man began to build and was not able to finish.' Or what king going to make war against another king, does not sit down first and consider whether he is able with ten thousand to meet him who comes against him with twenty thousand? Or else while the other is still a great way off, he sends a delegation and asks conditions of peace. So likewise whoever of you does not forsake all that he has cannot be My disciple"* .

EXTRA READING

EXODUS 32:26-28	NUMBERS 25:12-13	PSALMS 89:30-34
ISAIAH 24:1-6	ISAIAH 24:19-20	ISAIAH 54:10
MALACHI 2:5-6	MATTHEW 19:27-30	MATTHEW 24:35

Luke does not tell us where Jesus was at the time He taught this parable, however He was just at the home of a Pharisee in the town. Luke said He had left and when He did, great multitudes followed Him. When He became aware of the people following Him, He turned and spoke to them.

Jesus told those that seemed to have a desire to be with Him that it was not just a matter of following after Him. Those that made the commitment to walk in His footsteps would have to *hate* everyone else involved in their lives. Their lives would include *taking up their cross* in order to be His disciple. He then spoke the parable we intend to study today.

He reminded all those followers that none would begin to build a tower without first figuring out the complete cost. A man that had the intentions of building anything needed to know ahead of time if he could afford to finish the project. Or a king would certainly need to know the strength of an opposing army before he started to war against them. He then added that it was the same; if they were to choose to follow Him and be His disciple then they absolutely must consider the cost of that commitment.

This parable bothers many Christians. It seems to be quite inconsistent with all the teachings we have already studied. What in the world does He mean, "Hate your father and mother?" How on earth does He expect us to first follow the commandments that tell us to" Honor your parents "and at the same time He tells us here to HATE them? Why would anyone hate his/her siblings (for longer than a day or two, anyway)? How can you live with a spouse day in and day out and hate him/her? To not love your own children certainly seems most unholy to me! And all of us living today have grown up listening to every talk-show host giving reason after reason for why we should love ourselves. Yes, these verses have confused many Christians, and those that are not Christians don't even try to understand them! But Jesus is firm; to do these things is what it takes to be His disciple!

Well, I am no smarter than those men and women that were actually there that day. These words seem to be just as harsh to me as they were to them. I am more than sure that at that point, many of those people shook their heads in utter disappointment and walked away from Him. They heard the surface meaning and knew they could not make the commitment that Jesus was asking of them. I'm sure that they were trying to compare these words with the words of love and compassion that they usually heard Him speak.

But I do not think for one second that Jesus was teaching *hate* as we use the word today. I looked up the word in the dictionary (Webster's New World Dictionary and Thesaurus). You can hardly believe how many other words we have in the English language that means "to hate." I listed a few on a scrap sheet, just so I could quote them to you. After I had written down twenty of them, I quit. I knew I was not going to list nearly that many in this paper! And even more interesting is that the word *hate* is often associated with the word *great*. I had always thought the word *great* had a good connotation! But read this list! Great contempt …great repugnance…great dislike…great aversion… great hostility…great disgust… And among the innumerable definitions I found this…the "opposite of love." Wow! Hate is the opposite of love! I don't think that shocked any of us! Apparently the word *hate* expresses one of the strongest emotions that a man can feel.

After that experience I decided to look up the word *love*. It too was a long list of other ways of describing a human emotion… adoration… affection… devotion… infatuation… All those ways we have for expressing how we feel about someone near and dear to us. But amazingly enough to me was one definition that actually included the mention of God's love! I will quote it here but I cannot give you page and verse for where it was found in that same dictionary, dear Ms. Sarah, because it is a computer program, not a book.

#1 LOVE IS GOD'S TENDER REGARD AND CONCERN FOR ALL HUMAN BEINGS.

#2 LOVE IS DEVOTION TO AND DESIRE FOR GOD AS THE SUPREME GOOD THAT ALL HUMAN BEINGS HAVE.

Isn't that simply wonderful that a book that most all people will use at least one time, would define "love" in terms that include God! Those two definitions have to be one of the most glorious things I have found in the secular world to date! It gives me hope that if we cannot persuade a person to read the Bible, maybe they will read the dictionary! This man, Mr. Webster found a way to witness in his work. There is no acceptable excuse for any of the rest of us now!

But back to the study:

I think that Jesus was speaking of a complete devotion of your love for Him that would exclude family and/or friends if there were some discrepancy. If you were placed in the position that you HAD to choose between your relationship with the parent, the child, or the other family member and your relationship with God, then you need to be prepared to choose your fellowship with God. Our love for God needs to be so much stronger that when laid down in comparison with our love for others, it seems to be like hate.

At some point in history, according to Revelations, we each may have to choose between our own life and our devotion to God. The horror of that may be that the mother may have to choose between the life of her child and her relationship with God. I think He is saying here that we must be prepared to answer these choices of our commitment to Him. I think that is what He is speaking of when He said be prepared to take up your cross and follow Him. Oh, what a cross to bear if you had to let your child die or deny God!

I know that there are crosses that aren't nearly so horrific to mention, but maybe those are harder to take up. A friend might want you to go walking with him each morning instead of doing your morning reading of scripture. So you walk and then don't have time to read before going to work. You promise yourself you will read in the evening, but somehow it is not the same, so you just gradually quit.

Perhaps you really feel bad, not sick, just feel down a bit and don't go to church Sunday. We all have those days occasionally. You watch a television show that you enjoy. Next Sunday a friend reminds you that you've already missed once, so why not go boating today? And you do. The next Sunday you feel ashamed and don't want to tell the pastor where you were the last two weeks, so you stay home again… You see where this conversation is headed, don't you? If you had born that first cross the day you felt just a bit out of it, and lived up to your commitment none of this other would have happened! A not-so-big-deal would not have turned into such a disaster!

Jesus tried to simplify this conversation as He often did by using a story about familiar situations. He compared this cost of discipleship to a man planning to build a tower and the plans he must make ahead of time. Do you remember the man that built the tower in his vineyard in the parable called "The Wicked Tenants?" He was a good businessman so of course he had figured the cost down to the last piece of wood. That's what you would do. I never started a sewing project that I didn't first be sure that I had every piece of material I needed. The pattern… the fabric… the zipper… the interfacings… the thread… the trims… and the time to complete it. I knew before I started what that garment would cost me, so I could then decide if it was worth the effort.

Jesus then spoke of a king that was having a disagreement with another. Yet before he would openly began a fight that might get all his men killed, he would investigate carefully. He would send men to spy and see just what was the strength of the opposing army. Then he could make an intelligent decision. He could see if the quarrel was worth the effort it might take to win the argument. He would know the cost of a war to his country. He could then decide if he might ought to consider seeking a peace agreement.

That's all Jesus was trying to show those people that day. He wants their commitment to Him to be an educated, thought-out decision. He would not be satisfied if it was an emotional, spur of the moment event in their life. A commitment like that is seldom lasting. A decision a person makes while in an excited emotional state usually fades when the emotion fades. (That's why it is so important for the members of a Church to follow-up on new members. We must be there to help them maintain the excitement of God's love during the days that Satan begins to weary them! And it is a solid fact he will begin to try as soon as he realizes they have made that commitment!)

Jesus knows that if we consider the cost, understand the decisions we have made, and still think God's love is worth it, then we will be strong enough to stand tall when the tribulations and trials hit us. We must believe and live by every word to be successful in a commitment to follow Jesus! Jesus wants us to make a thought-out, true from the heart, completely total decision to be His disciple for all time.

43- PRODIGAL SON

LUKE 15:11-32

Taught at home of Pharisee. Taught to all present at dinner

"Then He said, *"A certain man had two sons. And the younger of them said to his father, 'Father, give me the portion of goods that falls to me.' So he divided to them his livelihood. And not many days after, the younger son gathered all together, journeyed to a far country, and there wasted his possessions with prodigal living. But when he had spent all, there arose a severe famine in that land, and he began to be in want. Then he went and joined himself to a citizen of that country, and he sent him into his fields to feed swine. And he would gladly have filled his stomach with the pods that the swine ate, and no one gave him anything. But when he came to himself, he said, 'How many of my father's hired servants have bread enough and to spare, and I perish with hunger! I will arise and go to my father, and will say to him, 'Father I have sinned against heaven and before you, and I am no longer worthy to be called your son. Make me like one of your hired servants.' And he arose and came to his father. But when he was still a great way off, his father saw him and had compassion, and ran and fell on his neck and kissed him. And the son said to him, 'Father, I have sinned against heaven and in your sight, and am no longer worthy to be called your son.' But the father said to his servants, 'Bring out the best robe and put it on him, and put a ring on his hand and sandals on his feet. And bring the fatted calf here and kill it, and let us eat and be merry; for this my son was dead and is alive again; he was lost and is found.' And they began to be merry. Now his older son was in the field. And as he came and drew near to the house, he heard music and dancing. So he called one of the servants and asked what these things meant. And he said to him, 'Your brother has come, and because he has received him safe and sound, your father has killed the fatted calf.' But he was angry and would not go in. Therefore his father came out and pleaded with him. So he answered and said to his father, 'Lo, these many years I have been serving you, I never transgressed your commandment at any time; and yet you never gave me a young goat, that I might make merry with my friends. But as soon as this son of your came, who has devoured your livelihood with harlots, you killed the fatted calf for him.' And he said to him, 'Son, you are always with me, and all that I have is yours. It was right that we should make merry and be glad, for your brother was dead and is alive again, and was lost and is found..."*

EXTRA READING

I SAMUEL 15:24	II SAMUEL 12:13	PSALMS 51:4

This parable was told in the book of Luke only. It was the third in a series that Jesus taught at a dinner in the home of a Pharisee from the local Temple. The first two He told at the table were "The Lost Sheep" and "The Lost Coin." This one is called either "The Lost Son" or, most often "The Prodigal Son." All three have one theme, the lost sinner. And the Bible tells us that the tax collectors and the sinners gathered near to Jesus while He spoke. We need to remember while we are studying this that the Pharisees were present there that day too.

Jesus spoke of a well-to-do farmer that had two sons. Finally the younger son realized that he would not inherit the farm itself, but only the value of the single portion that the Jewish law allowed. So being young and it sounds like he was a bit restless, he asked his dad to go ahead and give him his share and let him go. He was like our sons (and daughters) today and wanted to see the world and have an adventure while he was young. So the dad did as he asked and divided all he owned and gave the younger son his portion.

Jesus said in the story that not many days later, the son left the farm and went to a far away country. A far country ... to an unknown culture... an unknown peoples... even an unknown language most likely... all this equals adventure to the young man and terror to the father. We all raise our babies and try to make them self-sufficient but when the day comes that they declare their independence we cry. We mourn and grieve much like a death has occurred. I remember when my daughter left home. She was a mature young lady that I trusted to take good care of herself. I knew it was time for her to try her wings. But I went through all the stages of grief, sorrow, denial, and anger, and back to sorrow. I wanted my baby to stay my baby. And who could ever love her like I did? I suspect this dad in this story felt much the same as I did. And he didn't have the advantage of telephones that I had, so I can almost feel his pain.

The boy was enjoying his new life at first very much. There were new things to see. Many new experiences were just waiting for him. And there were lots of new friends perfectly willing to help him celebrate life by spending his money. And Jesus explains that all of his spending was not in his own best interest. In fact the word Jesus used to describe the boy's spending habit was "prodigal living." The word means *wasteful* or *to waste*. In other words the boy used much of his inheritance to experience a side of life his dad had always protected him from earlier. (That is a lesson within this lesson, if we will notice. Often times if parents are too protective, the child will "go wild" when they first leave the nest.) We need to let them see some the real world while we still have control of their activities. Maybe they can learn without getting hurt.

As the times changed and there came to be hard times for this country where the boy was, he too began to have hard times. There was a famine in the land and he had thrown away most of his funds on entertaining all his new friends. He had to seek employment just to survive. He found a man that was willing to "take him in" so to speak. However the job he offered him was probably the lowest job that a young Jewish boy could even imagine. It was his job to live far out of the city in a very rural area to tend the hogs. Everyone is aware of the smell a hog farm produces so this particular man kept his swine in an isolated area away from the other people. It was the boy's job to feed and care for the hogs. And as we all know, the Jewish considered hogs unholy. The only time I can think of them being mentioned where they lived in the Promised Land at all was when Jesus cast the Legion of demons from a man into some wild hogs. And they immediately jumped off the cliffs into the water and died. The Jewish were not pork eaters! They ate mutton and beef and fish.

So this was a horrible fate for this young man. He still had very little available to him for his own food. No one gave him anything. (All his new friends were no longer friends.) He became so hungry, he seriously considered eating the food that was provided for the hogs. That food was a product called 'husks'. It was a seedpod that grew on the carob tree. It was a tall evergreen tree that had seed pods that were six to eight inches long. The actual pod itself had a bit of sweet taste. And the seeds were flat beans. The trees produced a flower that looked sort of like a sweet-pea flower. I picture the whole tree much like our mimosa tree, except taller. If I described it, I would probably use the same words. The Israelite farmers used the dried pods as fodder for their cattle. It was a rare and extreme circumstance that would force a person into eating it. But the young man had met that circumstance. He was hungry.

Sitting way out alone as he was he finally took the time to realize what kind of mess he had made of his life. He knew that the servants in his dad's house were cared for far better than he was. His dad provided well for those that worked for him. He was humbled by the past events and decided it was better to go to his father and admit his guilt. There he would beg a position in his father's house as a servant. Even that was more that he deserved, but he would throw himself on the mercy of his fathers heart.

So he started back home, planning all the way of how to approach his dad. It was easy for his heart to admit the sins against God of not honoring his dad, and of all the adventures he had experienced in the strange city, and all the money he had wasted that his dad had worked all his life to provide for him. It was no problem for him to see how he had sinned against both God and his dad, and he was truly sorry. He was more than willing to repent and confess these sins, in hopes that his dad would forgive him enough to hire him as a servant. He had completely lost his way in life and the road back seemed to be a long hard one to travel. But he was totally ready to start the journey! And he practiced his speech to his father all the way home.

The dad had never stopped hoping and praying for his son to return. He had no reason that I found mentioned to expect the son would return, but he still must have waited. When the father sat watching down the road one day, his heart jumped a bit. He saw one coming that he thought might be his boy.

Don't you suspect he had thought that with nearly every traveler since his boy had left? But he saw him and as he realized it was indeed his son, he ran toward him. His heart was filled with joy and he ran and he ran and grabbed the boy around the neck. The Bible says he fell on his neck and I suspect that was exactly what happened. It sounds like he had run what would be a long distance for an older man. He had run as far as his eyes could see to recognize his son. He would have been nearly breathless and quite winded by time he reached the boy.

He looked on him with compassion Jesus tells us. I think the boy would have been wearing dirty, ragged clothing. He would have been unshaven and most likely considerably slimmer than when he left home. His feet were bare of all protection from the hot sand and stones that made up the road. His face would have shown the ravages of the time gone by and the lessons learned. He body was tired and hungry. All this the dad took in at a glance.

As soon as the dad reached him, the boy began to speak. He wanted so bad to tell his dad how very sorry he was that he had done the things he had done. He spoke his speech just as he had practiced now for a long time.

But his dad wasn't even listening. I picture it as both of them speaking at once, both probably with tears of joy and relief that this time had passed. The boy was back in the arms of his dad. His dad is feeling relief; his son is safe. And the boy is feeling the love and protection his dad's home offers to him. The dad orders the fatted calf to be prepared for a feast. There will be a celebration that cannot be matched in their home that day! The father ordered the servants to dress the boy in the best clothing with shoes to match and jewelry to befit the youngest son of his home. For not one instant did he consider treating this child as a servant! His son was home and alive and well!

It would be nice in some ways if Jesus had stopped this story at this point. It most certainly is at a joyous time right here. The dad's joy is beyond measure and the boy is home and happy. And most likely he is bathing and resting to prepare for the celebrations in the evening. Though Jesus has given us a complete lesson by now, the lost son was found. But that is not the whole lesson He intended for us to receive. So the story continued.

The oldest son had, during all this time, been a faithful, trust-worthy son and worked in his father's fields. He had done it before the younger son left and he had done it while he was gone. This day when he came in from the day's work, he saw a lot of excitement going on at the house. He heard music and saw dancing. The sources that I used expresses that we know very little about the kind of instruments that were used then to make music. The Bible actual speaks less about the dances they enjoyed. We have all seen in different movies and television shows what we imagine as the music and dance forms from back then. But we know they did have a form of entertainment that included music and dance. And the older son saw those things happening at his home that day. He of course, asked the servants what was going on.

They told him that his brother had returned and his dad had ordered a big celebration in honor of this event. He was not pleased. In fact he was very angry! He refused to go into the house and join the festivities. His father learned of his anger and went out to talk with his eldest son. But his response to his father was a bitter reply. He pointed out to his dad that he had been there with him and for him all these years. He reminded his dad that the younger boy had wasted and threw away much money. He also reminded him that even though he had been faithful and reliable, his father had never so much as given a goat to be enjoyed by his friends and in his honor, much less the fatted calf! He was very insulted that he had been slighted in this manner.

Any family that could afford it kept a young calf in a special enclosure and fatted for any feast or special occasion that might present itself. Beef was then, (much as it is today in our world) the preferred meat. And to kill the fatted calf was a true celebration indeed. And yet the young kid, or goat was more common meat and most families that grew their own meat ate it several times a week. It was not a particularly special occasion to cook a goat. But the oldest son was disappointed that he had been denied even that treat to share with his friends in a party celebration. He was bitter and very jealous concerning the treatment of his younger brother.

His father was compassionate with him, as he had been with the younger boy, and tried to explain to his eldest son that his anger was not appropriate. He told the son that he had always been there with him, and he recognized that. And he explained to the oldest that everything there on the farm, in the house and in the fields was equally his own as well as the father's. It always had been. There was no need for him to make a fuss over killing a kid, or the fatted calf, for his pleasure because it had always been his to do with as he wished! But the younger boy had been the same as dead to the family and he was living again. Since he had been lost to them, now that he was back it was fitting and right that they all should celebrate.

Jesus did stop this story at the end of the father's reprimand to the oldest son. We have to imagine how he responded. Did he accept his father's words as true and go give his brother a hug of welcome? Did he continue to pout and stay away from the party? Did he give the young brother a hard time each day afterwards or did he realize the boy had matured and wanted to be a help to his father now? There is nothing in the scriptures to lead our thought pattern toward any finish to this story. So why would Jesus leave it like that?

As I said earlier this parable was one of a series told that day to that particular group of people. And the scriptures said those people gathered near to Jesus, listening to every word. They were sinners and knew it. Even the tax collectors considered themselves sinners. And they heard the hope and joy Jesus expressed in these stories. They heard Jesus talking of love and happiness when they came into the fold under the protection of God. Suddenly the words "a father's love" meant something real to them. God was not just a Deity of extreme might and strength. He was a Loving Father, a Parent that would never desert his children! He was the Father that would celebrate with music and a feast when they returned to Him. As they had heard the story about this kind and compassionate man, they realized that they could look upon Yahweh in the same light. It was exciting to know that no matter what mischief they had experimented with, God would forgive them. They realized that they no longer wanted to live that life of adventure; they wanted to live walking in the footprints of Jesus. God celebrates as each young child returns to His love and protection.

Jesus left this story sort of without an ending on purpose. He wanted the Pharisees to see that this story was about them, as well as the sinner that was lost. In fact, I think He was very much including them in the *lost* category. In His parable the oldest son represents the Pharisees. When his father reminded him that he, as the oldest son had always been with him and that everything he owned had always belonged to him equally, this was the message Jesus was giving the Pharisees. There was no point for them to be jealous or resentful toward the new converts that were beginning to acknowledge God and His love. They, the Pharisees had always been under God's protection and love. They had taken their place in God's creation for granted and forgotten all the blessings He had delivered as well as those that were yet promised.

So Jesus did not finish the story. He knew that the ending depended on the decisions that the Pharisees would make. Would they understand and accept the new plan of salvation that Jesus was introducing to the world?

Would they try to prevent the spread of the gospel and continue giving the new Christians a hard time? Would they be willing to celebrate with God when a sinner repented of his sin? Would they join in the music and dance and feasting when a *lost child* was found? Would they realize that God really did want a personal relationship with each man? Could they ever have any idea that sin would be forgiven by repentance via the death and resurrection of Jesus Christ; and not by the animal sacrifices that they had performed? Do we yet know the ending to this parable?

44- UNJUST STEWARD

LUKE 16:1-13

Taught at the home of the Pharisee to different peoples including tax collectors, His disciples, and Pharisees.

"He also said to his disciples, *"There was a certain rich man who had a steward, and an accusation was brought to him that this man was wasting his goods. So he called him and said to him, 'What is this I hear about you? Give an account of your stewardship, for you can no longer be steward.' Then the steward said within himself, 'What shall I do? For my master is taking the stewardship away from me. I cannot dig; I am ashamed to beg. I have resolved what to do, that when I am put out of the stewardship, they may receive me into their houses.' So he called every one of his master's debtors to him, and said to the first, 'How much do you owe my master?' And he said, 'A hundred measures of oil.' So he said to him, 'Take your bill, and sit down quickly and write fifty.' Then he said to another, 'And how much do you owe?' So he said, ' A hundred measures of wheat.' And he said to him, ' Take your bill and write eighty.' So the master commended the unjust steward because he had dealt shrewdly. For the sons of this world are more shrewd in their generation than the sons of light. And I say to you, make friends for yourselves by unrighteous mammon, that when you fail, they may receive you into an everlasting home. He who is faithful in what is least is faithful also in much; and he who is unjust in what is least is unjust also in much. Therefore if you have not been faithful in the unrighteous mammon, who will commit to your trust the true riches. And if you have not been faithful in what is another man's, who will give you what is your own? No servant can serve two masters; for either he will hate the one and love the other, or else he will be loyal to the one and despise the other. You cannot serve God and mammon.*"

EXTRA READING

DANIEL 4:27	PSALMS 27:12	PSALMS 41:1-3
MATTHEW 6:24	MARK 14:57-58	JOHN 2:19-20
ROMANS 14:12	GALATIANS 1:10-12	I PETER 1:3-4
I PETER 4:8		

This parable was only told in the gospel of Luke. It is assumed that it was told at the home of the Pharisee because it follows the others that were told there. The scripture does not mention that He had left yet. Many times in the past Jesus has spoke of the blessings that the gospel offers the poor. In this parable He approaches that a little differently. He warns again here how hard it is for the wealthy to accept the gospel.

Jesus speaks of a very wealthy man that has heard from some of his servant staff that his estate manager (the steward) was cheating him. Since the tasks of the steward was to manager the money and make the financial decisions, it was probably easy for him to slip a bit into his own pocket pretty often. The landowner called the steward to him and asked for an accounting. Jesus does not tell us the whole conversation but He does tell us that the landowner gave the steward notice that he was to be let go. Apparently he was allowing the steward to work a notice of a week or so, to clean out his desk. I guess the landowner needed a bit of time to find a replacement too. Most people of today's world would not have shown the compassion the landowner showed. Most would have escorted him immediately off the property and maybe to jail. But this man allowed the steward time to prepare for his own future before he lost his job completely. (Isn't that a good idea? How many today would appreciate that courtesy in our world of unemployment?)

Of course the steward was extremely concerned that he was loosing such a good job. He admits he was not able to do physical labor that would require him to perhaps dig and toil. He has always had a pride in his life that would not allow him now to beg for food. So he set his mind to work on what other solutions might be available to him. And he quickly came up with a plan that he felt would give him a good life after this job ceased. And he set about implementing it right away.

He called all the debtors to him that owed his master. He asked each one, "What is your total debt to my master?" When one said, "One hundred measures of oil." He told him to write a bill for fifty measures. And as the financial manager, he forgave the other fifty measures. The next debtor was forgiven twenty measures of wheat. And so on, he made himself, if not loved by the debtors, at least very much appreciated by them. He had endeared himself to them so that after he was fired from this master's home, he would be welcomed into another's home easily. He was causing a situation that would indeed give him a bit of job security. Most people caught stealing from his job, and given the time to continue working as he was, would simply line their pockets further. But he was far more shrewd than that. He gave himself an opportunity to have another job working for someone else, and doing what he liked to do.

Even his master admired his cunningness. He was impressed that the steward had made a place for himself in the homes of the other potential employers, even though it was by abusing his authority and miss-handling the master's money. Of course the master was not glad that the steward had stolen from him, again, but the master was impressed that he had been alert enough to see this opportunity and to take advantage of it as he did.

Jesus then continues His conversation by telling those present that a man that is faithful with a little, can be trusted with much. But if like this steward, he in unfaithful with a little, then he will be unfaithful with much. He asks those present that if one deceived you with a little, would you trust more to him? And if a man cannot be trusted with the property of another, who would reward him with something to be his own? Jesus then said that no man could be faithful to two masters. Either he will hate the one and love the other, or he will be loyal to one and detest the other. And He ends this with the statement that one cannot serve God and mammon (wealth).

Jesus had two separate messages that I see in this parable. The first is fairly obvious to anyone reading the words of these verses. It teaches a trust one can have for another that is faithful in what he does. Or a lack of trust one will have for another that is unfaithful in some small matter. I am very much aware that when one lies to me, it seldom matters to me if it is a BIG MAJOR lie, or a little bitty white fib. If I determine it is a lie, my trust is standing at attention from then on with this person. If this person is a family member or some one that I have a type of personal relationship with, I guess I continue in the relationship on some basis. But if this person is a business relationship, or some impersonal acquaintance, then business is over. I have no need or desire to have anything else to do with them. There is always someone else that can offer the service I had expected from them.

Lying is not the only way a person can be disrespectful and unfaithful to a relationship. There are many other ways one can be a bad steward, such as the one in this story, by stealing or the fancy word of miss-appropriating funds. I don't have any funds to allow anyone to miss-appropriate, but I can imagine I would be very disappointed in someone I had trusted that much. But Jesus is plain in this story, if one thinks money is so important in their life that they are willing to steal it, then they cannot have God first in their heart! There is no way a man can think a thing, a product that is man-made, even a valuable piece of something, is worth breaking the laws God asked us to remember. We cannot love wealth and God completely! We cannot expect God to be devoted to us if we mistreat His children! Just as Jesus told us in a previous parable we can't even love another human with the commitment of love that we have for God, much less some inanimate object! I would say that verse 10 in this reading is the key verse for this teaching:

> *"HE WHO IS FAITHFUL IN WHAT IS LEAST IS FAITHFUL ALSO IN MUCH; AND HE WHO IS UNJUST IN WHAT IS LEAST IS UNJUST ALSO IN MUCH."*

Jesus has told us in this of the dangers of being untrustworthy in the eyes of other people. He has extended that warning to what God thinks of the man that is not faithful. He is also showing some of the temptations that go with a love of money and the dangers that go with wealth.

But as I said earlier, I see a different message here too. Jesus tells in the story that even the master of this unjust employee looked on him with a certain amount of admiration. Most certainly not because the man had stole from him, but because he had seen and acted on a handy opportunity almost instantly. The master was impressed that the steward had thought of such a good plan to endear himself to other possible employers so quickly. And then he had begun the plan to carry out this new program.

Jesus must have known the saying we have all heard grandma try to teach us. There is something good about everybody! Jesus saw a good side to this man. By saying that the master was impressed, Jesus was admitting to a certain amount of admiration for the steward Himself. He was impressed by his industrious and energetic nature.

Now we know that Jesus was not proud of the behavior of the thief, or the shyster he became. But He was proud that he worked so diligently toward his goal. Jesus admired the strength of commitment this steward had toward his lifetime goals. He wanted a certain lifestyle and was more than willing to do what ever it took to accomplish it. I think Jesus was wishing that all His children had that kind of devotion toward living as He has taught us. I think He wished we would be as alert to see the opportunities made available to us to witness, to study, to worship our God; and that we would be as quick to grab a chance to show our love and faithfulness by working toward our eternal home.

After all, if this steward was successful in his plan to acquire a new job; it was still only a temporary solution to his lifetime problems. He would get caught again. (And truthfully, I would not hire him if I knew he had cheated his former employer by lowering my bill. I would expect him to do it to me too.) But if we work as shrewdly and diligently toward our goal of living in the kingdom of heaven...that is an eternal home! No temporary solution there!

We have just got to stop wishing and waiting for the rich uncle to leave us his fortune! In the long run (eternity is a LONG run) it would do us no good at all to be rich now! Our true riches are to be in the company of God and His Son, for all time. Whatever the message you see in this parable, the fact is Jesus spoke plainly when He said:

"YOU CANNOT SERVE GOD AND MAMMON."

45- RICH GLUTTON AND LAZARUS

LUKE 16:19-31

Taught at the home of a Pharisee. There were a number of people present.

"There was a certain rich man who was clothed in purple and fine linen and fared sumptuously every day. But there was a certain beggar named Lazarus, full of sores, who was laid at his gate, desiring to be fed with the crumbs which fell from the rich man's table. Moreover the dogs came and licked his sores. So it was that the beggar died and was carried by the angels to Abraham's bosom. The rich man also died and was buried. And being in torments in Hades, he lifted up his eyes and saw Abraham afar off, and Lazarus in his bosom. Then he cried and said, 'Father Abraham, have mercy on me, and send Lazarus that he may dip the tip of his finger in water and cool my tongue; for I am tormented in this flame.' But Abraham said, 'Son, remember that in your lifetime you received your good things, and likewise Lazarus evil things; but now he is comforted and you are tormented. And besides all this, between us and you there is a great gulf fixed, so that those who want to pass from here to you cannot, nor can those from there pass to us." Then he said, 'I beg you, therefore, father, that you would send him to my father's house, for I have five brothers, that he may testify to them, lest they also come to this place of torment.' Abraham said to him, ' They have Moses and the prophets, let them hear them.' And he said, 'No, father Abraham, but if one goes to them from the dead, they will repent.' But he said to him, 'If they do not hear Moses and the prophets, neither will they be persuaded though one rise from the dead.'"

EXTRA READING

ISAIAH 66:24	ZECHARIAH 14:12	MATTHEW 5:29-30
MATTHEW 18:6-10	MARK 9: 42-48	JOHN 5:46-47
JOHN 12:10-11		

This is another of the parables that was taught at the dinner that Jesus attended at the Pharisee's home. Luke was the only writer to mention it in his work. The title of this parable is interesting even before you begin to read the words of it. I did not choose the title but I did accept it as I found it on one of the many lists I found. I suppose my reasoning for leaving it unchanged might be the same reason it was named as it was to start with.

There have been a good number of rich men mentioned in the different parables. It was beginning to be difficult to tell them apart. I would like for you to hear a title and have some idea which parable I am speaking of…but that was starting to be less and less possible. It became important that something was in the title that distinguished each rich man from the other.

Well, Jesus spoke of this man as faring *sumptuously*. That meant to me that he had food plentifully and it was prepared in a fine manner. In other words, he ate "high on the hog." At least if he had been a Southerner that is the way his life style would have been described. Since none of the other rich men had that description, he got the name of a glutton. I guess maybe the first person that called him that might have been from one of the southern states too. But I thought it was interesting to note the title.

Jesus told the listeners of a certain rich man that lived a life of luxury, dressed in the most noble clothing. (The color purple was a very expensive dye and usually used by royalty) and he only ate the finest foods. But at the gates of his beautiful home a poor man was brought by friends or family to beg his fare for each day. This was often the only way a person unable to work could survive. It was not good to be disabled then! This beggar was named Lazarus. It is sort of sad but his name means "one who God has helped" . He was covered with sores the scripture tells us. And we know God did help him, but at this point of the story he is having a bad time. Even the neighborhood dogs recognized that he needed attention. The dogs licked and cleaned his sores regularly. And that is most likely the only treatment he had for his body. I doubt he could in any way afford to go to a doctor. Or perhaps his wounds were beyond the help of a physician's care.

After a passage of time Lazarus died, and with God's mercy he was carried to Abraham's bosom by the angels. The phrase "Abraham's bosom" was a way the people of those days described heaven. It meant a place of honor and a place of comfort. With the life that Lazarus had lived, he needed both the honor and comfort he was now receiving. As a believer he had earned his spot in glory. And as the parable tells us, Abraham was right there with him. So Abraham's bosom was not just a figure of speech. It was a fact.

The rich man died about the same day that Lazarus died; but his eternal fate was much different. He was buried and his soul was condemned to the fires of Hades. He looked up and saw Lazarus in the arms of Abraham. He cried and shouted to Abraham, begging for relief. He pleaded that Lazarus be allowed to just dip his finger in water and bring that much to him. Abraham was compassionate but he explained to the rich man that he had had his good life. And that Lazarus had had a horrible time here on earth. Abraham tried to make the rich man understand that he had lived to please himself so now he was in torment. Lazarus had believed in God's love, even though his life had not been what he would have wished and now he was reaping his rewards. And in spite of any desire there might be to help the rich man, it was not possible. God had built a great chasm between the two places and no one could pass back and forth between them.

At that word the rich man, according to Jesus, then began to beg that Abraham would send Lazarus to warn his brothers of the horrors of Hades. He did not want them to be condemned to that place as he was. He felt for sure that if Lazarus, having died, were to return then for sure they would believe him and change their ways. Again, Abraham refused the request of the rich man.

He told the rich man that the brothers had the words of the prophets and of Moses to warn them of the place of Hades. He told him that if they would not trust and believe those words, then one rising from the dead would not convince them at all. The rich man could no longer influence his brothers. His time had passed. And he could no longer receive any form of relief or comfort. His eternity was decided.

To get the full message about this story, we need to know what kind of place Hades is. We all have the ideas that we have learned from our grandma. We've all heard a word or two in many different lessons. We have most likely heard a few preachers speak about that place. But all these references are just a word here and there. The idea of Hell is still a vague, almost unbelievable spot somewhere in the universe. But even then it is not a place we can find on an astrological map… so is it really *real* in our minds?

Our first problem in understanding that we have to deal with is the word "Hell" . I imagine that most of you have had the same experience with that word that I have had. I was NOT allowed to even say the word. It was one of the most gross bad words my Mama ever heard. (She has led a protected life.) And I was not allowed to even think it! Today's world of pastors were raised in the same gentile Southern world that I was (at least those that I have met) They KNOW better than to curse behind the pulpit! And when you hear that word come from their mouth… well, they might as well have said some of the other four-letter words we know, but don't say! It is practicality impossible to preach a sermon warning of the horrors of that place without saying the word. So they don't attempt it real often.

However, I did hear one good sermon on the rewards of disobedience to God. And that preacher gave a long list of the things we can expect if we earn that spot for eternity. He actually spoke the word ' hell' as he spoke. The words he used to describe the torments that the rich man was suffering were eye opening. I can't remember all the places he got his list from but I did write part of it down in the Bible I was using at the time. These things are the things we can expect in hell:

DARKNESS…we are all very well informed that Jesus is the Light of heaven. So we also know that Satan is the prince of darkness. There has always been the comparison of light versus darkness when comparing God and Satan. And there seems to be an inborn fear we have of darkness. No one is completely comfortable in the dark.

BURNING… Many references in the scriptures tell us about the pit of fire. In fact this parable we are studying today talks about it. And we know that where there is fire, we will be burned. Heaven will be cool and pleasant experience, like walking beside a stream of water all the time. But hell will be fire snapping at our bodies, from all sides, all the time.

CHOKING… I have to admit that this was the first time I had heard of this as being one of the torments, but if there is fire, there is smoke, and with smoke you would have choking, and your eyes would run water and your nose would run. At least these two things would happen until your body became dehydrated. Then those parts of your body would just be scratchy and miserable. Heaven will be a constant breathe of cool, clean air. Hell is different.

LONELINESS… There will be others there, and you may or may not see them, but there will be no communicating between you. No kind of relationship or companionship. Have you ever been lonely in a crowd of people? Maybe you were a visitor at a Church social or something like that. To be in a crowd and have no one to even speak to is the loneliest lonely ever! We will all enjoy the company and companionship of one another and Jesus in heaven, but not in hell.

FOREVER HOPELESS… in no way can you even think of a rescue. No matter what happens here on earth we know the pain or suffering will come to an end, even death is a relief to some thoughts. Especially if you are a believer. There will be complete peace and joy in heaven. But in hell there will be no relief!

SCREAMING and BEGGING… have you ever heard someone scream with absolute and total abandonment? Someone that has discovered something they know is a live-changing event. They have suffered something that cannot ever be repaired. I was in my house one day and heard my neighbor scream one of those screams. She had found her new baby (less than one month old) dead in his crib from SIDS. The thought of it still makes my skin crawl. It is not like I was good friends with her. I hardly knew her but that sound haunts me today if I dwell on it. That is a sound we will hear all the time in Hades. It may be coming from loved ones or it may be strangers but it will make the skin crawl no matter who it is. There will be no weeping or crying in heaven, there will be sounds of singing and praise. But this horrible scream will be all over Hades. All these people will be crying and begging God for forgiveness and redemption from this torment. But their fate is sealed.

FALLING… This one I particularly remember. This is the one I think of when I think of the true horrors of Hell. I have always been very much afraid of heights. I have never been able to stand on a footstool and reach up into a cabinet. And just forget the idea of changing a light bulb! So the idea of a bottomless pit through which I would continue and continue to fall…oh my! To always be in that situation of not knowing where the floor is… or never being able to feel solid ground beneath you feet again; that is indeed hell to my mind! Falling and your body tossing and tumbling and never landing on any surface…In heaven we are told of streets of gold and fields of lilies. But in hell there will be no streets of gold…in fact there will be no bottom at all.

ALWAYS REMEMBERING… Can you imagine that you will always think of the times you could have witnessed? …of the times you could have trusted God to care for you and tithed as you were supposed to do… of all the times you could have hugged that child instead of fussing because he broke the knick-knack on the table…of the times you could have attended a worship service instead of watching that golf tournament on television? I have sometimes mentioned to the class that on occasion I will wake up with a past sin on my mind that still haunts me. I know that I have repented, over and over. And I know that God has forgiven me. But this is just a taste of the power of Satan trying to convince me that God does not forgive. Imagine if you have been judged and condemned to hell, because you did not believe. Satan then has all the power of his world to bring all these things back to your mind and torment you forever! I understand there will not be this 'memory' in heaven. We will not be aware, somehow, that there were loved ones that are not there with us. But then hell is the absolute opposite of heaven, isn't it?

HELL… a summary of these torments…First your body is tossing, turning, twirling toward the bottom of the pit…but wait, there is no bottom. So this activity is eternal. The flames of a fire that never goes out is grabbing at your flesh, a blister here, a busted blister there; what moisture you have left is oozing out a drop at the time. Beside you somewhere (you can't see exactly where for the darkness) you hear the screams of someone. It sounds like your own daughter. You think for hours on end about the times you didn't take time to tell her what you knew about Jesus. So now her fate is the same as yours…this horrid place! But you are choking and your eyes are filled with smoke and you can't concentrate on her. It takes all your strength to get through the next few minutes…Oh no! its not going to be over in a few minutes. It's not going to ever end! You are forever going to be here. There is no chance of leaving and even going back to earth… much less Heaven! You wish you could find your daughter in this darkness and hold her one more time. It is so lonely suffering all this alone, and it's a special torment of it's own to know it is your fault she is here too. God had blessed you with her in your care, and look at what you have done with that responsibility! This is hell and it certainly feels real now!

HELL IS NOT A TEMPORARY PLACEMENT. IT IS REAL AND PERMAMENT...FOREVER AND EVER. AS IN THE PRECIOUS SONG, "AMAZING GRACE" WHEN YOU'VE BEEN THERE TEN THOUSAND YEARS... THAT STATEMENT FOR HELL IS TRUE TOO.

YOU'VE ONLY JUST BEGUN!

And this is the lesson the rich man had learned. These are the things he realized that he did not want his brothers to suffer. This is not an experience he wanted to share with those he loved. So he begged a second chance for his family.

Isn't it just a bit ironic that he suggested to Abraham to send one that would be returning from death to warn his brothers? And he was surely positive they would listen in that case. As the story of Jesus' life continues to reveal itself to these people; that is exactly what He did. But Abraham told the rich man that day that the brothers had the words of many prophets, including the word of Moses, to persuade them to trust God. If they refused to trust those words, then nothing else would convince them.

I think he was telling them in his own way that they must be a people of faith. If they could not have the faith to trust the words of God from those honorable men, then why would they believe a lowly beggar? They wouldn't. And in spite of the fact that since then, the most Honorable Man has died and returned, there are those that still do not believe! In fact I would venture to say there are more that do not believe than there are that do! What else could God do to convince them to see His love and His gift of eternal life with none of the horrors of hell ever being a threat again? This parable is as clear a message of warning as Jesus could have told. With it He has given us a glance into a place we could have seen no other way. His words are our only chance to really know what the consequences of disobedience are.

Are we listening?

46- TRUE VINE AND BRANCHES

JOHN 15:1-11
_____

Taught in the Upper Room during the Last Supper to the disciples

"I am the true vine, and My Father is the vinedresser. Every branch in Me that does not bear fruit He takes away and every branch that bears fruit He prunes, that it may bear more fruit. You are already clean because of the word which I have spoken to you. Abide in Me and I in you. As the branch cannot bear fruit of itself, unless it abides in the vine, neither can you, unless you abide in Me. I am the vine, you are the branches. He who abides in Me, and I in him, bears much fruit: for without Me you can do nothing. If anyone does not abide in Me, he is cast out as a branch and is withered: and they gather them and throw them into the fire, and they are burned. If you abide in Me, and My words abide in you, you will ask what you desire, and it shall be done for you. By this, My Father is glorified, that you bear much fruit; so you will be My disciples. As the Father loved Me, I also have loved you; abide in My love. If you keep My commandments, you will abide in My love, just as I have kept My Father's commandments and abide in His love. These things I have spoken to you, that My joy may remain in you, and that your joy may be full."

EXTRA READING

PSALMS 80:8-13	MATTHEW 3:10/13:12/15:13	JOHN 5:20/6:24/7:13/ 14:13-16/15:11
I JOHN 1:4-5	COLOSSIANS 1:19-24	JEREMIAH 2:21

This is the last of the parables I will put in this study. And it is again, as the other one from John's book, disputed by most Biblical scholars as not a parable at all. I won't present the arguments again that I did before. I will just say I think it is one so I will put it in this study.

It was told in the Upper Room during the Last Supper and the celebration of Passover. Most authorities think this supper took place on Thursday before Jesus was crucified on Friday. Only the twelve disciples were present at this meal, so it was one of the very last intimate times Jesus had with His disciples.

This was one of the longest discourses I have found in any of the Gospels. John wrote nearly one-third of his gospel in complete devotion to the last twenty-four hours of Jesus' life. Chapters thirteen, fourteen, fifteen, sixteen and seventeen, all discuss this conversation at the Last Supper.

Those chapters have more of the realistic details of those last few hours than any of the other gospels. If you read it with your heart you can almost feel the love Jesus had for these men. He was so concerned for them to go through the next few days. He wanted so much for them to understand the *why* as well as the *what* of what was going to happen.

It had finally sunk in to them that He really was going to go away and the disciples' hearts were breaking. They had many questions and Jesus tried to answer them all. He saw their pain and tried to comfort them as best He could. They wanted to know where He was going. They wanted to know if they could go with Him. They wanted to know when He was returning. The questions were coming from hearts that could not bear to loose His companionship, even for a few days. They were convinced that He would indeed return within their lifetime but for Him to be gone even a short time was almost unbearable!

As He was identifying Himself for who He truly was (and IS), He told the parable we are studying today. Jesus immediately began to interpret the parable as He told it. He did not tell a story in such a way that it needed a sort of translation to be understood. He told it as He meant it to be understood. He was speaking to His dearest friends and as He normally did, He explained the parable to them.

Right away in the first words He said, *"I am the true vine, and My Father is the vinedresser."* He continued by telling us that every branch on the vine that does not bear fruit is taken off, and every branch that does bear fruit is pruned. He was speaking directly to His disciples. (Thus He is speaking to those of us that are believers…we are today's disciples and followers.) And He assured them that they were already *clean* because of the words He had already told them. (Isn't that a comfort to know our sins are washed away? We are clean.) Then He said that they should abide in Him. A branch cannot bear fruit unless it abides in the vine. Here He was identifying His disciples as the branches. He goes on by saying that those that abide in His word will bear much fruit. And those will glorify God. He then explains that those that do not bear fruit will be cast away into the fire. He continues by telling His disciples that He loves them as His Father has loved Him. And that if they will continue to abide in His word, as He has obeyed His Father's commandments, then His joy will continue. And He has told them those things so that His joy could remain in them and that their joy could be made full.

As I said He pretty much explained this parable as He told it, but to make it more understandable I will give you a bit of history on some of the phrases He used. First, the Old Testament prophets often called the Israelite people "the vine of God" Jeremiah quotes God as saying "Yet I had planted you a noble vine, a seed of highest quality." (Jeremiah 2:21). And Psalms 80:8-13 talks of that vine being brought out of Egypt.

So in the verses we are looking at today Jesus identifies Himself as that Vine. He uses one of the "I am" phrases. John told of a number of different times that Jesus said, "*I am…*" For example He said, "*I am the bread of life.*" "*I am the way…*" These quotes are simply to us, a way of expressing His role in our lives but it meant much more to the Jewish people. Remember they only had the first five books of the Bible so they might have been a bit more familiar with those particular books than we are. They remembered in the Book of Exodus (3:14) that God had identified Himself as "I Am Who I AM" . And here this Man called Jesus was calling Himself, "*I AM…*" Those words were upsetting to the Jewish leaders. Even non-believing Jews (or pagans) realized this Man was calling Himself God.

These phrases Jesus used caused the ongoing dispute between Him and the ones that were suppose to be the religious leaders of the day to simply escalate and continue. In many of the parables as well as other teachings that Jesus had used, He often showed how *unfruitful* the Jewish leaders (Pharisees) had been. It seemed that everyone in that time was outraged by His claims. (That apparently was one of the requirements that allowed God's plan to work.)

As in many of the other parables He used references to facts of nature to describe the thought He was showing the listeners. A vine that bears fruit is most often, to my mind, a grape vine. In order for a grape vine to be productive it needs a good bit of care and attention. As He told us, the old withered limbs and branches must be cut away. You do not want the life of the vine to be sapped away trying to support that branch that is already dead. It is no use in thinking that limb can ever bear again. All it will do is entangle itself into any new growth and become diseased. As it grows full of some fungus it will contaminate the other branches. To cut it off is the only solution. You certainly want to burn the diseased branch.

The good branches have to be pruned and cut back regular to make them grow strong enough to support the weight of the fruit. I do not know the exact time they are to be cut but I think a branch will only bear fruit after the second year's growth. If it is not pruned it will grow slim and weak and break under the burden of the grapes. But if it is cared for properly it will build up a stronger limb and hold pounds and pounds of fruit. Jesus is referring here to the believers that need discipline on occasion. To be corrected in some fault we have, allows our faith to become stronger. We cannot grow unless we are pruned back once in a while. God will often discipline us for our own good because He loves us. When we punish a child for going into the road, we do it to protect the child; out of love for the child, not because we wanted to hurt him/her. But the cared for vine is very productive. It can and does produce more fruit than one ordinary family can eat. The cared for believer will produce fruit up to one hundred fold; Jesus told us that in another parable.

God is the Vinedresser. Jesus came to teach us how to walk in obedience to God. He came to tell us the laws that God wants us to follow. The Vinedresser is in charge of the orchard. He oversees everything that goes on there. He recognizes and loves His Vine and knows it to be productive. The Vine in turn, knows and recognizes the branches; he knows that with the right care they will produce the fruit needed.

Jesus tells us He knows His followers and loves them as He has loved His Father. In other words He has shown His love for His Father through His respect and obedience. At all times He has conducted Himself according to the will of His Father. Everything He has ever done, He did with the wishes of His father as His guide. And His Father has always, every minute loved Him. God told us of His pride in His Son. When John the Baptist baptized Jesus God spoke for all to hear, "This is my Beloved Son, in Whom I am well pleased." (Matthew 3:17.) There are other times that God expressed His love for Jesus in an audible manner for all to hear, but He always expressed His support and love for Him in other ways. And Jesus told us in this parable that He loved His followers as God loved Him.

He then asked us to *abide* in Him. In other words He wants us to trust Him and remember our commitments to Him. He expects us to honor His word and respect His commandments. When we act as we should, like any parent, it gives joy to His Heart. He told us that in these words. And like any parent, when we act in a way that does not respect His word, then He is disappointed. And His joy is lessened. Often our parents would show their hurt, anger, or disappointment in our behavior. Jesus asked us in this parable to allow Him to keep His joy. He did not want to show that disappointment.

And as the parents (or Jesus) has joy in our behavior, we have joy that we have pleased them. It always made me feel good to know I had done something that my Daddy was proud of! He had dark, dark brown eyes. You wouldn't think they would show emotion. But they did. When he was proud, his eyes would sparkle and almost dance. I loved that look and it never failed to give me great joy to know I had put that dance in his eyes. My daddy was a joyous person, usually happy and pleased with his world; but it was so special to know I made him smile. That is the emotion Jesus wishes for us in the last sentence of this study. And I think I could not have ended this work better if I had planned it. (I didn't, the Holy Spirit did.)

"THESE THINGS I HAVE SPOKEN TO YOU, THAT MY JOY MAY REMAIN IN YOU, AND THAT YOUR JOY MAY BE FULL." JOHN 15:11

AMEN.

ABOUT THE AUTHOR...

MARY BULLOCK CARTER ...obstinate...stubborn...hard-headed

(Biblical definition as well as the description of those that know me pretty well)

I guess it is only fair that I tell you a bit about me too. After all, at this point, I am acting like a writer. And with my opinions being a part of this work, well, I guess you might understand my work better if you knew me too.

I was born MARY ARMATHA BULLOCK in Loris, SC on January 4, 1947, sometime in the early morning. So you can figure out how old I am by now. I won't try to tell you because I have no idea how long it is going to take me to finish this, or how much longer it might be before you decide to read it.

My parents were hard working people from hard working families. Daddy was raised a Methodist. Mama was Southern Baptist. As time passed, Daddy attended church with her. I really don't know if he ever joined a Baptist Church but I do know he was very active in working at her church for a period of time.

Mama taught at church a number of years. She was a Training Union leader for a long time. I bet there are not many of you that even remember Training Union, is there? Well, for you youngsters, it was Sunday night's version of Sunday School for young people. That was where we learned Bible verses and all the songs that children sing in church. I think that the program they have now called <u>Bible Drill</u> came out of that. And somehow it was more fun; maybe because we didn't call it school! And we didn't have to wear our Sunday best. We just wore our jeans, no little white gloves or hats with ribbons, or white patent leather slippers. Remember?

Now for at least twenty years (maybe more), she has been the Director of Vacation Bible School for an Association of about 68 Churches! In case you can't see it in my writing I'll tell you; I'm kind of proud of her!

As for Daddy, back when cassette tape recorders became so very popular Daddy would often make me a tape. He used it as a letter. The tapes would be a combination of him talking to me and music that he wanted to share with me. One of those tapes stands out and I'd like to tell you about it.

It started like all the rest, with a few songs, some country (I mean old country like Mac Wiseman or Ralph Stanley bluegrass), and some Southern gospel. And then he started talking. He was in the automobile body shop he operated then and he told me about the car he was getting ready to paint. I used to sand them for him when I was in high school. He said my hands were softer than his so I could feel it and get a smoother sanding done.

But I will get back to the tape. He was alone that day and somewhere in the conversation Daddy was no longer talking to me, but to God. It was almost a very private time for Daddy with God and yet I was being given the gift of sort of being the fly on the wall that everyone wants to be at times.

Daddy told God all about his day, just like he had started telling me. And he thanked Him for his family and for his wife (he was proud of her too) and all the other blessings such as the work he had to do, such as the collards they planned for supper that night. He asked His protection for all his children and he named each of us, with some little something that each of us had going on in our lives right then. I didn't realize he kept that close an eye on my life. After all I lived nearly 200 miles away. I guess I told him more than I thought I did on my tapes to him. Then he apologized to God and begged God's forgiveness that he was not able to do more of the things that people called working for God. He couldn't go be a missionary. He had a family to support. And the apology went on until he said, "So God, I guess I'm just praying man. At least I can do that, Lord."

I cried then when I heard the tape, because he did send it to me. And I cry today when I remember it. I think he had probably forgotten that all that was on it. But it was certainly a blessing for me! How many times are you blessed to hear a testimony like that? I don't think he ever knew how important and comforting that was to the rest of us. No matter what kind of mischief we got into, we knew Daddy was calling us by name to God and asking forgiveness and knowledge. I guess that's where I first learned what it really means to have someone intercede on my part with God.

But this is supposed to be about me...I was the oldest of five children. I was the babysitter and any other help that I could be to keep our family functioning. Mama worked a full time job and needed help around the house. That's the way it was for every family back then. Children were not just living for their own pleasure or excitement. Everyone was to carry his or her own weight, according to his/her ability and station in the family.

My siblings called me "Sister, "in truth everyone in town called me "Sister" and still does. (To my nephews and nieces I am "Aunt Sister"). We moved around a lot, so having friends was not easy for us. There were years that we attended church regularly and there were years that we didn't go at all. But I always had Grandma in my life and she ALWAYS attended church.

When I was at her house on Sunday I knew where I would be; and I knew if I woke up at her house any day of the week, I would hear her read some verses of scripture before I ate any breakfast. There were times (especially as a teen) that I resented that interruption to my plans for the day; but it was a fact of life and no exceptions were ever made. As I matured and grew to have some curiosity about the Bible and its true meanings, Grandma always knew.

It amazed me the simple and basic understanding she had, when all she had to study was a King James Version, no Study helps, no more recent translations, just her and the Holy Spirit!

I married in March before I graduated high school in June, and when my daughter was born in June of the following year, I suddenly began to see the importance that Grandma had tried to show me.

My daughter was born on a Saturday. She was in church the eighth day of her life. (I thought that was very symbolic for a Gentile girl!) I had good intentions. But I had to work. I had a husband that needed a certain amount of attention. I had a son born eighteen months later. I still had to work. My husband was going to school and trying to work. I lost my determination to be in Church with my children every Sunday. Like in my family, there were periods of time we attended regularly, and times we didn't go at all. As you can expect, things went downhill during those times when we ignored God. Eventually my husband and I separated. Our children were grown and I guess we figured we did not need to be together any more. We really did not seem to bring out the best in each other.

Nearly ten years later I met and married my husband today. We both wanted God back in our lives and we started attending church regularly. God has blessed us over and over. With the grace of God and the influence of some very good people, my son is now a deacon in his church. His wife and five children are busy with their activities. He is a strong Christian man that is *Head of his Family*, and his wife is a strong nurturing partner.

My husband is a deacon in our church and I am the adult class teacher. But that is just what we do. It is not who we are. God has been there through serious illnesses with each of us. The gifts He has given us is beyond measure! We have a loving and caring church family. We have a pastor that is strong and knowledgeable! We have the love and pride of our biological families. We have a nice home and what ever we need to live comfortably. But that's just things. I've never been hungry that I didn't know I was going to have food to fill me before long. I've never even considered the idea that I might be cold from lack of clothing. Even back when I was not living as God wanted me to live, He was still there for me.

As I re-read this I see it sounds like the typical fairytale where every thing is roses and sunshine. Nothing could be further from the truth. Life hands us bumps and bruises almost daily, but listing them or dwelling on them long enough to type them out here is a waste of energy. I choose not to even acknowledge those things! As I said in the last paragraph, God is there for us, no matter what else is going on. Sometimes I feel like maybe He is attending to someone else and I'm out in the world on my on, but eventually I come around and remember He has given to me the Holy Spirit and He lives inside my heart. I am never alone! Not one second!

And now He has shown me what He wants me to do for my part to accomplish His goal, my way to help spread the gospel! I truly thought that teaching was fulfilling that job. But now I know God has a little bit more for me to do. So here goes! If one person can come to a closer understanding of His word through this work, then I can know my life has had a purpose! Maybe this is just taking *teaching* a step further up the road. Maybe my class just grew a bit!

Thank You Jesus

LETTER FROM AUTHOR

Dear Friend,

I certainly hope that you have been able to read this project and that you might have learned a bit of what Jesus is about; and what He might want us to know about His teachings. But this is a note to say so long for now. I feel like you have been a part of my life for several years now, and I'm going to miss spending time with you. Perhaps I need to start another project? There are so many people I could say thank you to if I could remember all of them: encouragement...suggestions...proof-reading...etc...printing lessons so I could spend my time studying. But some that have to be named are:

Earnie Carter... My most impatient and bored husband. The hours he has spent alone with no company but the television has been uncountable! I thank him with all my heart for the times he gave his blessings for me to work at the computer or read the books that I had to keep referring back to. I could never count the cups of coffee that he made! (He has tried to keep count, and says I now owe him 476 cups.) And I beg his forgiveness for the times when he didn't give his blessings but I did it anyway! To me, it was worth any thing I had to do...but I know it might not be so with him. I love you dear man! And I thank you for loving me...in spite of....more than I want to list here!

Reverend Mike Catoe...I can imagine reading this with me and for my assistance has been a true revelation to him, as a properly educated pastor. He was most likely shocked at how simple a mind can be as mine has proven... especially in reference to interpreting the Word of God. It has to be amazing to him! I thank him for all the phone calls and all the hours reading and re-reading, not to mention the hours he must have spent not paying his dear wife any attention. She's been precious to allow his time to be even more taken from her than it usually is! I could not have done this without their support!

W.J. Ryan...one of the students at church that has been more than encouraging and put his encouragement into action as he helped me try to do two things at once; taking my time to be correct as I can while I write this; and at the same time being prepared to teach each Sunday morning… Bless his heart for doing the printing. He freed me to have what I needed most, time. Thank you Ryan…

Mrs. Eva Cullom… our senior member at Church…a long time teacher that so many of my students grew up in her classes. Mrs. Cullom has from the first day I taught here been a source of inspiration and comfort to me. From day one she stopped me and told me she believed I was here for a reason… she didn't know, or wouldn't tell me the reason, but she has continued to insist it was true. I have never discovered her reason except that I needed to know her in my lifetime and I wish all of you could too. She is a blessing just to speak to and I love her much! Some day we will all gather together and I'll introduce you to this grand lady!

Mr. James Adams… the one student that has been completely faithful and present at every class through this project. I know there were times he would make a choice to be in class when he felt he needed to be somewhere else, like at the church where he is a lifetime member! Thank you, Mr. Adams! Your support has been a gift!

There are others but at some point I must stop listing them. I guess this is as good a place as any that I will come to. I do want to thank all of you that have read this and studied God's word with me.

Today the Pastor taught on the time that Moses was on the mountain with God for 40 days. Can you imagine… he was in God's presence for so many days?

I tried to tell the Pastor how I felt Friday when I finished the last parable, I cried and felt a good bit sad, a good bit proud, and a good bit lonely, like a dear friend had gone away. The pastor easily related it to his sermon…and told me I had been on the mountain. I knew when he said that, that it was exactly what I felt! God blessed me and gave me that special time on the mountain; and now I must come down for a while… but I have all intentions of going back up!

Thank you for traveling this journey with me, and I'll watch for you when I start the next trip! Love you All,

Mary B. Carter

OTHER (OLD TESTAMENT) PARABLES

A few pages ago, maybe 50… maybe 100, maybe even 200, I told you there was ten parables found in the Old Testament. I made that statement because I had counted the ones listed in <u>one</u> my very reliable sources. So when I started to actually type the list, I checked another source. OH MY! Not a good idea! Just like the parables that Jesus used, there was a different list. Some matched with different titles and some were not there at all. Anyway, since I have decided a long time ago, (weeks and weeks) to only TRY to study the parables of Jesus, I have simply listed some of these others. I did not study them. I did not try to verify them. I did not name them. I have just listed them. If you decide to do more with them, good luck. I wish you well. At least I have let you know they do exist. And that is more knowledge than I had when I started. I thought the only parables were the ones Jesus taught!

NUMBERS 23:7/23:18/24: 3/24: 15/24: 20/24: 21- 23
MICAH 2: 4-6
HABAKKUK 2:1-8
I KINGS 20:35-43
ISAIAH 5:1-30
EZEKIEL 15:1-8/16:1-63 /17:1-24/19:10-14 /20:45-49/23:1-24:14
PSALMS 49:4/78:2
MALICIAH 13:35

Since I have failed so completely with the "other" parables, I will give you an extra gift. Below is a partial list of some of the <u>PARADOXES</u> in the Bible.

Most of these are in the New Testament but there are many in the Old Testament too.

MATTHEW 8:22
MATTHEW 10:39
MATTHEW 10: 34 38
MARK 10:34

MARK 10:43
LUKE 14:26
JOHN 12:24
I CORINTHIANS 3:18-19
II CORINTHIANS 4:18
II CORINTHIANS 12:10
PROVERBS 13:7

BIBLIOGRAPHY

GOSPEL PARALLELS: A Synopsis of the First Three Gospels, Revised Standard Version, Third Edition, Arrangement Follows Huck-Lietzmann Synopsis Ninth Edition,1936; Camden, New Jersey, Thomas Nelson And Sons, 1967.

HOLY BIBLE Old and New Testaments, King James Version / Red Letter Edition, Self-Pronouncing, References, and Translations, Giant Print,544BG; Nashville, Tennessee; Thomas Nelson Publishers, INC., 1976

HOLY BIBLE Our Family Bible, King James Version / Red Letter Edition, Nelson / Regency 702WM, Royal Publishing, 1971.

THE BIBLE ALMANAC: The Guideposts Edition, Carmel, New York, 10512, Copyright by Thomas Nelson Publishers: Published by Special arrangement With Thomas Nelson Publishers, 1980.

THE OPEN BIBLE Holy Bible, New King James Version; Red Letter Edition, Copyright by Thomas Nelson INC. 1982, Nashville, Tennessee, Thomas Nelson Publishers, 1997.

*THE STUDENT BIBLE*_New International Version, Grand Rapids, Michigan, Zondervan Bible Publishers, Copyright by New York International Bible Society,1986.

WARRINER, John E. and GRIFFIN, Francis. *ENGLISH GRAMMER AND COMPOSITION*: Complete Course: Revised Edition: Atlanta, Georgia: Harcourt, Brace, & World, INC, 1965.

WEBSTER'S DICTIONARY: "Home, School, and Office Edition" ; Baltimore, Maryland, Copyright by Ottenheimer Publishers, INC, Harbor House Publishers INC, 1984.

WEBSTER'S NEW WORLD DICTIONARY and THESAURUS, Fourth Edition, (Windows Computer Program) Simon and Schuster Interactive, division of Simon and Schuster Inc., publishing operation of Viacom Inc., 2003.